W9-BIH-443

BEST BATHS

BEST BATHS

BUILDING REMODELING DECORATING

BY THE EDITORS OF
CREATIVE HOMEOWNER PRESS
WITH
CONTRIBUTING EDITOR: JAY HEDDEN
CONTRIBUTING AUTHOR: JANE CARY

CREATIVE HOMEOWNER PRESS™   A DIVISION OF FEDERAL MARKETING CORPORATION, PASSAIC, NJ

COPYRIGHT © 1980 CREATIVE
HOMEOWNER PRESS™
A DIVISION OF FEDERAL MARKETING CORP.,
PASSAIC, NJ
This book may not be reproduced, either in part
or in its entirety, in any form, by any means,
without written permission from the publisher,
with the exception of brief excerpts for purposes of radio, television, or published review.
Although all possible measures have been
taken to ensure the accuracy of the material
presented, neither the author nor CREATIVE
HOMEOWNER PRESS is liable in case of misin-
terpretation of directions, misapplication, or
typographical error. All rights, including the
right of translation, are reserved.

Manufactured in United States of America

Current Printing (last digit)
10 9 8 7 6 5 4 3 2 1

Editor: Shirley M. Horowitz
Contributing Editor: Jay Hedden
Assistant Editors: Marilyn Auer,
  Gail Kummings ·
Art Director: Léone Lewensohn

Technical Assistance: Ivan Nagode, Super-
  visor, Human Engineering and Installation
  Services, The Kohler Company.

Cover photograph: Tom Yee, photographer

ISBN: 0-932944-20-5 (paperback)
ISBN: 0-932944-19-1 (hardcover)
LC: 80-67154

CREATIVE HOMEOWNER PRESS™
BOOK SERIES
A DIVISION OF FEDERAL
MARKETING CORPORATION
62-72 MYRTLE AVENUE, PASSAIC, NJ 07055

FOREWORD

The bathroom as we know it today is a phenomenon of the 20th century. Until indoor plumbing became common, a bathroom was just that — a room in which one took a bath. Most homes, however, did not even have such a space. The bathtub was stored in a shed and dragged in for the Saturday night bath — usually in the kitchen in front of the stove. Modern bathrooms became common and then nearly universal in the early part of the century. In older homes, closets were converted into bathrooms. In new homes space was allotted for the tub, the toilet and the lavatory. It was a utilitarian space; the only luxury was that it was indoors.

Hollywood elevated that bathroom in the 1920's. The stars of elegant movies took elegant bubbling baths in marble tubs, sunken tubs, screened tubs, and raised tubs. From that point on Americans have wanted both utility and style in their bathrooms.

Best Baths provides an opportunity to discover, plan, design and build the best bathroom for your home. In some cases, this best bath will be a new bath created in an old space, or a new bath created by shifting space or adding a hanging bay to your home. For some readers, however, the best bath may be a very practical one for a very special person. *Best Baths* provides much-needed information and requirements for creation of bathrooms for the elderly and physically handicapped. A special section features information and suggestions for bathrooms used by small children.

For the do-it-yourselfer, this book goes beyond dreaming and planning to the pipes-and-wrenches stage. Step-by-step instructions enable the homeowner to determine the quality of the plumbing system and then extend or add pipe lines, or remove and install fixtures and faucets. Lighting needs include how-to steps for removing old windows and enlarging the space for a new window and adding skylights. Chapters on materials include moving walls, installing wallboard and paneling and tiling all types of surfaces. Directions are given for building tub and shower enclosures or adding storage and medicine cabinets. You will find ideas, answers, and information needed to make large and small adjustments to your bath — from changing fixtures to starting from scratch, from adding a light to extending cable, from constructing new walls to resurfacing existing ones. We have tried to keep in mind the various levels of background knowledge our readers are heir to, and have included projects and details to help the novice homeowner and inform the experienced worker.

Pg. 40

Pg. 46

Pg. 38

Contents

1 Bathroom Planning and Design

Unfinished attic space was remodeled into a small, practical bath. A skylight provides light, but retains privacy. Vinyl wallpaper appears to be grasscloth, but is more durable. Space is saved by installing towel racks on a sliding shower door.

When you plan a new, updated or remodeled bathroom, first work out your ideas on paper. You will discover your priorities and limitations, and will feel more confident about how to proceed. A host of factors can influence the success of the project. Unless you have a complete plan of what you want to achieve, you could end up with a hodge-podge of shortcuts and compromises.

Money, of course, is one important consideration. What will it cost to have the kind of bathroom you now visualize? What is the best way to use all available space? Will the new bath have all the conveniences the family needs? Bathroom planning calls for relatively permanent choices. Unlike tables and chairs, fixtures can't be moved around to give the room a new look.

The best way to protect your investment and to have the kind of bathroom you envision is to set up a comprehensive planning guide, including a project checklist of materials, costs and scheduling. A three-phase guideline like the one below will help make the work flow more smoothly. This also will avoid unpleasant surprises when all the bills come in.

Phase One of the checklist should cover the kinds of materials to be used, and the cost for each in quantity and quality. This list should include materials for covering walls, floors, ceilings, as well as identification and prices for new faucets, vanity tops or window treatments.

Phase Two deals with all possible major alterations, such as structural changes, built-in closets or shelf systems, new plumbing lines and fixtures such as a tub, shower, toilet or bidet.

Phase Three pulls the whole project together. You can see total costs and can judge how long the job will take. It will help you figure out how much outside help you are likely to need and enable you to compute the labor costs.

The checklist should be specific about equipment and supplies. If you need to buy a caulking gun, that should be included. List the costs of paint and brushes, likewise spackle, adhesives, paper, carpeting, tiles — all materials. Everything must be included in the budget. All materials, even small ones, should be on hand in ample supply before the work begins. Stopping in the middle of a job to buy more screws or paint becomes more than just a bother, it causes delays which are expensive.

You will benefit further from a checklist as you shop for information and prices. You will discover what is new in bath design and decorating, from light switches to bathtubs. More new concepts exist for bathrooms than ever before. You should make the most of unusual room features or interesting design touches which add style but not excessive cost. Bathroom projects rarely are exactly alike. Each should reflect individual and

While the bathroom was structurally sound, it had no style except for color coordination.

A dramatic bath was created in the remodeling with few structural changes. An enlarged window as installed; a shampoo niche cut into the wall; new fixtures installed. Ceramic tile and mirrored ceiling, combine with towels, rug and shower curtain to make the room look large and bright.

family needs and wants. Put your ideas to work through a checklist similar to the one below.

PROJECT CHECKLIST
Phase One
A. Walls will be: Painted_____
Papered_____Tiled _____
Paneled_____Mirrored _____
Other_____
Areas in square feet for each treatment

_____
Amounts of materials needed _____
Total cost of the above_____
Cost of outside labor _____
    Total Cost_____

B. Ceiling will be: Painted_____
Papered_____Other_____
Area in square feet to be covered _____
Amount of material required_____
Cost of material _____
Cost of outside labor _____
    Total cost _____

C. Floor will be: Tiled _____
Carpeted_____Other _____
Area in square feet to be covered _____
Amount of material needed _____
Cost of material _____
Cost of outside help _____
    Total Cost_____

D. Related equipment and materials (include all brushes, paint, paper, adhesives, spackle, plaster, drop cloths, tools and equipment you have to buy or rent)
    Total cost_____

E. Accessories and cost of each:
Shower curtain_____Window shades, curtains, or shutters _____
New faucets _____
New tub-shower controls_____
New vanity_____Vanity top _____
New lavatory_____Towel bars_____
Dispensers _____
Seat cover_____Shelves_____
Towels_____Face cloths _____
Wastebaskets, etc. _____
    Total cost_____

Phase Two
A. Major alterations will include:
New tub_____New shower_____
New toilet_____Bidet_____
Heated towel racks_____
New heating_____New venting_____
New lavatory_____
New (structural) Walls _____
Ceiling_____Floor_____
Built-in closets _____
Tiling_____
Other structural work _____
New lighting _____
Total fixture and material costs _____
Cost of outside help _____
    Total cost_____

Phase Three
A. Time estimates include:
Number of hours of your own time and/or unpaid helper to complete steps you will undertake in Phases One and Two_____
(break down by job) _____

_____
    Total hours_____

B. Written contracts for outside help must include: Itemized list of all materials, cost for each_____Labor costs _____
Payment terms; list dates _____.
Agreed date for starting actual work _____Agreed date for completion of all work _____
    Total cost _____

C. Expected final total of all costs for the project _____

THE DECORATIVE SOLUTION

Redecorating is the simplest way to enliven an age-worn bathroom. A fresh coat of paint, or a new shower curtain and towels, can suffice — for those on modest budgets. With more dollars, you can add luxury with wall-to-wall carpeting. Choose a color that picks up the dominant hue in new accessories.

Other quick refreshers are new towel bars and soap holders, interesting switch-

The needs of the wheelchair bound are met here. Turn-around space is left at the sides of the counter. A corner toilet takes up little floor space and permits grab-bars on both sides. The sink height allows the wheelchair under it. Tilted mirrors provide an unobstructed reflection.

plates, or a new window shade. Bath shops contain many provocative ideas and objects. Do not buy on impulse. Browse and fix in your mind the colors and materials most likely to suit your needs and budget. Work out a decorating plan geared to the problems you want to solve and the look you want to achieve. Follow the guidelines in Phase One of the checklist. No set rules should restrict you, because decor is a matter of personal taste. However, every problem bathroom has to be treated individually. Your general guideline will help you in planning.

The Current Situation

First, consider the existing fixtures. They may be outdated, but if they work properly you may not wish to change them. However, fixtures are an important part of any decorating scheme. The decor will be influenced subtantially if the fixtures are colored. Pastel or dark-toned fixtures and wall tiles will force you to follow their lead. All new colors should match large color areas or else blend with them compatibly.

Since you cannot take the fixtures with you when you shop, collect paint samples

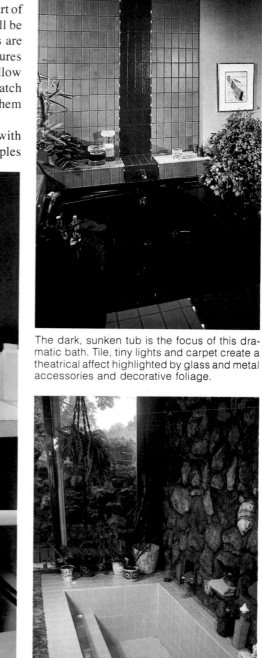

The dark, sunken tub is the focus of this dramatic bath. Tile, tiny lights and carpet create a theatrical affect highlighted by glass and metal accessories and decorative foliage.

This bath is for the handicapped but ambulatory person. An assist bar is provided at the toilet and a rolling chair at the sink. The single lever faucet can be operated with one hand. Storage is provided in open shelves and swing-out bins that are easier to open than drawers.

This sunken tub was created by an enterprising homeowner. He created the plans and laid the tile. He also built the garden wall.

Under-stairs half bath uses mirrors to give the impression of more space. Carpeting extends up the side of the stainless steel vanity. A large yellow light brightens an otherwise dark area.

A mirrored closet makes this well coordinated bath seem larger. The sheltered view can be enjoyed from the sunken tub, adding an indoor-outdoor feeling to the room.

and fabric swatches to make color comparisons at home. You will be surprised by how many different tones of blue or beige exist. Some are pink tinged, others are more grey or green. A near-miss in color value is equivalent to a ten-mile detour in an otherwise well-planned decorating route. Plan your color scheme well and accurately, before you buy.

On the other hand, white fixtures invite a bold use of color if that is your pleasure. Walls, floor, accessories can be light or dark, pale or vivid. Accents can contrast or blend with major color areas. However, an all-white bathroom can be spectacular with, for example, fluffy white wall-to-wall carpeting.

Style Starters

Immovable as they are, fixtures also can suggest whole decorating themes. A truly old fashioned bathroom with tub on legs, frumpy old basin and toilet becomes a challenge. You can combine it with 20th century flair or go all-out Victorian, a fashion trend still in vogue. Use burgundy red or deep blue paint for background color on walls and ceiling, or a paper patterned with big roses. Add bric-a-brac if there is room. Hang mirrors framed in shiny brass or curlicued wood. Cover the floor with a patterned rug over vinyl-asbestos tile in solid colors. Cover lighting fixtures with new shades of stained glass or silk-look fabrics.

Existing fixtures in the majority of homes and apartments have no particular style, are functional and efficient, yet neutral. This gives plenty of decorating latitude to go in any style direction you like — traditional or contemporary, using paint, wallpaper, floor coverings, and lighting. Once you decide about the major areas, carry out the basic theme with such items as curtains, towels, wastebaskets, or tissue boxes. You can find them in Early American styles as well as Oriental, French Provincial or crisp modern. The little touches bring a decorative theme into total harmony.

Attention Restorationists

The antique look is back in new fixtures. Since so many persons are restoring vintage houses, it makes sense to carry turn-of-the-century themes into the bath as well. Such attention to detail increases the aesthetic value of the house as well as its real worth. Available to you, then, are pedestal sinks, pull-chain toilets, tubs on ball-and-claw feet, even fittings and faucets in gleaming polished brass.

MINOR REMODELING

To provide extra space or greater convenience, a bathroom often needs more than fresh paint. Sometimes one new fixture may make the difference between an unsightly bath and one that is neat and attractive. A new vanity top and base cabinet might also be all that is necessary, since it will look better than the old wall-hung sink, be easier to clean, and provide extra storage space as well.

If a loud, out-of-date toilet creates a problem, a qualified plumber can replace it with a new one in four to six hours. (Or see Chapter 8 for how to do it yourself.)

New faucets also can make a difference, especially the dripless washerless ones. Manufacturers now make them for do-it-yourselfers.

Packages and Kits

If tub or shower needs overhauling, look into the ready-to-assemble prepackaged systems. Kits contain wall surrounds of marble-like acrylic or preshaped fiberglass panels. Other kinds of wall-surround kits include: square panels or pregrouted ceramic tiles; thin sheets of paneling coated with tough plastics that are impervious to water; coated plywood paneling in wood tones and colors that withstand moisture and heat. You will find these materials, and the supplies for installing them, in home centers or at building supply dealers, or from mail order firms such as Sears and J C Penney. Collect brochures and leaflets about the latest innovations. Study floor displays for new ideas and decorative effects.

Calling in the Plumber

Unless you have had considerable previous experience with plumbing you may wish to call in a professional for any job requiring removal of large fixtures and connection of complicated new ones. Keep in mind, too, that old drains and lines inside walls and floor may need to be replaced. If so and you have the financing, do it. Otherwise, you may find your new decor spoiled shortly, patching up damage to the new remodeling job.

Include in your remodeling budget the plumber's fees as well as cost for the new valves, pipe, connectors. Get at least two,

This sunlit bath is done in beige and white. The square lines of the large tub and the storage unit are softened by carpeting. The sheltered courtyard offers sunbathing privacy.

and preferably three, written estimates for any project, large or small. Make sure the estimate and written contract contain a provision for taking the old fixtures off your property, not just out of the house.

MAJOR REVISIONS

Sometimes an old bathroom becomes intolerable. Fixtures are stained, ugly, and not working properly. Walls, floor, ceiling and lighting seem hopeless, and the spatial arrangement inconvenient. The problem may be one of these, or several. A major overhaul may be the only solution.

In such a case, you might consider calling in an architect, designer, or remodeling contractor to handle the whole job. Their fees must be added to the costs of materials and supplies, but for many homeowners — who prefer not to cope with the work — it's money that must be

spent. Again, get several written estimates, have a written contract, and a time schedule with dates for starting and completing the work.

Above all, compare fixtures and materials. Learn what the items on your checklist will cost. The better informed you are about prices, the better you can control the cost of your project.

Bathroom fixtures are priced like most durable goods. Quality and style vary according to cost — high, medium, or low. Take advantage of any price break you can. Some building and plumbing suppliers buy up odd-lots from wholesalers and manufacturers. These are not seconds or damaged goods. Usually they are overruns or discontinued styles or colors. Look over the discount stock. You might find a good buy. Naturally, nothing is a bargain if you can't use it once you get it home. To be sure a new fixture will fit existing connections, measure the old and the new, inside and outside. Or, check with your plumber before you buy. He may have to see the fixture himself, and may charge for this time. On the other hand, he may be able to judge simply by having the manufacturer's name and model number.

EXTRA SMALL SPACES

Powder rooms and extra-small baths can be tucked into surprisingly small spaces. All you need is a minimum of 16 square feet for an attractive powder room. To visualize how tiny such a dimension really is, consider that a room 4 by 4 feet is adequate for two fixtures. Or how about this: a space that is one yardstick wide and two yardsticks long — 3 by 6 feet, or 18

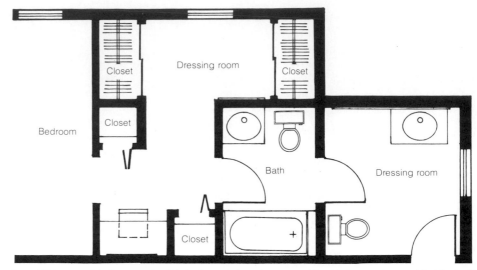

An addition provided space for this bath and dressing room. Closet storage is provided for both clothing and linens. The double, compartmented bathroom is accessible from the bedroom and the back of the house. The back portion also serves as a general powder room.

An antique Victorian washstand was converted into a vanity for a modern bath by the owner/designer. The heavy wood cabinet and choice of accessories give the room a masculine look.

This view of another compartment of the same bathroom shows a modern sink in a style and color compatible with the strong colors of the walls and the Victorian style of the room.

square feet — is sufficient for a powder room under a stairway.

Many old homes, for example, have a back stairway inside the house. Because such structures usually have high ceilings, often enough space exists under the stair for one or more compartments — a 3 by 6 foot powder room, a compact laundry center — or at the lowest part of the slope, a pantry or a closet for boots and rainwear.

Once you and your plumber have determined that a small bath or powder room in a new location is technically and economically feasible, you can find fixtures designed specifically for small spaces.

Shower stalls in enamel-finish steel or seamless plastics are available in 32 by 32 inch sizes as well as 36 by 36 inches. Larger dimensions include one-piece units that are just 36 inches deep (front to back) and 48 inches or 60 inches wide (side to side).

Tubs in small sizes are less easy to find, though most well-known manufacturers do produce one or two models for restricted spaces. Such tubs generally have two basic configurations: a short rectangle 42 inches long, 34 inches wide, and 14 inches high (the Standish by Kohler); and an in-corner square-looking tub with a bathing well set diagonally, such as American Standard's Restal tub that is only 39 inches by 38 inches. Plumbers, architects, and designers are likely to know of other sources for tubs of unusual shape and design.

Toilets generally have to be designed within certain limits to conform to the human anatomy. However, all makers now have low-profile compact models which take up less space than the conventional designs of 10 to 15 years ago. The new one-piece designs with unobtrusive tanks are especially well suited for spaces with low or sloped ceilings.

Lavatories offer the most flexibility for creating attractive baths in small rooms. Vanity base cabinets 30 inches high, 18 inches wide and just 16 inches deep (front to back) are available ready-made, in a wide variety of traditional and contemporary styles. Exquisitely designed one-piece pedestal washbowls are the best to use when two fixtures must be placed close to each other. Small washbasins for base cabinet or countertop installation are also readily available. American Stan-

This small basin is useful in areas with limited space. The unit is 21 by 13 inches and self-rimming for easy installation in a countertop as shallow as 15 inches from front to back.

This attractive oval basin is also designed for use in small areas. It can be set into a countertop only 19 by 22 inches. High-style faucets add visual interest.

This small sink is identical to one shown above except for color and faucet style. The brushed gold-tone fixtures give a richer, heavier look to the installation.

The angled mirrors in this bath create the illusion of greater space than exists. The super-graphic over the tub is created with ceramic tile. A project such as this takes careful planning and tile setting, but it is not beyond the skill of the homeowner.

dard's Spacelyn lavatory measures 20 inches side to side, and 12 inches front to back. Kohler's Boutique is 21 inches by 13 inches; their Farmington is just 19¼ inches by 16¼ inches.

Visual Dimensions

Mirror Use. Decorating tricks can give small bathrooms the illusion of more space. Mirrored walls and ceilings are the most effective. The amount of space to be covered may determine what you will use, big sheets of plate glass mirror or easy-to-handle lightweight tiles. Plate is best, and safer to handle, for doors, walls above lavatory cabinet or countertop. Mirrored tiles, on the other hand, can be installed over larger areas like wall-to-wall, floor-to-ceiling. For crisp, clear brilliance, use plain mirror tiles. If you

prefer a more subtle gleam, select tiles that are etched, decorated, or smoke-toned.

You can find mirrored tiles in mail order catalogs, at home centers, and building supply dealers. Most are sold for DIY installation and come prepackaged. Some have peel-and-stick adhesive backings, others need special adhesives. Read the instruction sheets before you buy in order to determine if any extra work will be needed to prepare the walls for mirroring. Adhesive applications need a smooth, firm surface similar to preparation required for paint; metal or plastic anchor clips (for holding big plate glass mirror) need to be firmly anchored in plaster, masonry, or wood studs.

Texture and Pattern. You can add greater interest to a small-space bath with

a pattern or texture on one wall and a complementary solid color on the others. Walls of the same pattern and hue seem to move closer together, causing the space to appear smaller. This holds true whether the wallcovering is paint, paper, or paneling. Pale colors and subtle patterns make a space seem more open than do dark colors and strong patterns. However, if you want the space to feel cozy and enclosed, use strong pattern and vivid color on all four walls and the ceiling. Some people prefer the visual and decorative impact of a small bath or powder room bursting with vivid imagery.

Storage. Storage inside small baths is as essential as it is in conventional ones. Often, it is even more crucial since many powder rooms are located some distance from linen closets or other accessible storage areas. Your best bets are a vanity base cabinet, modular wallhung shelf systems, or in-wall shelves and cabinets built between the existing studs. (See Chapter 7, section on "In-wall Storage").

Floor Plans

The floor plan for a small bath must be carefully thought out. To make the most of the space you have, place the fixtures for the best plumbing connections and use, and for easy care and maintenance as well. Often one aspect receives too much emphasis, to the detriment of the other. You might save money on labor and materials, for example, with the fixtures grouped closely together on one wall. But if this arrangement makes the room uncomfortable, inconvenient, or almost impossible to clean, it will be less valuable to you in the long run. Shown are some powder room floor plans suitable for small spaces.

COMPARTMENTING THE BATH

A popular design concept divides the bathroom into compartments or zones of privacy. Instead of a single room that must be shared by members of the family one at a time, compartmenting makes the bath areas available to more persons at the same time.

In theory, such zoning makes good sense in convenience and luxury. Keep in mind, however, that compartmenting requires more space and construction materials than does the average bathroom. It requires more accesses to the different zones. If you plan to enlarge your home to include a privacy-zoned bath in the master suite, for example, place compartments and fixtures according to sensible traffic flow. Take into account the entrance and exit patterns. In large family homes, a centrally located room might be plumbed and compartmented, with each zone having its own entrance. True privacy zoning may involve new construction or extensive remodeling that only a reliable contractor or an experienced do-it-yourselfer could do.

Avoid being sold on the concept of compartmenting an existing bath as simply a fashionable thing to do, especially if there can be only one entrance into it. A toilet enclosed by walls or partitions is a compartment, but it does not offer the privacy zoning you may be expecting. In addition, most such spaces are difficult to

Half Baths

Master Baths

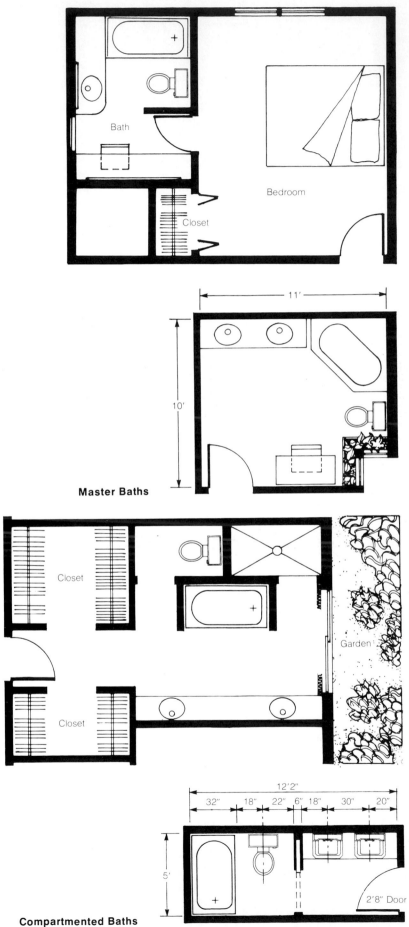

Master Baths

Compartmented Baths

clean. If your remodeling or new building plans include privacy zoning, allocate enough space in each compartment so fixtures can be repaired with ease whenever necessary. Take into account how you will clean the areas with brushes, mops, or vacuuming equipment, which is often ignored in planning. The ultimate in privacy zoning has compartments that are free of such things as noise, vapor or odor.

Good privacy zoning will look like the representative plans given here. You will notice that each provides for separate entrances to the compartments, and aims for compact arrangement of plumbing lines.

Three-Zone Privacy. One of the best arrangements is the T-plan. Each zone has its own entrance, and the generous-sized compartments are easy to clean. Plumbing lines radiate from one wall.

Three-Zone Deluxe. Many variations of the T-plan are possible, depending upon the amount of space available.

Two-Zone Privacy. A rectangular plan has two-wall plumbing. Emphasized are separate entrances, a center divider door (sliding), and a generous-sized grooming table in one compartment.

Full-Zone Privacy. Two baths back-to-back share one plumbing wall.

Modified Two-Zone. This plan has one entrance, with an interior privacy door. To achieve back-to-back plumbing, however, tub and toilet are set together. The unused areas are for storage.

Example of poor compartment planning. Two privacy zones have been forced into a small space. Tub and toilet are too close together. Whichever way the door swings, it will be awkward to maneuver around. A redeeming feature is the one-wall plumbing arrangement, which saves time and labor costs.

FLOOR PLANS FOR NEW CONSTRUCTION

The most complete bathroom project is, of course, a new one. This offers the best opportunity to add the designed space, comfort, and beauty. Some of the exciting features a new bath can incorporate are a steam room, sauna, greenhouse, dressing room, exercise room, wooden soaking tub, sunken tub, pool-sized spa tub, or a whirlpool bath. As you study the following pages you will see how to coordinate and integrate these unusual possibilities.

Once you have settled upon the kind of

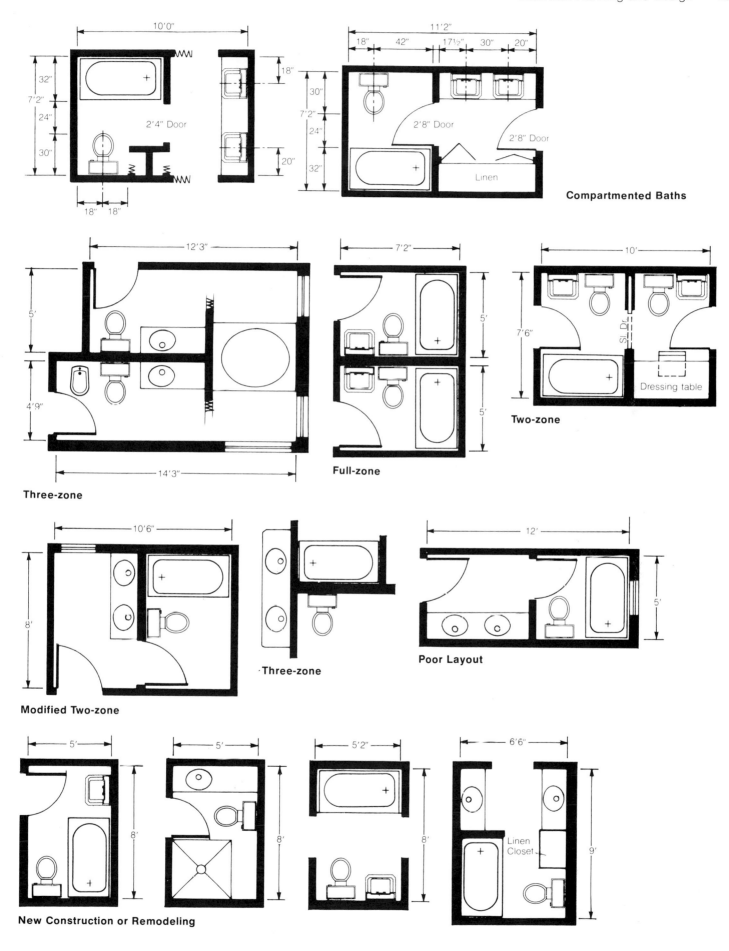

Compartmented Baths

Three-zone

Full-zone

Two-zone

Modified Two-zone

Three-zone

Poor Layout

New Construction or Remodeling

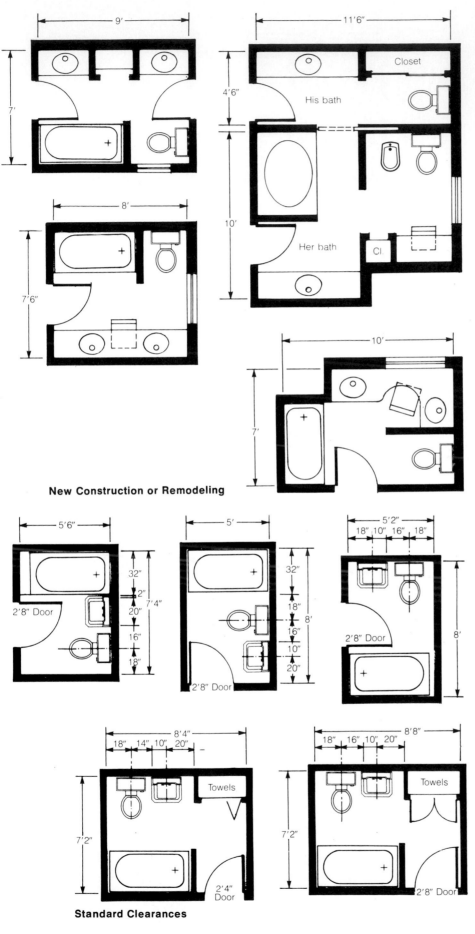

New Construction or Remodeling

Standard Clearances

bath you want, and the amenities it will have, select a floor plan that makes the best use of space and plumbing techniques. Take into account how best to situate the new bath for family use, as well as the room's relationship to the rest of the house. Shown are some popular plans you will find helpful. They are suggestions, to be used as starting points rather than as rules to be slavishly followed. From these suggestions you can develop your own plans to show to contractors or suppliers. Remodelers also will find these plans workable for most renovating projects. (Note: Each square in a plan represents one square foot. These plans are adapted from those provided courtesy of American Standard.)

Layout Guidelines

When space is limited, select a small tub with a finished end; it needs no third wall enclosure. If the door must swing inward, place it opposite the fixture that has the least amount of protrusion, usually the lavatory.

Receptor-tubs offer spatial choices. They are low, and fit into space not much bigger than that needed by a shower stall (about 39 by 38 inches). Free space can than be used for storage shelves and cabinets.

For a bath between two rooms, ample-walk through space should be provided. Doors should be hinged to open outward to simplify access.

Try to avoid placing the tub under a window unless you plan a bath-garden combination (discussed in a following section). This plan makes better use of space in a small narrow bathroom.

If you have any extra space, you can have twin but separate lavatories (with extra storage space), plus a linen closet.

Twin lavatories can be arranged to permit the addition of a dressing table between the base cabinets. If possible, hinge door to swing outward.

A modified compartment plan will allow the toilet and bidet to be enclosed, with walls and sliding or double swing-out doors.

Twin vanities can be separated by a floor-to-ceiling linen closet, with access to the bathroom from rooms on each side.

One possible arrangement for twin lavatories offers a curved in-corner dressing table. The toilet area can be compartmented off if desired.

Large-scale bathrooms give opportunities for his and her bathrooms, with specialized privacy. The toilet and bidet areas can be enclosed. A pool-sized tub can be shared. In one such design shown the pool-sized tub has been enclosed by sliding doors.

A GARDEN VIEW

While privacy dominates bathroom design, a view into a garden has appeal. To get the simplest and least expensive garden inside the bath, install a greenhouse in an existing window. Small prefabricated types you can install yourself. You may also consider building your own shallow-projection window greenhouse of wood and acrylic panels from mail order plans like the one adapted here from a Stanley Tools project.

More ambitious projects include large greenhouse add-ons fastened to an existing exterior wall. Entry from the bathroom into the new solarium could be through a sliding glass door. If you have all, or a large section of the bathroom wall removed, the attached greenhouse then becomes a room-extender, a walk-in mini jungle filled with trees and plants that thrive on warmth and high humidity.

Naturally, large greenhouse additions are for ground-level bathrooms or those having a sturdy structural projection on which to build, such as an adjacent terrace, porch roof, or one-story room.

Investigate local codes and regulations governing built-ons, especially rules concerning greenhouse glazing and framework. If the greenhouse, large or small, will be open to the room, carefully study the distributor's recommendations for making the unit watertight in your location.

In cold climates, heat loss may be countered with solar heat captured during the day, especially if the greenhouse has a southern exposure. During the night and on cloudy days, warmth can be supplied by supplemental heating. Look into the merits of double glazed windows as well. Initial costs may be offset through the long-range savings.

Another way to impede heat loss during winter months is with the new double-walled plastic insulating film that can be applied like wallpaper. Just peel off the film and rinse adhesive from the glazed surface. One brand cuts heat loss by 35 percent and reduces light by only 12 per-

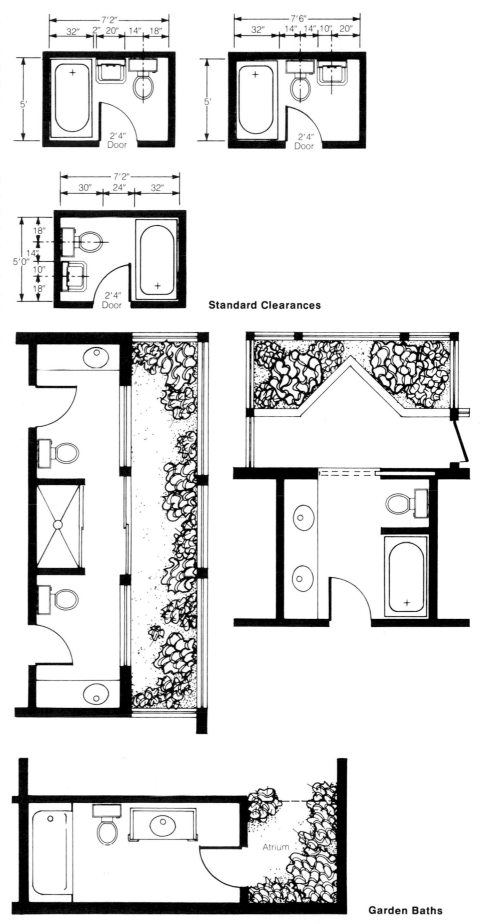

Standard Clearances

Garden Baths

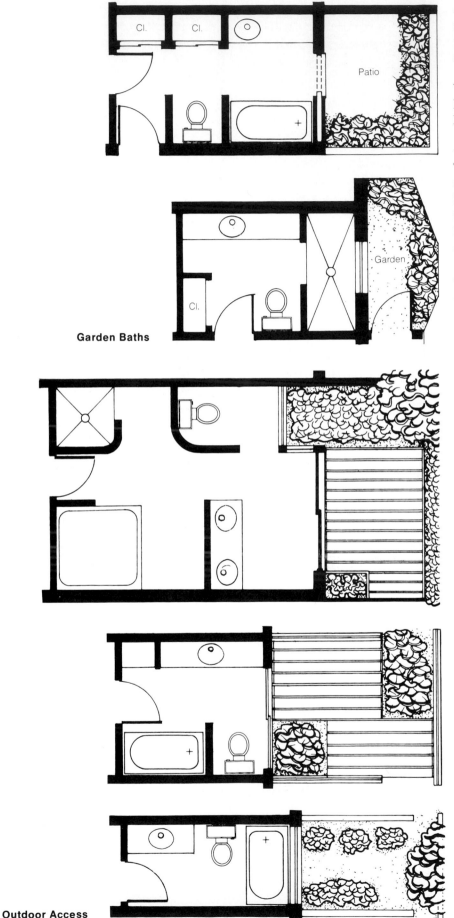

Garden Baths

Outdoor Access

cent, according to its manufacturer. For more information about greenhouses and insulating film, see the manufacturers addresses list in the appendices.

Double-walled Insulating Film. Write to Lord & Burnham, Division Burnham Corporation, 2 Main Street Irvington, New York 10533.

Window greenhouse. Stanley has developed plans for a window greenhouse. The company says you can install the shelf garden without removing double-hung windows. For a set of plans, write to: Stanley Tools Window Greenhouse New Britain, Conn. 06050. Include 25¢ for handling and postage.

The outdoors can be transported indoors in a variety of ways. Here are some alternative plans from which to choose.

Adjacent porch or deck

A bathroom that opens directly onto a deck or patio is especially convenient. Sunbathers can refresh themselves in a shower that is only steps away. Family and guests can bathe and dress without having to stalk through the rest of the house to get to the bathroom. An end-wall of insulated glass increases the indoor-outdoor atmosphere and keeps the room filled with natural light. For privacy, cover the glass door and wall with narrow-slat louvered blinds, or use wavy glass for light without visibility.

Bath-Atrium Combination

A ground-level bath can be joined to an enclosed atrium for a high level of luxury. The court can be left open if you live in a warm climate; elsewhere, cover it with a sloped glazed roof or skylight. An interior wall and sliding door of glass keep the appearance of open space, yet keep the bath free from drafts.

If the atrium is tiled and fitted with a center floor drain it will be easy to keep clean by hosing. Nearby plants will benefit from frequent hosing and misting.

High Privacy

Take advantage of a sloped site by situating a tub and shower on one side of a glass-walled bath. Beyond there will be open air, sky, and (hopefully) a good view. The tub can be sunken fully or partially, depending on ground conditions, or it can be a standard floor-mounted one. Either way, have its rim level with the lower edge of the glass wall.

Privacy Fencing

Almost any bathroom on an exterior wall has potential for a garden view. The object is to visually open the room to lawn or deck that is surrounded by an attractive 8 foot privacy fence. This suits homes and lots of any size or shape, and is one that the experienced amateur home remodeler can handle. Suppliers of quality lumber for fences and decks have excellent idea sheets and plan booklets for do-it-yourselfers. So do manufacturers of ready-to-install windows and doors. A few of these plans are given in Appendix A.

Before you become seriously involved in a bath-garden project, check out local codes concerning enclosures, setbacks, electrical wiring and related regulations.

For this type of outdoor building, plan on using pretreated lumber, galvanized postcaps and hangers, and other exterior hardware. Concentrate on obtaining high-quality glass panels and doors, with tight seals around the frames. Keep finishes and designs in mind, also. Close neighbors will see the outside of your garden enclosure; it should be attractive to them as the interior is to you.

MEASUREMENT GUIDELINES

Bathroom fixtures vary in size. Tubs can be big enough to hold two or more people. In modern low-line toilets, tanks have nearly disappeared. Since distances between fixtures and walls affect your comfort, room arrangement, and ease of maintenance, consider these standard dimensions. Take them into account as you plan your new bath and when you shop for furnishings.

Lavatory

The standard dimensions of a vanity base cabinet are 30 inches high, 30 inches wide, and 20 inches deep. Tops that are sold separately usually increase the height to 31 inches. Because this is too low for many adults some manufacturers have created "back-saver" models that are 34½ inches high.

Countertop lavatories can be installed at any height you prefer since they are custom installations. The average top should be 20 to 24 inches deep (front to back) to accommodate standard lavatory bowls. However, since there has been recent demand for smaller fixtures, you can find lavatories as narrow as 16 inches.

Allow at least 6 inches of space be-

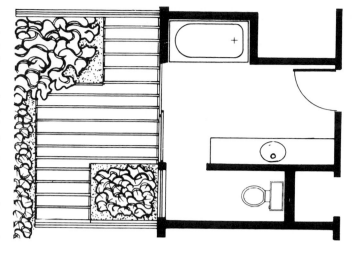

Outdoor Access

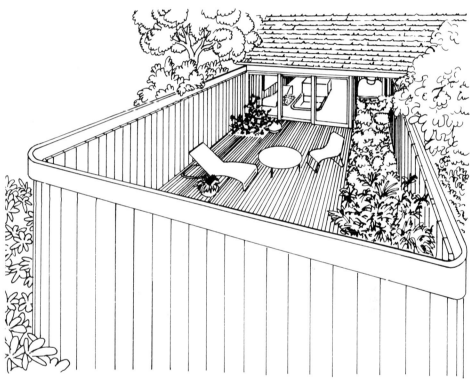

Privacy Fencing

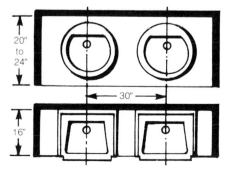

Standard Dimensions

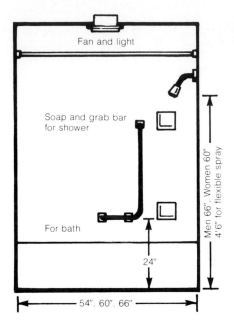

tween an end wall and the edge of the lavatory, otherwise your elbows will bump the wall when you move about.

Standard towel rack lengths are: 18 inches for hand towels; 24 inches for bath towels.

The top of the mirror or medicine cabinet is 72 inches to 78 inches from the floor. This allows 8 inches clearance between cabinet bottom and lavatory top.

Twin lavatories, whether in a counter-top or vanity base cabinet, should be at least 30 inches apart.

Standard placement for the showerhead is 66 inches above floor level for men, and 60 inches for women. Since this may not please everyone, you may have to compromise. You might settle on a point half-way between the two standards, or play it safe with a flexible coil and showerhead that can be adjusted. The soap dish for a tub should be 24 inches above floor level, and at 54 inches for a shower.

A safety grab bar (install one if at all possible) should be 24 inches above floor level for the bath, and 56 to 60 inches for shower. A grab bar can be L-shaped as shown or long and straight mounted on a downward slant from shower to tub.

Shower curtain rods usually are placed 78 inches above floor level; however, for people of medium height or less, 74 inches would be more comfortable.

Toilet

In most installations, the toilet tank will be one inch from the wall. How far the entire unit will project from the wall varies according to style and make. Some are more elongated than others, so take this into account if space is a problem. The suggested minimum distance between the fixture and the side walls, or to another fixture, is 15 inches on each side, measuring from the center of the bowl. There should be no less than 18 inches between front edge of toilet and a facing wall (to allow for knee room).

EXTRA SMALL SPACES

Powder rooms and extra-small baths can be tucked into surprisingly small spaces. All you need is a minimum of 16 square feet for an attractive powder room. To visualize how tiny such a dimension really is, consider that a room 4 by 4 feet is adequate for two fixtures. Or how about this: a space that is one yardstick wide and two yardsticks long — 3 by 6 feet, or 18 square feet — is sufficient for a powder room under a stairway.

Many old homes, for example, have a back stairway inside the house. Because such structures usually have high ceilings, often enough space exists under the stair for one or more compartments — a 3 by 6 foot powder room, a compact laundry center — or at the lowest part of the slope, a pantry or a closet for boots and rainwear.

Once you and your plumber have determined that a small bath or powder room in a new location is technically and economically feasible, you can find fixtures designed specifically for small spaces.

Shower stalls in enamel-finish steel or seamless plastics are available in 32 by 32 inch sizes as well as 36 by 36 inches. Larger dimensions include one-piece units that are just 36 inches deep (front to back) and 48 inches or 60 inches wide (side to side).

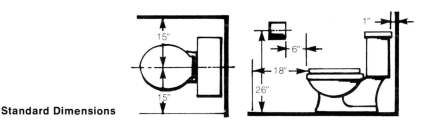

Standard Dimensions

2 The Bathroom Plumbing System

The bathroom plumbing often seems mysterious to homeowners because components are hidden in walls and floors. The only visible signs of your bathroom's plumbing system are at the bathroom fixtures. However, a complex water supply system feeds into these points from the city (or well) water system.

WATER SUPPLY

The water supply enters a house either from a city main or, in rural and some suburban areas, from a line from a well. If the supply is from a city main, the water first passes through a meter valve, then a water meter and then a stop valve. It is the stop valve — also called "main water shutoff" and similar names — that you would shut off when water to the house must be stopped for a repair. In colder parts of the country the water meter will be in the basement or crawl space, while in more moderate climates the meter may be in a "dry well" out in the yard.

Hot and Cold Water Lines

Shortly after the main supply line enters a house it splits into two lines. One runs to the hot water tank, while the other is routed directly to the cold water faucets in the various sinks and basins, and for the toilets. If there is a water softener required because the water is very hard, one line will run to it, and from it to the hot water tank. In this setup only the hot water will be softened, while all cold water will remain hard. Softened, treated water is generally bland and does not make good coffee, tea or other beverages. Running treated water out through an outside faucet to sprinkle a lawn or garden can also be expensive.

If you do not mind your plumbing system becoming somewhat complicated, you can provide untreated water to the kitchen sink and perhaps a bar, while supplying softened water — both hot and cold — to the bathroom, the dishwasher and the laundry room.

Main water shutoff valves are located near or next to the water meter, usually in the basement or a heated crawl space. Or the water may be turned off at the cold water inlet on the gas or electric water heater.

Pipe Layout

The water lines that run vertically — from the basement or crawl space to the first and second floor, for example — are called risers. Additional risers function as air chambers, although these are not found in every system. These are vertical lengths of pipe fitted into the walls behind fixtures. Air in these vertical chambers acts similar to shock absorbers when the water is turned off suddenly. With air chambers, instead of banging and shaking pipes when the water pressure is suddenly stopped, the piping pushes the pressure into the air chamber where the air compresses and absorbs the water hammer. Eliminating the water hammer not only makes for a quiet and peaceful house, it also prevents damage to the piping. Constant hammering on a joint can cause it to leak, and that same hammering can cause leaking at a faucet.

In order to use the shortest possible water lines and therefore assure the most economical installation — as well as a

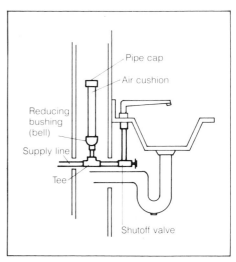

Air chambers to eliminate water hammer generally are hidden inside walls when the plumbing is installed. The air chamber is a vertical length of pipe larger than the line to the fixture, which traps air to provide a shock-absorbing cushion.

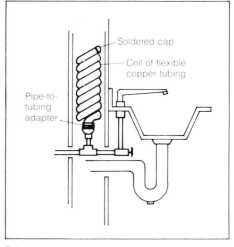

This alternate style of air chamber is a coil of copper tubing positioned vertically above the supply line to the fixture. As well as containing air to provide cushion, the coil flexes like a spring to further absorb shock of water hammer. This, or any other type of air chamber, can be installed in the cabinet below to avoid cutting into the wall.

minimum of line friction — fixtures (sinks, vanities, bathtubs, toilets) should be located as close together as possible. This is not always possible when adding a new bathroom some distance from existing bathrooms or the kitchen. But the

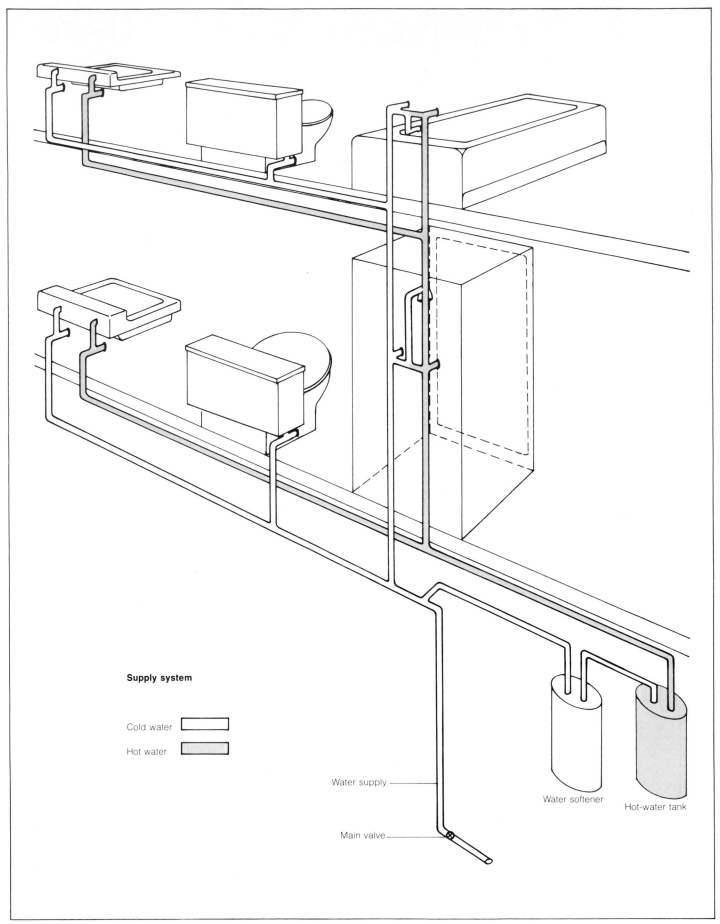

Supply system

Cold water

Hot water

Water supply

Main valve

Water softener

Hot-water tank

Here is a diagram of a typical water supply system for a two-story house with basement. It shows how water enters through main valve, is routed to the hot water tank and to various fixtures.

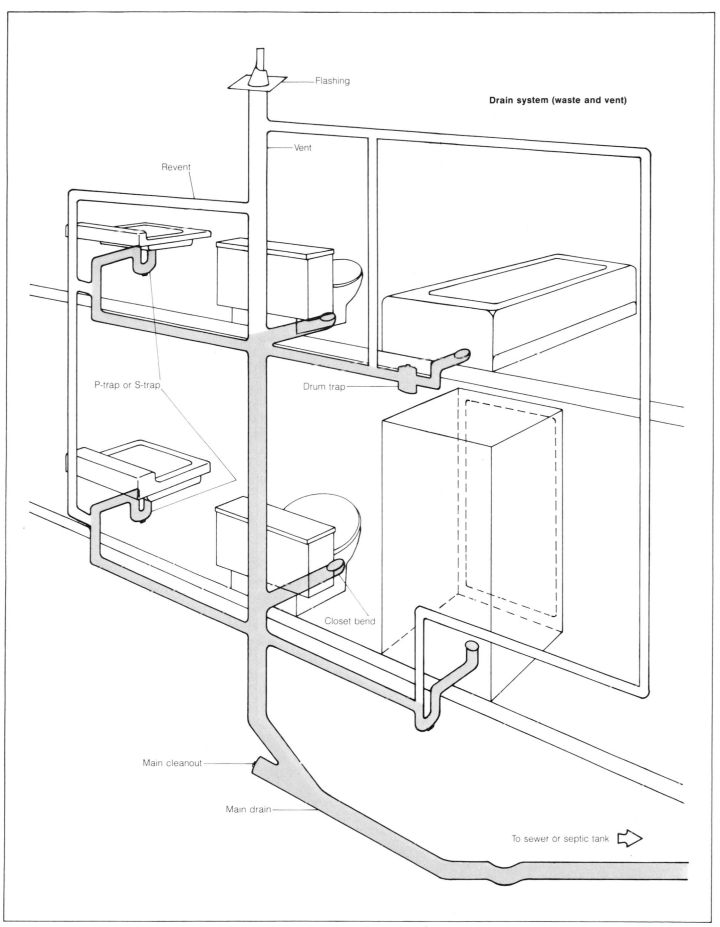

Flashing

Drain system (waste and vent)

Vent

Revent

P-trap or S-trap

Drum trap

Closet bend

Main cleanout

Main drain

To sewer or septic tank ⇨

The drain system includes waste and vent lines. Note that toilets must drain directly into main stack, which is generally 3 or 4 inches in diameter, while sinks and vanities can drain into smaller waste lines that run to the main stack.

ideal situation is to have rooms with fixtures back-to-back, so the plumbing in one wall supplies both rooms. Such an arrangement also makes it possible for one main drain line to handle the waste water from both rooms.

Note that toilets must empty directly into a main drain line, while bathtubs, basins and other fixtures can drain indirectly through smaller lines. Usually these smaller lines are 1½ or 2-inch pipes. They empty into a much larger vertical drain line which is called a "stack." This will be a line that measure 3, 3½, 4 inches or larger, and it will run vertically from the basement or crawl space right up through the roof. Although the vertical stack may be plastic, rigid copper tubing or cast iron soil pipe, the line that enters the ground and empties into the city sewer system, or into a septic tank in the case of a private system, will be cast iron. The main reason for this is that cast iron pipe is stronger than other types and so resists crushing and soil pressures.

Traps

All fixtures that drain into the stack are fitted with traps. These traps consist of curved sections of piping under each fixture so that there is always a water seal to keep out sewer gases, which can be unhealthy as well as causing very unpleasant odors. The water seal also discourages strange creatures from crawling into a fixture from the sewer line. You will see the chromeplated traps in the shape of a "P" or a "J" or even an "S". Toilets have a built-in trap. Bathtubs generally will have a "drum trap," which will be located under the floor beneath the tub. It has a screw-on cover that must be removed when the trap needs to be cleaned.

Vents

The main drain line will not only have a trap in it just before it leaves the building, it will also have a vent stack.

The vent stack allows atmospheric pressure into the drains, which assures that water drains easily with no partial vacuum in any of the lines. When you hear a "glug-glug" in a drain line, it generally means the stack or the drain line is plugged and atmospheric pressure is not flowing into the vent behind the dropping water.

The opening in the vent on the roof lets dangerous sewer gases escape into the air,

well above any people; if you have ever worked on a roof and come close to a vent, you know what a stench is expelled from it.

The venting also prevents draining water from backing up into a fixture below it that also is draining. If you note that a downstairs basin has water backing up into it when a basin is draining upstairs, you can be pretty sure the vent stack is plugged — it is not unheard of to have a bird build a nest on top of a stack.

At the lower end of every vent stack there is a cleanout. This is in the form of a plug that unscrews. If you cannot clean the drain from a fixture, very often you can get at it from below by running a snake up from the cleanout to the stoppage. These cleanout plugs do tend to rust shut, which makes them difficult to open. We will describe the method to free these plugs in a later chapter.

Besides the main vent there also are "revents." The drain line from a sink or basin will run directly to the main vent, but there will be a smaller vent that runs up from the fixture, then across to the main vent. Such an arrangement assures that air is pulled into the drain line as the waste water runs out the drain. This keeps the water seal in the trap from being siphoned out thus creating a health hazard.

Valves

There are three main types of valves used in the water supply system of a house: globe, gate and check. There also are variations of these valves, as will be explained. The majority of the valves found in the bathroom are globe valves.

The globe valve is used to shut off the water to fixtures and appliances, and is also the type used for the meter valve and main shut-off valve. Globe valves are found where the water supply needs to be reduced or controlled, as in the case of individual vanity, tub and shower valves. Single-level faucets are variations of the globe valve. Note in the drawing that a globe valve does offer considerable resistance to water flow, as the water must make two right-angle turns when it passes through the valve — this is why you should never install a smaller valve than can be handled by the piping.

Gate valves are not often found in bathroom plumbing because they only function fully open or fully closed. If a valve is

partially opened, it will vibrate. In most cases, the vibration will cause the valve to leak. Check valves, which allow water to flow in only one direction, are used occasionally. If the pressure in your hot and cold supply lines is unequal, install check valves and there will be no chance of hot and cold water mixing when only one faucet is turned on.

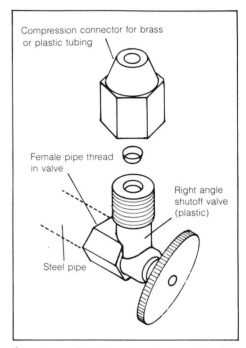

One type of right-angle plastic valve has female pipe threads on the inlet, and a plastic compression fitting on the outlet side that goes to the fixture. In effect, the valve is a steel-to-plastic adapter.

Right-angle shut-off globe valve from Genova has pressure under the disk because of its configuration. It is used under sinks and toilets to shut off water to the fixture.

90° Globe valve

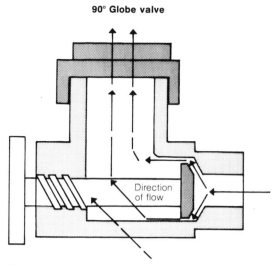

Direction of flow

A globe valve is used to control the flow of water. Note, however, that there are two 90-degree direction changes in flow of water, creating friction in the water flow. The valve should be installed so that water pressure is above the disk closure when the valve is closed.

Globe valve

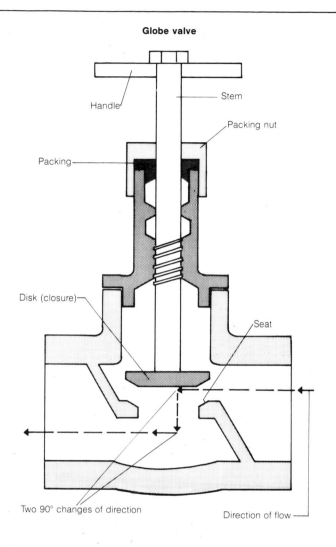

Handle

Stem

Packing nut

Packing

Disk (closure)

Seat

Two 90° changes of direction

Direction of flow

Check valve

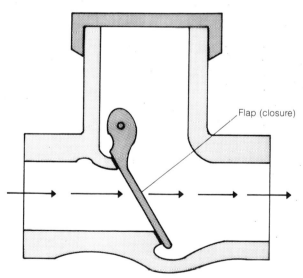

Flap (closure)

A check valve is used mostly on private water systems where it prevents backflow of water from house when pump shuts off. Check valves are also used in lines at the bottoms of wells (called a "foot valve" in that application) to prevent lines emptying when pump shuts off.

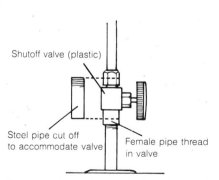

Shutoff valve (plastic)

Steel pipe cut off to accommodate valve

Female pipe thread in valve

If you do not want to use plastic valves and fittings in steel piping, you must cut out a section and fit in a shutoff valve. No union is required, as pipe-to-tubing adapter provides the same action as a union. A short pipe nipple in the valve allows use of existing pipe-to-tubing adapter, with female threads.

Shown are floor plan and final remodeling of a compartmented second-floor bath in a Victorian home. Originally a bedroom (opposite page, above) framing was added to support the plumbing. A pane of translucent glass in the wall separating the shower from the water closet area lets in light, but not image. The result is a sunny and spacious feeling throughout.

Perched 150 feet above the Pacific, this simply decorated bathroom incorporates the view as its most compelling feature.

3 Decorating Options for Walls, Floors, Ceilings

WALLS

Any wall finish chosen for use in a bathroom must resist moisture without drooping, peeling or warping. Although ceramic tile continues to be widely used in bathrooms, some paints, papers, paneling and solid woods make effective substitutes on walls and ceilings.

For homeowners who plan to add walls or partitions to a bathroom, a gypsum panel made especially for high-moisture areas can be used. It has a water-resistant gypsum core with chemically treated face and back paper. These 4 by 8 foot sheetrock panels are available at most lumber yards and building supply centers.

Paint

Paint is the most economical wall finish, provided you select the right paint for the job and for the condition of the existing wall. Paints differ in cost, durability, and the way in which they behave when subjected to water and to the steamy atmosphere of a bathroom.

A paint labeled washable may not be ideal for bathrooms. A flat no-sheen paint, for instance, will hold moisture in its blotterlike surface and, if scrubbed, will permanently change color. The color pigment in the compound sits unprotected on the surface. When you attempt to rub away water spots or steam streaks, some of the pigment comes off. Another point to remember is that scrubmarks will not show up prominently on pale pastels or white, but they will on dark and bright colors.

If you want medium or deep-toned walls, choose a paint having a certain amount of gloss. The most durable and moisture resistant are high-gloss enamels. They are the most expensive liquid coatings, but you can wipe them down with a soft dry cloth without damaging either the sheen or the color. Enameled surfaces reflect glare spots of light, which some people find annoying. From that point of view, semi-gloss paints are more

Paint is the least expensive material you can use to restyle a room. Here, the blue of the bathtub provides the accent color for the design. The color is repeated on all the moldings applied to the tub enclosure, shelves, closet doors, and walls.

comfortable to live with and are almost as tough and durable as the wet-look finishes.

Matte-finish or low-sheen paints are less durable and easy to clean than enamels but are worth considering, especially if a soft, warm-looking surface means more to you than being surrounded by hard-finish glossiness.

You also should be aware of the different kinds of paint and their characteristics. Knowing how compatible they are with each other, and how each is likely to affect the existing wall material, can save you money and time — and can prevent future problems.

The two major classifications of paint today are oil, or solvent-thinned paint, and water-thinned paint. Alkyd paints are solvent thinned; Latex paints are water thinned. The two are compatible with each other only under certain conditions.

Alkyd applied over Latex will bond well. Latex applied over an alkyd paint will not bond well.

A brick wall that would be intrusive if left in its original condition, is here painted white to minimize its texture.

Latex. Latex is popular because it can be thinned and brushes cleaned with water, is easy to use, and is odorless. All other types of paint can be applied over latex. It can also be used over fresh plaster patches, cinder block, or even unprimed wallboard.

Latex does not work well over paper-type wallcoverings since the water in it eventually soaks into the paper, causing it to pull away from the wall. If used over raw wood, the water will cause the fibers in the wood to swell and roughen the surface. The paint will then look gritty rather than smooth. Latex does not bond well to surfaces previously coated in alkyd paint, and it will peel off nonporous surfaces such as glass, ceramic tile, or metal. You can use it over high-gloss enamels only after you have roughened the gloss with chemicals or by sanding.

Caution for remodelers and restorers of houses 65 years or older. The surfaces in your house, and especially the ceilings, may have been coated originally with a compound known as calcimine. Though no longer seen or heard of these days, this primitive substance may still lurk under coats of old paint. The water in latex can soak through and reach the calcimine, causing it to blister and, in time, fall off. If you want to repaint with latex and are not sure if calcimine exists, brush or roll on a test patch of latex. If bubbles appear within fifteen minutes or less, calcimine is there. Use instead a solvent-thinned paint.

Alkyd paints. These almost odorless paints have a synthetic-resin base. However, alkyds must be thinned with solvents that, though low in odor, are nevertheless flammable and toxic. Make sure you have adequate ventilation in the room and that the solvents are not exposed to open flame or sparks. Manufacturers usually list on the paint label the kind of solvents to use for thinning and clean-up.

Alkyd paint does adhere well to bare wood, wallpaper, latex, and to the high-gloss enamels once the surface has been roughened by sanding. Alkyd paints do not adhere well to bare plaster, unprimed wallboard, or bare masonry.

Urethanes and epoxies. Recently developed in the plastic paint category, these require specially formulated solvents for thinning and clean-up. They are more elastic and resistant to abrasion, moisture, and household chemicals than any other interior coating; they are well suited for bathrooms.

They are more expensive than either latex or alkyd paints, but are so durable and easy to keep clean that they are worth the investment. Because these coatings dry very quickly, you have to work fast, otherwise the painted surface can look patchy. Experiment before you tackle any large-scale project.

Although epoxies and urethanes are listed together in the solvent-thinned classification, they have totally different uses for bathroom projects. The epoxies, for instance, are used for covering nonporous surfaces like old ceramic tile, porcelain fixtures, glass, or concrete. Epoxy will not adhere well to surfaces previously covered in latex, alkyd, or old oil paints.

Urethanes, on the other hand, do adhere well to old oil paint, alkyds, and latex, and can be used on bare wood as both primer, sealer, and final moisture-resistant finishes. The clear, colorless urethane varnishes are excellent for walls, woodwork, base and storage cabinets. They provide a tough, long-lasting water-resistant finish.

Metal primers and paints. You will find metal primers and paints worth investigating if you want to freshen the look of an old radiator, radiator cover, or metal wall hamper.

Rust causes paint to chip and crack off the basic metal. Before applying rust-inhibitors, scrape off all loose paint, scrub off rust with a metal-bristle brush, and sand the surface until the sharp edges of the old paint blend smoothly into the areas of bare metal. Apply metal primer, then paint.

Wallpapers and Coverings

Wallcovering describes both paper and other wall material more accurately. Untreated papers do not hold up in the steamy atmosphere of most bathrooms. The vinyls and some foil wallcoverings are better suited for bathroom decorating.

As to durability and washability, the

Wallpaper applied to cabinets and accented with painted lath augments the colors in the resilient flooring. Mirrored inset panels decorate the free-standing vanity.

A closet has been opened to become part of the bathroom and the handbasin fitted into an old chest. Decorative moldings on the chest pick up the plum-colored figure in the wallcovering.

Unusual wallpaper designs can add interest to a strictly utilitarian area. This whimsical pattern is created from old patent medicine advertisements. A pattern such as this is not difficult to hang if care is taken to begin on a true vertical.

even for "prepasted" materials. Others require application of adhesive. Brush it on with a wallpaper brush. In either case, make sure the adhesive is a mildew-resistant vinyl compound labeled or marked as suitable for use in high-moisture areas.

Natural Wood Walls

Solid wood 1x6 tongue and groove paneling of redwood or cedar creates walls and ceilings of unusual beauty. In addition to being highly durable, wood provides something extra — heat and sound insulation. These qualities alone make the initial cost of wood paneling worthwhile. You can produce interesting patterns by mixing wood grains, lumber dimensions, grades and texture of individual boards.

Some of the bathrooms shown indicate how the color variation of Sap-wood streaked Clear grade redwood can be used diagonally and horizontally on walls and base cabinet. Spaces and structural shapes within the room become design elements in and of themselves when color-streaks and wood grain are used as decorative tools.

In another bathroom design, 1x6 Clear All Heart redwood tongue and groove boards are applied vertically and horizontally. Texture and pattern derive from the rich mix of natural grains: arch-shaped growth rings on the vertical boards, rippled grain on the horizontal ones. The interior of the room becomes a sculptured entity when all surfaces are covered in wood boards arranged in planes and angles.

Knot-free Clear and Clear All Heart redwood lumber grades are best for bathroom paneling and should be specified Certified Kiln Dried for maximum stability. Individual boards are light-weight and easy to handle and machine. Clear All Heart redwood is cinnamon brown in color, naturally decay and insect-resistant. The Clear grade has lively sapwood streaks that are creamy in color.

A Lasting Finish. For redwood and cedar lumber around sinks, tubs, and showers, apply four to five coats of flat or satiny sheen polyurethane clear varnish. It will withstand waterspots, humid heat, and hard scrubbing. Clear alkyd resin varnishes also will produce tough, lasting finishes that are moisture-resistant. Wax applied over the final coat of varnish will produce a soft rich luster. You should use

fabric-backed vinyls are the most dependable and the easiest to work with if you plan to apply the wallcovering yourself. A good second choice is a vinyl-coated paper or a paper-backed vinyl. Unbacked vinyls are durable and washable, but are not as easy to apply as coverings supported by paper or fabric. (Fabric backings look like fine-grained cheesecloth.)

Metallic foils with fabric or paper backings are also serviceable, and are dramatically effective in bathrooms. They crease easily during handling, however, and are more difficult to work with than other coverings. With a little practice you can soon learn to use them. If you are doing the work, and have not used foils before, buy and extra roll to have on hand in case of mistakes.

In many bathrooms, the lower portions of the walls are covered with ceramic tile, so maybe you can splurge to cover the rest of the walls. If so, buy a small amount of expensive wall covering having exceptional pattern, color and quality. To figure how much to buy, keep in mind that a single roll of wallcovering is calculated to cover 30 square feet of wall. Use this measure as a guide to the number of rolls you will need. Measure the wall areas to be covered. Do not deduct for windows or doors. You will need the extra amount for the matching pattern and for correcting mistakes. Any leftovers can be used to cover switch plates, tissue boxes, or wastebaskets. Compute wall measurements in square feet — width of each wall times its height from baseboard to ceiling, or from ceramic tile border to ceiling. Total square feet for all walls and divide by 30. This number will be the number of rolls you need to buy.

Some wallcoverings are prepasted, ready to be moistened with water and then hung. We suggest a coating of adhesive

Wood is an excellent choice for this soaking-tub area because it is nearly maintenance free. Prefinished paneling is combined with several wood textures; together they create an atmosphere of warmth and simplicity. The gold-framed mirror and wall sconces add an unexpected touch of elegance. Wood can be an inexpensive design option if you install it yourself.

a polyurethane vapor barrier under the paneling, and noncorrosive nails and fastenings to install the tongue and groove boards. Use top-quality hot-dipped galvanized, stainless steel, or aluminum nails. They may cost more, but will last longer than other nails and will not rust or deteriorate.

Ceramic Tile

No other material repels water as well as ceramic tile. This characteristic, along with tile's wide range of designs, patterns, and colors, is the reason behind tile's longtime popularity. When properly cared for, tile never loses its sheen or color. Clean it with an abrasive-free cleanser, or with mild detergent and warm water, and wipe with a soft cloth.

Sheets or Panels. American Olean makes a "Redi-Set" system which consists of sheets of tile to aid and speed installation. These are for use only on

Tile and wood can present exciting contrasts. Rather than isolating the shower, the designer chose to surround it with clear glass so that it became a visual extension of the tiled tub.

interior walls, vanity tops and floors. The sheets come pregrouted, and grout is also applied at the sheets' adjoining edges to bond them together.

Colored Grout. For many years grout was available only in white, and many older bathrooms are evidence of this limited color selection. However, use of colored grout has become widespread in recent years, for functional as well as for aesthetic reasons. Not only are more designs and effects possible, but the colored grout hides signs of dirt and age much better than does the white grout. In cases where white grout has deteriorated but the tile is still in good shape, the grout can be removed and new, colored grout applied (see Chapter 5).

Older homes often have the lower part of bathroom walls tiled and outlined in a tile border of some color that pleased only the original owner. Sometimes the hue of this accent is so bothersome a new owner wishes it would disappear. One possibility is to replace it with a favorite color using epoxy paint that dries to a high-gloss resembling the polished sheen of ceramic tile. Often, however, the border color can be made less obtrusive by covering the walls above it with a multi-patterned wallcovering. Choose a combination of colors that include, in minor amounts, the same shade of the border color.

Prefinished Paneling

Natural looking woodgrain patterns, finishes and colors resembling ceramic tile, and fabriclike textured prints are available for fast bathroom updating in economical 4x8 foot panels that have durable water-resistant finishes. One style in the Marlite brand from Masonite Corporation, a prefinished hardboard material double-coated with melamine, can have the pattern, texture, and coloring of ceramic tile.

Marlite panels can be applied to a full wall, used as wainscot, or to surround tub/shower. Panels are pressed into place over any solid surface — new or old walls of plaster, plasterboard or plywood — that has been covered by adhesive rather than over studding or furring strips. Because the melamine finish cannot be nailed into, panel edges must be slipped into molding strips designed for the material. Moldings and adhesive assure a watertight fit and give the finished paneling a

This child's bath is made bright and inviting by using 4 x 8 foot sheets of prefinished paneling in bold, primary colors. Mirrors on the right-hand wall help the room seem wider.

finished look. Surface patterns and finishes come in many colors.

You can also find the look of expensive wood in easy-to-install 4x8 foot panels. These are panels you install over studs or furring strips with nails. The woodgrain finishes are coated in protective resins to make them resistant to water, heat, and humidity. Plan to use the expensive-looking woods such as pecky cypress, handsome burled-patterns or deep textures, as an accent on one wall. Cover remaining walls in your favorite colors with a vinyl wallcovering highlighted by a deep border at the ceiling. To create interesting border treatments, staple or glue on fabric cutouts made from window and shower curtain material.

Mirror Power

Mirrors manipulate space, and have the added ability to reflect pattern and color. But consider also that a mirror is as impervious to water as ceramic tile. If installed flush with lavatory countertop, no backsplash is needed. (See also "Extra Small Spaces" in Chapter 1.)

USING COLOR

Color creates atmosphere and a style, and manipulates space and disguises structural flaws. It can add warmth, or make a bathroom seem cozy or large, or bright and cool. In bathroom design, color gives harmony to a space filled with three or more large objects which are totally dissimilar in shape — the major fixtures.

Whether you are remodeling or building new, color becomes your primary decorating tool. It can be used to produce a variety of effects. Basically, color may be warm or cool. Both categories contain shades — light, medium, or dark — and tone — strong, moderate, or pale. Warm colors are the reds, yellows, oranges, purples, browns. Cool colors are the blues, greens, and white. While the choice of cool or warm colors is a matter of personal taste, climate often helps determine preference. People living in hot climates generally select cool colors. Those in cold-weather areas usually prefer warmer hues.

Shade and tone cause color to appear to recede or advance. For instance, light shades of color in pale tones make a room seem larger; walls, floor, and ceiling look farther apart. Dark shades of the same color will cause a room to appear smaller; the large flat areas seem closer together.

Color Schemes

You can fill the room with several different colors and use them over and over. If you have a bath with white fixtures and wall tile, a wallcovering boldly patterned in bright colors such as sharp pink, orange, and black on white background, will give flair and style. In this scheme, you might add a shiny black shower curtain, a Lucite bench with an orange pillow, and a fluffy carpet of sharp pink.

Another possibility is to use one color throughout. This may be difficult to do unless you are able to select fixtures and wall tile at the same time. If you choose light blue, for example, cover walls and ceiling in medium blue, with the floor, towels, and shower curtain in dark blue. The one-color approach helps make structural flaws, such as irregular beams and odd angles, less noticeable. If wall and ceilings are the same color the irregularities fade into the background.

Pattern also contributes to the color scheme. Big, bold patterns, such as florals, stripes or geometrics with sharp color contrasts, will camouflage structural problems, pull walls and ceiling closer together, and give decorative impact. When the pattern is used behind fixtures grouped on one wall, the fixture appears more as related shapes than as random forms.

Small geometrics, delicate florals, subdued stripes and prints also disguise architectural irregularities, and give a room balance and harmony. Being small and light, such patterns can make the room appear brighter and more open.

Pattern mixing can produce refreshing decor. If you try prints with stripes or checks, polka dots with stripes, or geometrics with florals, remember that the trick to making pattern mixing work is use of color. No matter how many elements of pattern you use, the colors must share the same color field. Two examples illustrate the technique: to mix successfully the pattern in blue and white delft porcelain with a pattern, the blues must match each other. The greens and beiges in an Oriental bamboo pattern should match those in a companion pattern of

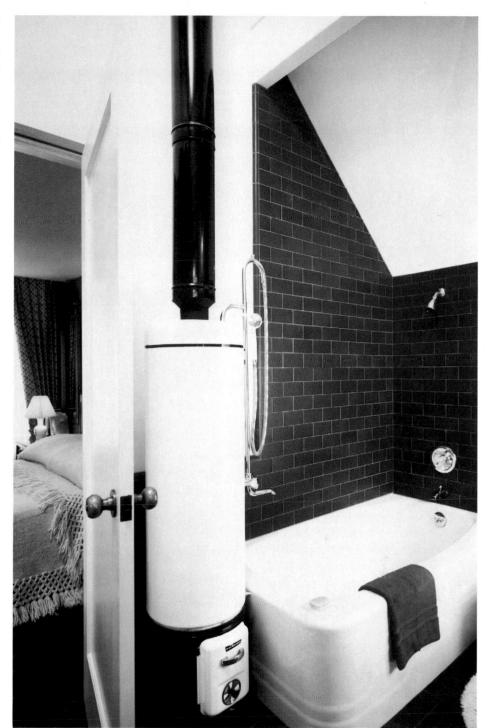

Attic spaces can be dramatic spaces, as in this small, guestroom bath. The slanting gable wall is painted white to contrast with the burnt orange tile, while the waterheater's tall, black vent pipe dramatically emphasizes the room's height.

cane or stripes. With the color principle to guide you, you can move toward mixing patterns that contain three, or even more, different colors.

Texture can be important for bathrooms because the fixtures are high sheen. Their shiny surfaces can be played up with gleaming foils or wet-look enamels, or brilliant mirror and chrome. Such textures create an atmosphere of crisp coolness. If you want softness and a feeling of

warmth, add textures that are coarse, fluffy, or velvety.

Accent colors will stimulate a color scheme; an accent pulls all the elements of the group together. No rule governs what or where an accent should be. A shower curtain, the ceiling or floor, or a cushion may do it. Generally it is a color that springs from the message, or statement, of the major color scheme. That is, the accent becomes a pleasing contrast,

A small porthole window brings natural light to the dressing room beyond the bathroom. The molding around the window repeats the warm wood tones of the cabinetry.

like a touch of stark white in a bath that is basically black (Kohler produces a complete line of fixtures in dense, gleaming Black Black). In a room of natural woods and sand-color fixtures the accent could be cinnamon red. A bathroom with bone fixtures (an American Standard color) with brown walls could be accented with a fiery red carpet. A colorful fixture, such as lavatory bowl in Tiger Lily (by Kohler) can be the color accent itself in a bath that is predominately Harvest Gold or Mexican Sand (also from Kohler).

If walls and shower curtain have a multi-color pattern, the accent usually picks up one of the secondary colors in the print. From a mix of barn red, deep green, pale blue, and lemon yellow, the accent color should be the brighter one — lemon yellow. In a room that has two colors, it is generally safe to introduce a third color as accent. With three or more colors, however, choose for accent a color that is already present. Introducing an alien color accomplishes little and may even disrupt what could have been a well-ordered color scheme.

Your best sources for ideas about color, accents, and exciting ways to combine them are magazines, room displays in stores, and decorating shops. You will discover color trends that will suggest ways to create your own personalized, individualistic touch.

FLOORS

Bathroom floors are similar to those in other parts of the house, but the crucial

requirement is moisture resistance. Whether the subfloor is of wood or concrete slab, the primary or top surface must fit over it like a tough seamless skin and allow no moisture penetration.

This preformed soaking tub was enclosed with platform framing, after which the entire structure was covered with tile. The tub now appears to be a sunken tub, though in fact it is not.

Tile

Ceramic tile. Durable, easy to clean, and available in a vast array of colors, shapes, and patterns, this is the floor material preferred by most homeowners for bathrooms.

Prices vary according to shape, color, and finish. If the color was applied to the face of the clay before it had been hardened by firing, the tile is referred to as glazed. If the color goes all the way through the clay body, it is known as quarry tile. Quarry tile comes in natural clay colors — earth browns, beiges, reds. Tiny mosaic tiles that are just 1 inch square also have color throughout. They can be white, black, or nearly any other color.

As a rule, quarry or mosaic tiles for floors are chosen because they will not show wear. Glazed, or surface-colored tiles are best for walls and countertops. They are also often used on the floor, but since floors should offer an element of traction to prevent slips and falls, choose ceramic tiles with a matte (low sheen) finish, or with a crystalline (pebbly) finish. These will be less slippery.

In making your bath design and decorating decisions, always choose fixture colors first, then shop for tile colors that harmonize. If you are buying new fixtures, ask for a sample color chip. Take this, along with your paint color samples, fabric swatches, and a sample of your wallcovering material, to select tile colors and accents that will round out your decorative scheme.

Resilient vinyl flooring. A relative newcomer to the bathroom remodeling market, resilient tile offers advantages for both new and remodeled bathrooms. It is formulated of materials that are waterproof, colorful, and attractively patterned. Vinyl flooring is available in two forms: sheet material that comes in rolls up to 12 feet wide, and in individual tiles that are 9 inches or 12 inches square. Tile are easy to install yourself. You can use the peel-and-stick kind that are precoated with an adhesive. Just peel off the treated paper shield and press the tile into place.

This apronless tub is specially designed to be built into a supporting platform. The decorative bamboo, rattan, and resilient flooring combine to create a tropical look.

Blue and white are the unifying elements here, bringing into harmony the four different patterns chosen for this room. The white wicker chair echoes the free-form shapes of the tub and the pedestal basin.

Other types of resilient tile can be installed with a special waterproof mastic which is applied to the existing floor with a grooved trowel, padded roller, or brush.

Sheet material, being wide, allows the floor to be covered by a single seamless layer if the bathroom is small, or with a minimum of seams if the room is large. As a permanent flooring, most sheet material is laid with a mastic adhesive. But there are varieties that can be stapled into place. Other types have a cushioned backing and often can be cut-to-fit like carpeting and laid without anchoring. Such floorings cannot be considered permanent, but they are a quick way to update a bathroom, especially if you rent your home rather than own it.

Cushioned flooring material is easy to walk on and cuts down on noise. In addition, the top quality have no-wax finishes, exquisite colors, and patterns to give a bathroom a durable, long-lasting and attractive floor.

Wood

Always favored for its warmth and comfort underfoot, technological advances in wood processing and watertight finishes have made wood even more valued today as a permanent bathroom flooring.

Decorative possibilities include narrow strips of solid hardwood laid on the diagonal in a contemporary bath. Parquet would be especially suitable to an ornate bath with touches of marble. If Early American or Colonial stylings are a favorite of yours, have a floor of random-width planking. For a pegged look, anchor the boards with countersunk screws capped with wooden plugs.

With development of the sturdy polyurethane clear varnishes and alkyd resins, your wood floor can be made water-resistant and still exhibit its natural color and graining. Urethane coatings come in low luster or glossy finishes. Apply six coats to assure a tight seal and long wear (see Chapter 5).

Prefinished wood flooring. Available in plank, strip, or parquet forms, all such flooring material is surface-protected by water-resistant vinyl film or one of the durable polyurethanes. For do-it-yourselfers, there are the handy and good-looking prefinished wood parquet tiles with peel-and-stick backing. For extra comfort underfoot, check out prefinished wood flooring having a resilient

Light-colored wood is used throughout — for walls, cabinets and ceiling — in this bathroom tucked beneath a sloping roof. Tile sheets were added for areas where extra waterproofing was needed. Wood is sealed against moisture.

foam backing. Such cushioning makes the floor feel warmer and tends to muffle sound as well.

Because of the different kinds of cushioning material and adhesives formulated by various manufacturers of prefinished flooring, not all types will adhere well to every kind of existing flooring. Always read package labels and manufacturer brochures before you buy, and again before you begin installation.

Carpeting

Carpeting establishes mood, color emphasis, warmth, and is one quick way to update a tired old bathroom. For the best decorative results, bathrooms should be carpeted wall to wall and cut to fit around the fixtures. Choose carpeting that will lie flat without anchoring at the edges and has a non-skid backing. Check that it can

be machine-washed at home. The face material and backing are made of synthetics that resist odors, mildew, and moisture.

Water-resistant indoor-outdoor carpeting can be used in bathrooms, but it cannot be machine washed and used over and over like the synthetic plushes. If you want to use it in a bathroom select the economical grades that can be replaced with a new piece from time to time. Note: If a wheelchair user prefers to have his or her bath carpeted, use the indoor-outdoor kind. It is thin, dense, and easier to wheel over than thick plushes and shags (see also Chapter 9).

Other Floorings

Some of nature's own materials make superlative bathroom flooring. Stone, slate, granite, and marble are some of the more expensive, and heavier materials.

Mirrored walls not only help this narrow bathroom appear wider, but dramatically reflect the three kinds of ceiling lights. The vanity is lighted by a single fluorescent tube combined with direct spotlights. A lightbox with a translucent panel illuminates the rest of the room.

Installation and final finishing are also more involved, but if you have the desire and budget for such long-lived beauty, you will have made a good investment.

Brick works well in bathrooms, too. Its porosity can be sealed and water-proofed with the clear urethane coatings applied in several layers. Six coats are recommended.

CEILINGS

A bathroom's ceiling must be as resistant to moisture and humidity as are the walls and floors. Often, the ceiling material and surface coverings are identical to those of the walls — lath and plaster or wallboard covered in paint, wallpaper, solid wood, or prefinished paneling. Other ceilings, however, can be totally unlike what has been applied to walls and floors. Sound-absorbing tiles, for instance, or back-lighted translucent panels in a suspended ceiling grid, or bright vinyl wallcovering. Your choice of ceiling material and covering will be determined in large part by your overall decorative theme.

If you are starting from scratch with a "blank" room — either brand new construction or an old bath ready for a major renovation — your alternatives are many. If your walls will be covered in solid wood cedar or redwood boards, the ceiling can be covered in wood, too. The room will have great visual appeal and you will have a ceiling which is easy to maintain. The major difficulty will be in applying the six coats of sealer overhead.

If you will paint the walls, a ceiling covered in an exciting geometric print may furnish the necessary dramatic effect. Conversely, a painted ceiling teamed with print-covered walls is attractive, and

Construction grade 2x4s were used throughout this bathroom. Framing was built for fixtures and storage units; the 2x4s were then nailed to the frames. Spacers placed between the boards and removed after nailing keep the boards equidistant. Note that all corners are mitered.

easy to achieve. Walls and ceiling covered in the same print, color, and pattern will create dramatic interest in a bathroom of any size.

Ceiling Tile
Select ceiling tile labeled as having a washable surface. Regular acoustical tile is too porous and soft to stand up very long in a humid atmosphere. Washable ceiling tile is not as moisture-resistant as treated wood, paint, or prefinished paneling, but it is fairly serviceable and can be coated later with paint or vinyl wallcovering. (Before painting the tile or paper, seal the surface with a waterproof primer sealer.)

Some ceiling tile can be glued into place if the ceiling itself is firm and smooth. If the existing ceiling is damaged, or scarred, the tile can be stapled to wood strips which you first fasten into the old ceiling.

Suspended ceilings
A lightweight wall-to-wall metal frame, or grid, can be hung from supporting wires attached to the ceiling. The outer edges of the grid are fastened to the walls for stability and extra support. Plain or decorated tiles (12x12 inch) or panels (up to 4x4 feet) are then tipped in and simply laid in place within the grid frame. You can paint or paper the removable tiles and

panels to create all kinds of interesting pattern and color displays overhead. Or you can intersperse transluscent panels and strips to make interesting room lighting effects.

Add strip lighting fixtures (fluorescent) to the old ceiling behind the grid system of translucent panels to create an illuminated ceiling — a continuous wall-to-wall glow of light.

Whatever kind of material you select as a ceiling cover, keep in mind that it should be smooth and easy to wipe clean from time to time. Pebbled, and sharp, gritty textures will hold moisture, dirt, and mildew. They should not be considered for bathroom ceilings.

4 Tubs and Showers

Tubs and showers have progressed from functional, dull fixtures to major design elements in the bathroom. The following projects and arrangements range from luxurious to very simple practical tub and shower installations.

TUBS
Enclosed Tub

An enclosed tub can have a surround that is open at one end and side, or the tub can be enclosed on all sides. A large, modern fixture, whether of steel or fiberglass, will be heavy when it is full of water, so the framing under it must be strong. Framing can be a low stud wall, similar to that which holds up the first or second floor of a house — it will easily support the tub.

One of the advantages when building an enclosed tub is that a deep soaking tub can be used. The framing can also support a bench.

If the tub is fiberglass, the rim must rest firmly on the stud wall at all points. It doesn't hurt, of course, to shim up under the underneath projecting "feet" (if you can reach them). Fiberglass flexes a little. A steel tub, however, definitely must be supported from below.

For the installation shown, a soaking tub has been installed above floor level to avoid heavy construction work. Allow for the thickness of any facing lumber when building the frame. The best bet is to place the tub in position on the floor and then level it. Measure every few inches to see how high the framing should be. In this case, you can shim under the top 1x4

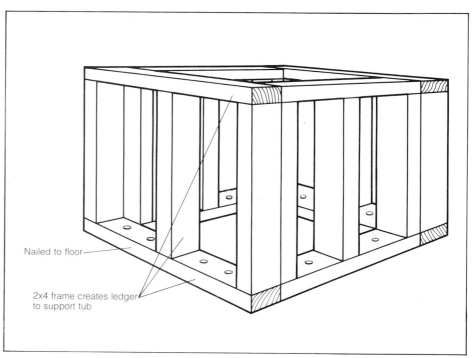

Nailed to floor

2x4 frame creates ledger to support tub

A strong frame of 2x4s supports a heavy tub. Be sure to allow for an access door through which you can reach the plumbing after the tub is installed.

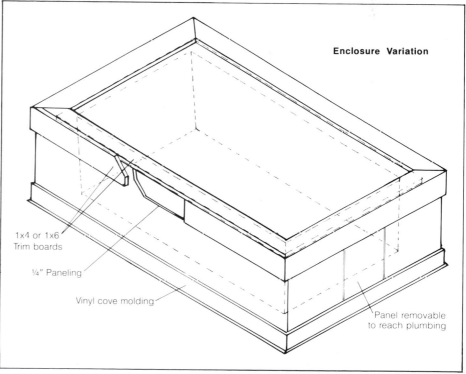

Enclosure Variation

1x4 or 1x6 Trim boards

¼" Paneling

Vinyl cove molding

Panel removable to reach plumbing

The "skin" of this tub enclosure is paneling; the trim at the top and upper edges is 1-inch lumber. The color of the vinyl lower-edge cove molding can be chosen to complement the flooring.

A raised, platform tub (a type of enclosed tub) can be made to look like a sunken tub without having to cut into the existing floor. The surfaces can be covered with nearly any water-resistant material, such as Corian or tile.

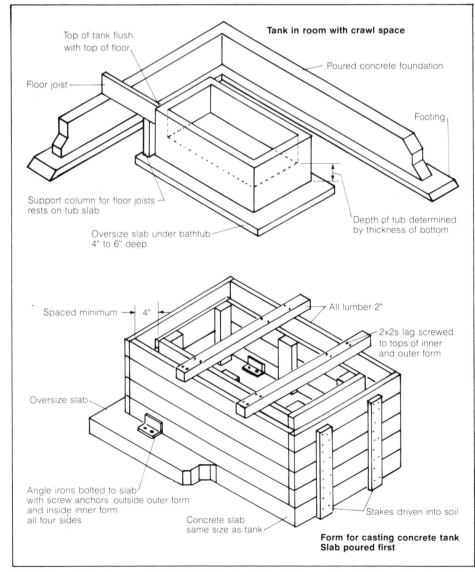

Tank in room with crawl space

Top of tank flush with top of floor

Floor joist

Poured concrete foundation

Footing

Support column for floor joists rests on tub slab

Oversize slab under bathtub 4″ to 6″ deep

Depth of tub determined by thickness of bottom

Spaced minimum → 4″

All lumber 2″

2x2s lag screwed to tops of inner and outer form

Oversize slab

Angle irons bolted to slab with screw anchors outside outer form and inside inner form all four sides

Stakes driven into soil

Concrete slab same size as tank

Form for casting concrete tank Slab poured first

If the room addition for your bathroom will have a crawl space, pour the slab for your sunken tub at the same time as the foundation. It is a good idea to form up and pour the complete tank before you install the floor joists. If the slab for the tank is oversize, support posts for the floor joists can rest on it, as in drawing shown for crawl space.

(or wider lumber if necessary) before attaching the side trim.

Paneling is installed after flooring is in place. Apply the paneling and then the side trim. Use vinyl cove to trim the lower edges of the paneling, installed after the flooring.

Sunken Bathtub

For the ultimate in luxury consider the installation of a tile-lined sunken tub in your remodeled or added-on bathroom. True, a sunken tub (called a "plunge" in the trade) is not a project for the faint of heart. It takes a lot of hard work, and considerable planning.

First, you can't hang it in the floor over a basement. The tub is very heavy, and a projection down from the basement ceiling could be awkward and a hazard. If an upstairs bathroom is located on an outside wall, you can build a footing and foundation somewhat like that required under a fireplace to support the tub. The wall of the foundation then would appear to be just an offset in the basement wall.

If the bathroom is over a crawl space, it would be necessary to cut a hole in the floor and pour a foundation on the ground under the house.

Concrete Tank. Sunken tubs usually are built over several kinds of "shells" or "pans." One type is of copper, another is lead. Neither of these containers is practical for the do-it-yourself homeowner. Instead, the sunken tub will be, in effect, a miniature swimming pool. The 1980 Handbook for Ceramic Tile Installation, issued by the Tile Council of America, Inc., shows this miniature concrete pool as the preferred installation. Properly waterproofed concrete is rigid enough so it does not flex under the weight of water, as do other materials used for sunken tubs. This eliminates the leakage problems that plague so many sunken tub installations. If you discuss sunken tubs with professionals, however, you will find that they insist that metal lined pans are preferred over concrete tanks. Even current owners of sunken tubs will insist on this fallacy. In one case, my discussion was with a man who had owned two homes with sunken tubs, and in both houses the tubs leaked and had to be rebuilt several times. On the other hand, a homeowner who had built his own sunken tub, using a concrete tank, had had no problems at all.

The size and shape can be whatever you

wish, keeping in mind that the tub should be a size that is reasonable for the bathroom in which it is located. It obviously will help you to have had some experience at building forms and pouring concrete. Oval and circular shapes require more difficult form construction. Unless you are truly experienced, it is recommended that you stick with a square or rectangular shape.

As mentioned above, you must build a strong foundation and footing under the concrete tank. If you are adding a room for your bathroom, make provision in it for a tub foundation at the same time. If a crawl space will be under the room, pour the foundation slab at the same time you pour the foundation walls. When you install the floor joists, at the minimum, box in around the slab with doubled headers. Even better, make the tub slab oversize so that columns to support the floor joists could be set on it. Another alternative is to form and pour the walls of the tank for the tub before you install the floor joists. This would allow easy working around the form for the tank. The tub tank may be recessed only a few inches into the floor, while the walls project up above the floor about 1½ feet. This means that even if the crawl space is shallow, a tub can be partially sunk into the floor. This same arrangement could be used for a room addition that has a floor slab of poured concrete. The section under the tub is deep enough to allow pouring a smaller slab at least 6 inches deep (check local building codes), and recessed to whatever depth you want.

If the house is in a cold climate, the soil around the tub will rapidly chill the tank and the water in it. Before the slab is poured, rigid insulation 2 inches thick should be placed underneath, on a bed of sand 4 inches deep. Rigid insulation (2 inches) should be adhered to the outside of the walls of the tank to prevent rapid loss of heat from the tub.

Shown is how to form up for one type of concrete tank, with reinforcing called "rebars" (reinforcing bars) ½ inch in diameter. The rebars are positioned near the bottom of the concrete, wired together in a cross-hatch and positioned as the concrete is poured.

If you have had no real experience with reinforced concrete, find a friend who has. Otherwise, get a concrete contractor to form up and pour the tank for you. The

A sunken tub is considered by many people to be the most luxurious, desirable bathtub option possible. Access to a private garden area is also popular, since it adds even more enjoyment to a relaxing ritual.

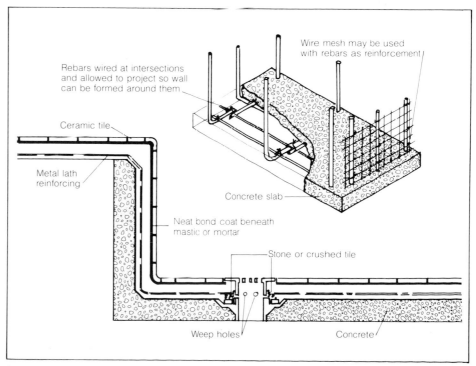

A concrete tank is a recommended container for a sunken tub where there is crawl space under the room addition, or where the floor is a poured concrete slab.

A standard tub can be given the look of sunken tub by building steps up to it. Make the simple frame of pressure-treated lumber and Exterior grade plywood, over which ceramic tile can be applied using mastic.

If you are not ready to tackle the major job of building a sunken tub, you can create the same feeling by building tile-covered steps up to the tub so you step down into it. Because this tub is under a window, the outside surface of the tub is insulated. Thick insulation is concealed in a false wall that creates an extra wide window-sill shelf.

A partially recessed tub gives the look and feel of a sunken tub. Installing a partially recessed tub is less work, less costly, and less disruptive during construction. The piping and the fittings, however, require careful planning and placement.

tank will be in your house as long as it stands, so you don't want a leaking tank. After the concrete has set, and the contractor (or you) pulls the forms, (machine oil application before pouring will make this easier) examine every square inch and remove any projections or ridges caused by spaces in the forms, using an old cold chisel. Be sure to wear safety glasses or a face shield. Fill in any recesses or imperfections, using a thick mix of cement and water.

The "neat bond coat" indicated in the drawing on page 47 can be replaced with a concrete sealer, such as those sold by Standard Dry Wall Co. When the sealer has set the required time (see the instructions on the container) an epoxy thin-bed mortar can be applied and your ceramic tile set in it. Again, read the instructions on the mortar container. As an alternative, a mastic can be used to install the tile, but it must be the type for use underwater.

When the mastic or mortar has set the required time, rub grout over the tiles with a squeegee. Pack it into the joints with a rounded dowel to smooth the grout and slightly recess it. You do not want deep grout lines, since this makes it harder to keep clean.

You will have cast around a form for the drain, which now can be installed. The water supply faucets should be above the tank, thus eliminating one potential source of leaks. The drain should be a flange type with weep holes. The weep holes allow drainage of any minor water leak behind the tile and/or mortar.

Plywood Tank. Another tank within the capabilities of a homeowner is one built of wood and Exterior grade plywood. This is a wooden box with heavy framing to support the plywood. The lumber used should be pressure-treated, and the specification stamp on the lumber should state that it is for "in ground use."

The waterproof membrane in this case can be two layers of fiberglass cloth, which you will saturate with three coats of polyester resin. Position the second layer of cloth at right angles to the first. Saturate each layer of cloth with resin, letting dry between coats. When the resin on the second layer has set up hard, apply one more coat of resin.

Trowel mastic or epoxy mortar onto the surfaces and set the ceramic tile in the mortar or mastic. Because the drain in the glass-lined plywood tank is not installed until after the fiberglass has been applied, partly fill the tank with water after resin has set. Let it stand two days, then check around the tank for any leaks. You will need a small pump to remove the water. Mop out the tank and let dry before boring the hole for the drain.

Use a hole saw to bore the hole for the drain. If the drain is in an unheated crawl space, wrap it with insulation to prevent a frozen drain in winter. The drain should be considered in the planning stage, not as an afterthought. Don't wait until the tub is complete before you discover you will have to run 30 feet to the main drain line. You can dig a trench (or have a plumber do it) and install the drain so it is right under

the tub. This assures a minimum length of drain exposed to the cold.

Curves. One advantage of the lumber and plywood tank is that you can create curves and shapes that are difficult to form up in concrete. Using ¼ inch Exterior or marine grade plywood (or pressure-treated plywood as used for wooden foundations and basements) bend a reasonable radius. Then apply two more layers of ¼ inch plywood, nailing and gluing with construction adhesive for the required ¾ inch thickness.

Recessing. If you do not desire a tile-lined sunken tub, the plywood and lumber construction can be employed to partially recess a standard steel or cast iron bathtub. The area around the tub then is covered with ceramic tile for a "sunken tub" effect.

Supply Lines. Sunken tubs are larger than standard tubs so they require more water. Increase the size of the supply lines to the faucets, making them ½ or ¾ inch lines, rather than the usual ⅜ inch.

Platform Tub

Platforms can be built around new (or old) tubs with less trouble and expense than most homeowners realize.

Using an Old Tub. In the first project given here, an old-fashioned bathtub on legs was framed into an enclosure.

Build the frame of the enclosure using 2x4 (or heavier) 2 inch lumber. Cover the frame with Exterior-grade plywood, to which ceramic tile is applied (see Chapter 5). When assembling the enclosure, be sure that your measurements take into account the space necessary for application of plywood and tile.

The ledger strip must be positioned to fit under the rim of the tub to support it. You will probably have to shim at some points to assure the rim sets solidly at all points. Before covering the framing, fit shims under the feet as necessary to make them all set firmly on the floor. The surface of the tile should be just under the lip of the tub. Run a bead of clear or colored bathtub caulk around the top of the enclosure so that when the tub is lowered into the opening the rim will bear down on the caulking for a watertight seal.

Include an access hatch in the construction plans so the plumbing can be connected once the tub has been lowered into the enclosure. The hatch also permits future repairs if they become necessary. Be-

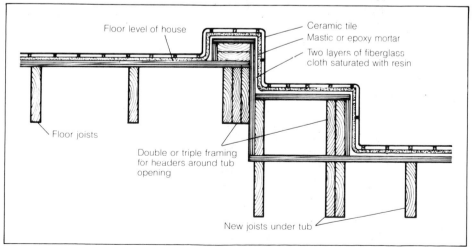

An alternative container for a sunken bathtub is a strong box assembled from pressure-treated lumber and Exterior grade (or pressure-treated) plywood. This container is much lighter than concrete and can be safely suspended in the floor framing above a basement or crawl space. There must be sufficient headroom in the basement, or the tank must be adjacent to a basement wall. A storage cabinet may be built under it.

Floor level of house

Ceramic tile
Mastic or epoxy mortar
Two layers of fiberglass cloth saturated with resin

Floor joists

Double or triple framing for headers around tub opening

New joists under tub

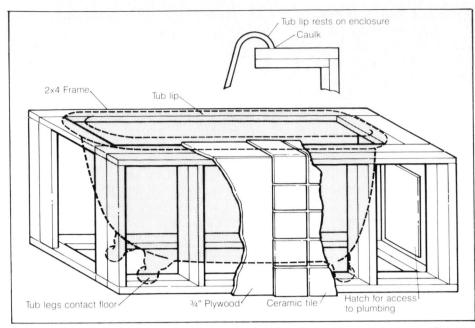

An old-fashioned bathtub on legs can be given a new look by framing it into an enclosure. Build the frame of 2x4 (or heavier) 2 inch lumber. Cover with Exterior grade plywood, and then apply ceramic tile; Corian sheets may be substituted.

As an alternative to the footed tub at left, an apronless bathtub can also be framed into an enclosure. Placement of fittings will vary.

fore applying covering to the enclosure, check the drain and supply lines to the tub to assure there are no leaks.

Variation: Color. For a new tub finish, check the Yellow Pages for a service that reconditions bathtubs. They may have a pickup and delivery service (most do) or you may have to take the tub to their location. The service treats the inside and outside surfaces of the tub, and

applies a polyurethane or epoxy finish inside and outside. For an old-fashioned tub you will want white inside, and some dark color on the outside. For the installation shown any color outside will do, because it will be hidden.

Variation: Laminate. The top of the shelf on which the tub sets can be covered with plastic laminate (Formica, Micarta, Textolite, etc.) instead of ceramic tile.

Since plastic laminate is only $1/16$ inch thick, it rarely requires height adjustment. If there is a slight problem, scraps of laminate can be slipped under the feet of the tub as shims.

Adding a Fiberglass Bathtub

Modern fiberglass tubs have two important advantages for the homeowner/remodeler: (1) the 5-foot model (used in this project) fits through any door, including 30-inch interior doors; (2) they are lightweight and can be carried by two persons. One person probably could handle the weight, but the size makes it an awkward package to handle alone.

The enclosure in which the bathtub is to be located must be planned and assembled so that the walls are plumb and square. For a 5-foot tub, dimensions must be as detailed on the drawing. Because even a new home seldom has walls that are plumb and corners that are exactly square, you probably will have to shim out at some points for plumb and square surfaces.

There are two ways to install the tub. The first is to level the tub using shims under the cast-in feet on the bottom. The second method requires a "ledger" strip that supports the rim of the tub. The best method is a combination of the two; that is, a ledger strip supports the rim while shims under the feet both level and support the tub. It is necessary, of course, to have access to the underside of the tub to

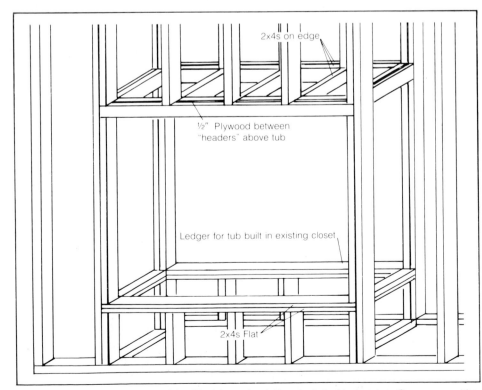

An old-fashioned tub was resurfaced inside and out, then installed in framing. Spaces on either side of recess could be closets. Space above the tub could provide storage or lighting.

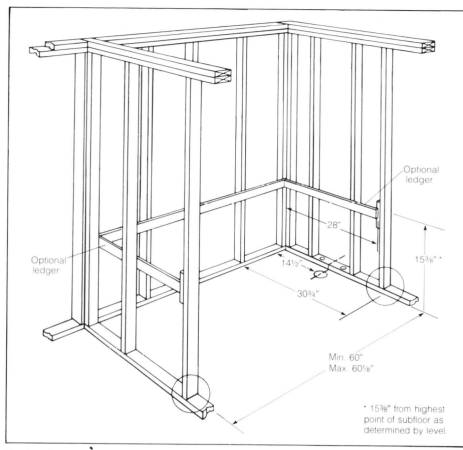

The framing (called stud pocket) for the tub must be plumb and square. To level the tub without shims, add optional 1x3 ledger, 15⅜ inch above the highest point of the subfloor.

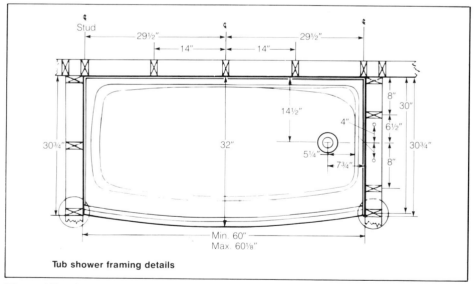

Tub shower framing details

When adding the tub against bare studs, the unit must be in place before the wall is finished. However, fire-rated wallboard and plumbing must be in position before the tub is installed.

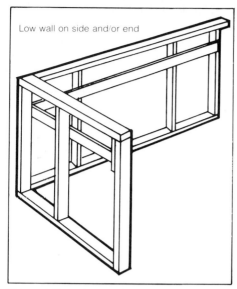

This variation, a low stud wall, can be built when enclosing the tub. This is suitable when placing stud pocket over existing wallboard or plaster, rather than new construction.

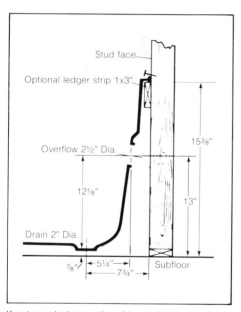

If using a ledger strip, shim so ledger and tub are in contact at all points on 3 sides. Shim under feet if accessible. If not using ledger, shim so all feet contact the floor.

shim the feet; this requires that the stud walls be open. If you are building a new room, this should not be a problem, although if the one wall is an existing exterior wall, it will be difficult to reach under the tub from the other two walls. However, we recommend that a bathtub never be placed against an outside wall. The cold outside wall will tend to cool the water in the tub, and condensation could occur on the side of the tub (outside) where it would run down and cause rot on the floor under and behind the tub. Fitting fiberglass insulation (without facing) into the void behind the tub would help. Insulation helps around any tub in an enclosure; it keeps the water warm.

After the enclosure is built, but before the tub is installed, rough-in the plumbing. This will include a standard 16-inch adjustable drain and overflow fitting for a bathtub, available at most hardware stores. The water faucets, whether double or single valves, are positioned in the wall above the tub — not in it.

As with other built-in tub installations shown in this book, the end walls, or an end and side wall, can be built low — just high enough above the tub rim to provide a vertical surface for locating the faucets. A single low end wall is a fairly common design for installing a tub.

As indicated on the drawing, when a

ledger strip is used the upper surface of the strip must be exactly 15⅜ inches above the highest point of the floor. Use a level and a straightedge board about 4 feet long to determine this high point. The ledger strip must be absolutely level, and the ends of the three pieces flush.

Slip the tub into place and shim under the rim of the tub at any point where it does not rest solidly on the ledger strip. The shims can be scraps of plastic laminate (Formica, Textolite, Micarta, etc.) for tight spots, and ⅛ inch hardboard scraps for the wider gaps.

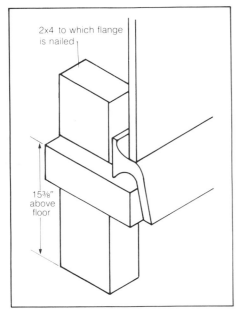

Tub hangers can be fabricated from 1x3 blocks attached to 2x4 studs with 2 inch wood screws. Use three screws for each block. Several blocks will be required for good tub support.

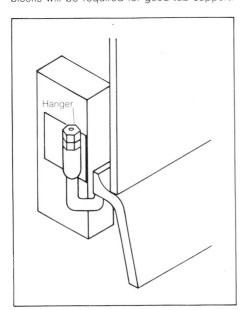

Prefabricated metal tub hangers are available for installing heavy tubs. These hangers attach to the studs with wood screws and provide the same support as the wood blocks.

Connect the drain at this time and make provision for an access door in the wall to reach the plumbing for future repairs. If the one end of the tub is on an outside wall (and we have owned a house where this was the case and the faucets and drain were on that end) consider this problem before you purchase the tub: buy one with the drain at the opposite end. The rest of the plumbing then also can be in the other wall, which is accessible for repairs.

After placing the tub in position, cut the top from the carton in which the tub was packed, and fit it into the bottom of the tub as a protector.

Note that the flange of the tub is nailed to the 2x4 studs, not the ledger strip, which merely provides support. If the tub is nailed to the studs, then wallboard (or tile backer board, which is water-resistant) can be nailed to the studs after being fitted down over the nailing flange. Position the uncut edge of the wallboard down against the tub, not the end or edge that is cut. Otherwise, the interior plaster is exposed.

After the tub is installed and the wallboard applied and taped, apply ABS plastic panels (see "Showers" below) or ceramic tile to the walls. When all work is done, remove the cardboard protector and clean off all stains and soiling. Use paint thinner (no smoking or flames, please!) sparingly, but avoid abrasive scouring powders and metal scouring pads. Heavy-duty detergents can be used for stubborn stains and deposits caused by hard water. Be sure to rinse the tub with water before anyone bathes, so that all cleansers have been washed away.

SHOWER STALLS
Installing a Shower Stall

Although fiberglass shower stalls can be installed in a bathroom remodeling job either before or after the plasterboard has been applied, it is best to apply the wallboard first, preferably tile backer board, which is a waterproof version of plasterboard. The surface provides a bearing surface for the walls of the shower stall and reduces any tendency for "drumming" of the relatively thin fiberglass when water strikes it. Be sure to mark the locations of the studs and blocking as you apply the plasterboard. Blocking is added to give a nailing surface for the top edges of the walls.

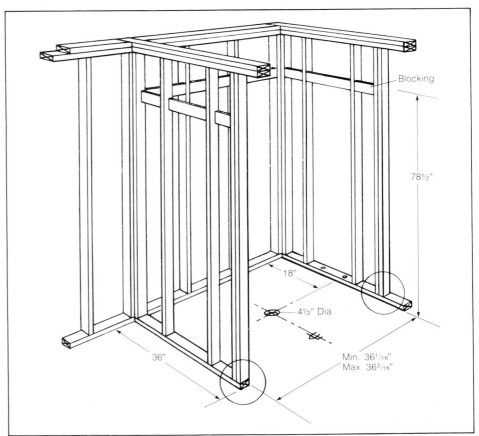

Studs circled in drawing (shower stall unit by Owens-Corning) must be positioned as shown. Pocket size varies according to size of unit purchased. If placing pocket against finished walls, adjust for thickness of walls and reposition circled studs accordingly.

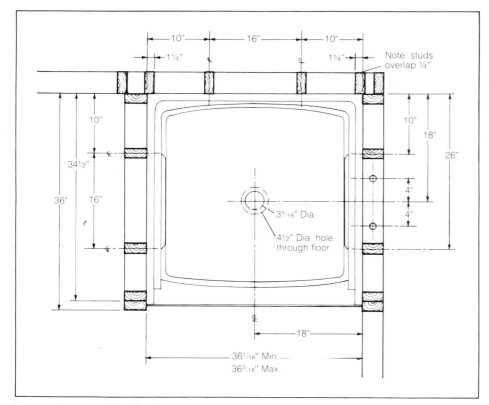

Here are the dimensions for shower stall installation of a unit whose dimensions are 3 feet x 3 feet. Note that the drain rough-in dimensions are 18 inches from the back wall and centered between side walls. This placement is mandatory.

The Swan Fiberglass showerall plus base is another alternative for the homeowner who wants the convenience of kit installation.

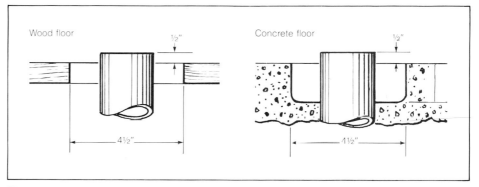

The openings in the shower pan of the unit floor will hold molded-in drains that are supplied with the kit. These openings and their sizes will differ, depending upon whether the floor is of wood or of concrete. The waste line should extend ½ inch above the subfloor or the slab.

Note that the drain for a 36-inch shower (the size of our example) must be 18 inches from the back wall, and centered between the side walls. A homeowner probably will install the shower on a wooden floor, but if a concrete floor is to be cast in the location of the shower (as in a basement) the drain is positioned differently. A recess must be cast in the concrete, as shown.

The drain line must project ½ inch above the floor, whether wood or concrete. The end of the drain fits into the perforated strainer that sits on the floor of the shower pan and seals it to the drain. Now rough-in the hot and cold water supply lines on one of the side walls. The

center line for the faucets is on the center line of the 36-inch wall. The valves, whether single or double, should be no more than 4 feet above the shower pan, or the floor. This showerhead should be no less than 79½ inches above the floor, which places it above the blocking at the upper edge of the walls of the shower stall.

Grab bars can be installed on the walls of the shower stall at the locations, indicated on the drawing. Where grab bars are desired at other locations attach 2x4s or 2x6s to the wall studs, 12 inches longer than the grab bars. The grab bars are fastened in place before the walls are fitted in place. The grab bars are backed up on the

back wall by fastening ⅝ x 3 inch spacers to the studs. Spacers for the side walls are 1⅜ x 3 inches. The locations shown on the drawing on page 54 are for grab bars 16 or 24 inches long.

Place the side wall that will have the valves into position. Mark hole locations for the single or double valves. Use a spade bit or a hole saw to cut the holes. This wall will be installed later; now remove it in order to put in the shower pan.

Before installing the shower pan, check the local plumbing code to see if oakum and lead are required. If the code is out of date, that method of sealing the drain will be required, and the ½-inch projection of the drain line is all right. If

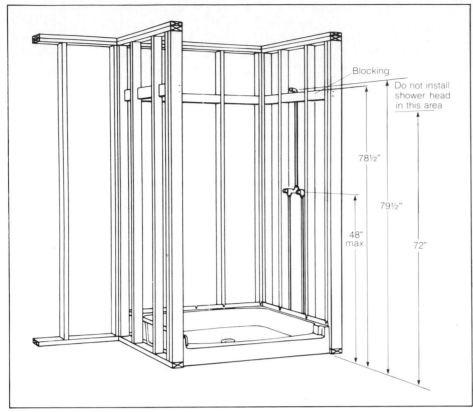

Blocking

Do not install shower head in this area

78½"

79½"

48" max.

72"

Mounting strips in the stud wall provide backing for grab bars. Mount the grab bars before installing the shower walls. Supply lines, showerhead supply line and valves should be roughed in and strapped.

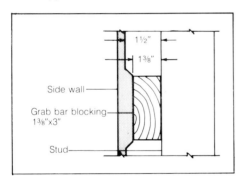

1½"

1⅜"

Side wall

Grab bar blocking 1⅜"x3"

Stud

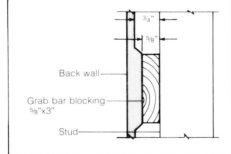

¾"

⅝"

Back wall

Grab bar blocking ⅝"x3"

Stud

Grab bars can be added in spots other than those shown. To attach grab bars to the studs in the side wall, fasten 1⅜ inch spacers to the studs at desired grab bar locations.

For back wall grab bar connection to the building structure, use ⅝ inch x 3 inch spacers for support. Mount the grab bars to the spacers after the wall has been installed.

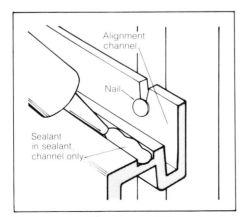

Alignment channel

Nail

Sealant in sealant channel only

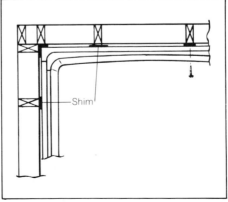

Shim

Fiberglass panels and base will fit snugly when properly aligned and level. However, a small channel is provided to hold the amount of sealant necessary to ensure a leakproof fit.

To achieve perfect level and plumb required for correct installation of walls and shower receptor, you will probably have to use shims between the walls and the studs.

code permits, use the modern plastic seal that is packed with the shower. In this case, however, reduce the projection of the drain line to ⅛ inch, as shown in the drawing on the opposite page.

Sweep the floor clean of all debris. Place the shower pan in place and level it, shimming under the legs and ribs. Nail the pan to the studs with No. 6 x 1½ inch big-head roofing nails. Before doing any of this, cut a section from the cardboard carton in which the shower pan was packed and insert it in the pan as a protector. While nailing, hold a piece of cardboard under the nail so that if the hammer slips it will not damage the fiberglass of the pan.

Use a vacuum or soft-bristled brush to clean the sealant grooves on the three upper edges of the installed shower pan. Using the sealant supplied with the shower, run a bead of sealant in the groove at the back of the shower. Position the back wall in place and seat firmly in the sealant. Do not fasten it yet. Apply sealant to the vertical channels in the back wall, and to the horizontal channels at the sides of the shower pan. Place each side wall in position and seat firmly into the pan groove. Clean off any excess sealant with a damp cloth. Shim the back wall at the upper edge as needed to bring the vertical edges of the back wall firmly against the side walls. Shim the side walls to make them plumb and square with the shower pan. Fasten walls to the studs and blocking using the screws supplied.

Cover strips are supplied with the shower for the screws that attach the flanges at the upper edges of the walls, and the vertical edges of the side walls at the open side of the shower.

Install faucets. Caulk any openings and fit bezels (metal trim) or escutcheons around the faucet stems, as provided with the faucets. Caulk around the stem of the showerhead; install the trim device supplied for it.

Remove the protective cardboard and clean away stains or dirt, using a heavy-duty detergent. Stubborn stains may require a solvent like turpentine or paint thinner. Do not use steel wool pads or abrasive cleaners.

A shower door to fit an opening 34¼ x 72 inches (or shorter) can be installed. If a shower curtain is chosen, fasten the rod above the shower walls on the wall surfaces, positioning the rod so the lower edge of the curtain hangs inside the front edge of the shower pan.

Shower Pan and ABS Panels
As an alternative to a packaged kit, flexible panels of ABS plastic may be applied with mastic, in combination with a shower pan. Lower panel edges are sealed to the shower pan; top and front exposed edges in the opening also are sealed. Plastic molding finishes edges at corners, top edges, and door opening.

REMOVING AN EXISTING SHOWER OR BATHTUB
Removal of an old tub or shower requires planning, and sometimes a lot of hard work. If the tub is the old fashioned kind with legs, it probably is too big to go through the door size common in older homes. (Interior doors should be 36 inches wide, although a 32-inch door can be used where space is restricted).

Measure the tub to see if removing the legs and turning the tub on its side would permit it to pass through the door. If not, you will have to break up or cut up the tub. Older, footed tubs are cast iron and can be broken up with a sledge hammer. Wear a face mask.

If you will be installing a new window, the required rough opening probably will be big enough to permit passing the tub through it. Therefore, plan to remove the tub at the same time as you are making the opening for the new window.

Disengaging the Tub
For the actual work of removing the tub, first turn off the water. Old-fashioned footed tubs are free standing; you can work around them to disconnect the faucets and to remove the plumbing. In the case of a tub that has been closed in to make it look more modern, you will have to tear off the plywood or other material used for the structure, and the covering applied to it. Some tubs have the plumbing inside a wall. There should be an access door to permit reaching the plumbing, but this is not always the case. You may be able to cut an opening to install an access door. If the plumbing is in an outside wall, and this is not uncommon, there is nothing to do but remove the ceramic tile or other covering. Then tear off the plaster and lath, or plasterboard. Leave the wall open until all plumbing has been done and checked for leaks.

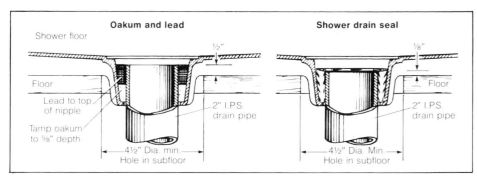

Codes may require a drain seal of a combination of oakum and lead, as shown on the left. If codes allow, use the elastic dry joint seal that comes with the fiberglass shower unit.

"Built in" bathtubs have a flange that rests on a ledger strip and may be nailed to the strip. Elongated holes in the flange permit movement of the tub as it fills and empties. This kind of installation means that at least that part of the wall down next to the flange of the tub will have to be removed. Check the condition of the wallboard or plaster when you remove the section above the flange of the tub. If it is damp, it is very possible that the moisture has worked its way through the wall for several feet. The most practical thing to do is remove the wall covering completely both at the ends and the back of the tub and replace it with new surfacing. Use a waterproof plasterboard or a tile backer board, either of which will resist damage from any moisture that might seep in under the bottom row of tiles.

Tearing Out a Shower
Removing an old shower is like removing a bathtub when you get down to the pan, where a flange will be under the wall covering and possibly on a ledger strip. If the pan is poured concrete, you will have to use a hammer and chisel and several hours of labor to break it up and remove it.

Because the walls of a shower are exposed to water much more than are the walls around a bathtub, you will do best to completely remove and replace all tile and wall material. Let the studs dry if they are damp. Replace the walls and then tile them. Use a waterproof plasterboard or tile backer board.

If the shower stall is metal or fiberglass, you will have to tear it apart in whatever way you can. Be careful with both metal and fiberglass; you may encounter sharp edges. Wear gloves — heavy ones with leather palms.

Even with a metal or fiberglass shower stall, check for water damage on the wall and the framing around the stall. Small leaks can allow a tremendous amount of water to seep through. If there is any sign of rotting in the framing and damage to the wall covering, replace the parts affected. It is a lot easier to do the work now.

Damaged Areas
When the bathtub or shower stall has been removed, examine the flooring and joists under it. Small leaks or splashes of water over many years can cause extensive damage. Remove any damaged flooring and replace it. If the joists show water damage, but not extensive rotting, fit a length of 2 inch lumber the same size as the joists alongside the affected joists. Spike or bolt the new lumber to the existing joists. The reinforcing piece of lumber must be long enough to extend a foot or two beyond the damage.

For extensive rotting, cut out the bad sections and spike or bolt lengths of joist material on each side of the removed section. In many cases you must support the ends of the cut pieces until you have added the two new pieces. As an alternative, bolt or spike a length of joist alongside the rotted section of joist, then cut through the damaged joist, stopping at the new joist. This is possible because the floor is removed and you can saw from above. After cutting out the bad section, add a second length of joist on the other side of the damaged joist. The new lengths of joist should extend at least 3 feet beyond the section cut away.

When replacing the flooring, allow for the offset of the new joists as you nail the flooring down. It might be possible to run some plumbing lines (new ones) up through the doubled joists for added support for the pipes. If the floor has seemed somewhat flexible (that is, it bounces when you walk on it), installing additional joists will remove this problem.

5 Materials: Installation and Repair

WALLS

Anatomy of a Gypsumboard Wall

Gypsumboard is a plasterlike material that comes in 4x8 foot sheets (standard). The gypsum core is wrapped in thick paper. The paper protects the gypsum and provides a smooth surface that is resistant to cracks. Gypsumboard is easier than

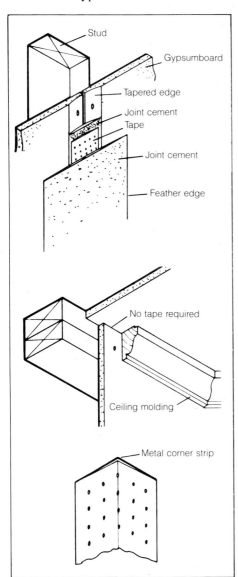

Reinforce inside gypsum wallboard corners with metal, or tape with joint tape. Reinforce outside gypsum wallboard corners with a metal strip for protection. Nail strip to the corner; add joint compound; embed the tape into the compound; smooth tape with scraper.

plaster to apply to the framing members of a house, which is probably why its use is so common.

Gypsumboard sheets are nailed to the studs and rafters with gypsumboard nails, and fastened every 16 inches on center (usually the spacing of the framing members), and the nails are spaced from 2 to 4 inches apart.

The edges of the gypsumboard are slightly tapered. The taper compensates for the thickness of gypsumboard joint tape that is applied over the joint and nails with joint compound. The compound is similar to spackling.

Inside and outside corners of gypsumboard walls often have a metal strip nailed to the gypsumboard, and the strips are embedded in joint compound. The strips add protection to the corners, especially the outside corners, and provide a straight and fairly square edge.

Gypsumboard varies in thickness: $\frac{3}{8}$, $\frac{1}{2}$, and $\frac{5}{8}$ inch thicknesses are standard. When making a patch or replacing a panel, know its original thickness. If the replacement material does not match the original, you will have a depression or projection.

Anatomy of a Plaster Wall

Plaster for walls and ceilings is applied over a wire mesh that has been nailed to the framing members. If your house is old, the plaster may cover narrow strips of wood called "lath."

Plaster is continuous in that it is not in sections as are gypsumboard panels. Nor is plaster covered with a paper wrapper, as is gypsumboard. When you dig into plaster, you are instantly into the wall.

You can patch plaster with plaster. Unless holes are huge, you also can patch plaster with spackling compound, which probably will be easier for you to buy than regular plaster.

Repairing Small Dents

If the damage is not deep enough to hold

even a small patch, you will have to enlarge the problem area.

If the wall is of gypsum wallboard, use a razor knife to score the paper covering the gypsum core, making a square or rectangular cut. Just cut enough of the paper to surround the entire damaged area. Then, using the knife blade, peel the paper back to the scored lines. Again with the razor knife, remove a quarter inch or so of the gypsum core, making a little void in the core. This area need not be smooth and finely cut; it is better to leave it rough because the rough edges will hold the patch better.

After this point the procedure is the same for plaster and for wallboard repair.

Mix a small amount of spackling compound in the mixing container. Add spackling to the water and stir it with the putty knife until the mixture is about the consistency of putty. Balance the mixture on the putty knife and press the spackling into the hole.

Fill the hole with spackling. You can probe into the patch with the tip of the putty knife to compact the mixture. When the hole is full, use the edge of the knife to smooth the fresh spackling. The putty knife serves as a trowel.

Leave the patch slightly higher than the surrounding surface of the patch. The spackling will shrink as it dries. Let the patch set for about two days.

Once the patch has dried, lightly sand it, working away the rough spackling and blending the patch in with the surrounding area.

Spot prime the patch with paint. Let the paint dry. Sand the area lightly again, and then apply a second coat of paint. If the wall has not been painted for some time, you may have to repaint the entire wall to hide the patch, since the new paint will not blend in with the old paint.

Nail Hole Repair

Mix a small amount of spackling compound with water. The spackling should

Looking straight on, nail pops are hard to see, so check the surface from an angle. Drive a screw-nail under the pop; slightly countersink the nail. Then drive in the popped nail. Fill dimples left by the hammer with spackling compound; sand and repaint.

be a stiff mixture, about the consistency of putty or stiff whipped cream.

Press the spackling into the hole, using the tip of the putty knife. Then, with the putty knife, level the spackling in the hole. Let the spackling dry an hour or so. Then sand the area with medium or fine grit abrasive.

Touch up the spot with paint. Try to feather out the paint into the surrounding area. Sometimes just a dab of paint on the spot works best. You can try both and decide which looks better before the paint dries.

Plaster Patches
Dents and cracks to plaster walls and ceilings are mended the same way as gypsum wallboard; check these techniques in this chapter. However, remember that plaster has several built-up layers which form the surface, while wallboard has a single core of gypsum covered with paper.

Clean the break with the razor knife, cutting back to the hard plaster. The patching area should be free of loose debris; don't enlarge the damage more than necessary. Clean the area to be patched with water and a brush. Mix the spackling compound (or plaster patching material

for a large, deep hole from which the metal lath is missing) to a fairly stiff consistency.

If the metal lath is still in place, you will follow these steps: Rewet the area to be patched; this prevents the plaster from absorbing water from the spackling mixture. Trowel in the spackling with a scraper. Level the patch and smooth it. After the patch has dried for several days, sand it smooth so it blends with the surrounding surface. Spot prime and paint the entire wall or ceiling.

For larger patches, substitute a mason's trowel for a wall scraper to apply and level the patch. Another possibility is to use a section of gypsum wallboard instead of spackling. The wallboard can usually be butted against the plaster and then taped and smoothed to match.

If the metal lath (a heavy mesh available in hardware stores) is missing, follow these steps. After cleaning the patch, as above, mix the plaster patch material according to instructions. Cut the mesh so it is a little larger than the hole — about 1 inch larger all around. Tie 5 or 6 inches of string through the center of the lath. Holding onto the string, bend the lath just enough to fit it through the hole, then

flatten out the mesh. Tie a pencil to the string, and twist so that the pencil spans the hole and keeps the metal lath in place.

If the hole is fairly small, apply plaster patching to within ¼ inch of the surface and let it dry. Once the patch is dry and holds the mesh in place, cut the string and remove it and the pencil. Then put on another coat; allow it to dry, and sand smooth. If the hole is large, you will apply three layers rather than two. Fill the patch so that it will form a bond between the metal lath and the wall; let it dry; remove the pencil and string. Add another layer, up to within ¼ inch of the surface, and let dry. Then apply the last layer, let dry, and sand smooth.

Large Hole Repair, Wallboard
Clean out the break with the razor knife. Try not to enlarge the hole, just cut away the loose gypsum down to the firm inner core.

Mix up a large batch of spackling compound and make the mixture stiff. Then stuff the hole full of mineral wool insulation. The fibers of the insulation will catch on the gypsumboard surface and hold in place.

Fill the hole with the spackling compound, being careful not to dislodge the insulation. You want to use the insulation as a backing material for the spackling. You may be able to tack the insulation to the back of the hole with small gobs of spackling.

When this initial job is finished, let the spackling dry a day or so. Then go back and fill the hole full of spackling. Level the spackling with the putty knife, but leave it a tad high for normal shrinkage.

When the spackling is dry, sand the area lightly so it is level with the surrounding surface. Then touch up the patch with paint.

Very Large Hole Repair, Wallboard
You must now make a decision. Can you patch the hole with a piece of gypsumboard, or is it so large that you should remove the gypsumboard panel and replace it with a new panel? The latter may be the easier plan.

Using the straightedge or square, outline the damaged area with a pencil. Include all the damage within the lines, but no more than this area. The patch should be adequate, but as small as possible.

Score along the outline with the razor

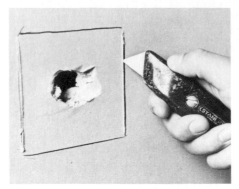

Mark a square or rectangle around the damaged area. Score with a razor knife. Cut and lift the rectangle from the wall. Slightly bevel edges toward the back wall. Now cut a patch.

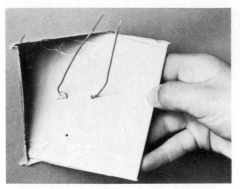

Run the wire through the patch, spread glue on it, and angle it through the hole. You may have to pull the wires toward you until the glue sets enough to hold the patch.

Before you continue with the patch, clamp the patch and let the glue dry for a day or so. Apply pressure by twisting the wires with pliers. Don't tighten too much, or you will damage the patch.

Cut another patch; this will fit on top of the patch already placed in the wall. Remove paper face on one side of the gypsum core. The paper comes off more easily if damp.

Glue the second surface patch over the first patch, paper to paper with the exposed gypsum core facing toward you. Wait another day while the glue dries before applying spackling.

Smooth the patch after the spackling compound has dried for several days. Try to feather the edges so they will taper into the surrounding wallboard. Then sand smooth.

knife, bearing down hard on the knife. If you can, cut completely through the gypsumboard at this time. If you cannot cut completely through the material, repeat the scoring procedure with the knife until you remove this part of the wall. You now should have a nice square or rectangular hole where the damaged area once was.

Measure the hole and transfer these measurements to the scrap piece of gypsumboard, plus 2 inches on all four sides. The extra material will be used for gluing. When you are done, you will have the patch for the wall.

Since you need to be able to hold onto the patch while you fit it into the wall, punch two holes all the way through the patch with a nail. Aim for the center of the patch and space the holes about an inch apart. Thread the wire through these holes so the ends of the wire come through the front of the patch.

Now coat the face of the patch with glue; use a lot of glue. Place the patch inside the hole, seating the patch in the glue. Pull the patch toward you with the wire so that the glue makes a good bond with the back of the wall.

When you are sure the patch is seated, wrap the wire around the 1x3 or dowel, which should bridge the patch. Then twist the wire around the 1x3 or dowel and tighten the wire with pliers. This will anchor the patch on the wall so that the glue makes a good bond.

Remove the 1x3 or dowel from the wall when the glue dries, after at least a day, and test the patch. If it seems to be wobbly in the wall, very carefully "tack" the recessed edges of the patch with a stiff spackling compound. Let the spackling dry a day.

When the patch is securely in place, fill the recess between the patch and the surface of the wall with spackling compound. Use the wide wall scraper for this, troweling in the spackling mixture and smoothing it level. Use the surface of the surrounding wall to help guide the wall scraper so that the patch will be level with the wall. Or, cut another patch of gypsumboard the same size as the hole.

Check that the patch fits, then peel off the paper covering on the front side of the patch. Use the razor knife for this. Go right to the gypsum core on the surface of

the patch that will face the room. You need not be too careful with the razor; the gypsum core should be a bit rough. Glue the patch into position. When the glue dries, fill the joints with spackling compound.

Once the spackling compound has dried — give it three days — sand the patch smooth, blending the patch into the surrounding wall surface.

Spot prime the patch with paint. Then paint the entire wall so the patch won't show.

Replacing a Gypsumboard Panel

When the hole is so large that you can't mend it with a spackling compound or gypsumboard patch, you will have to replace the panel. This is not especially difficult, but you need patience and must be careful not to damage the good surrounding panels.

Remove the base molding from the wall on which the damaged panel is located. Use a pry bar and hammer for this and take it easy when you pry; you want to save the trim and reinstall it after the repair has been made. When the molding

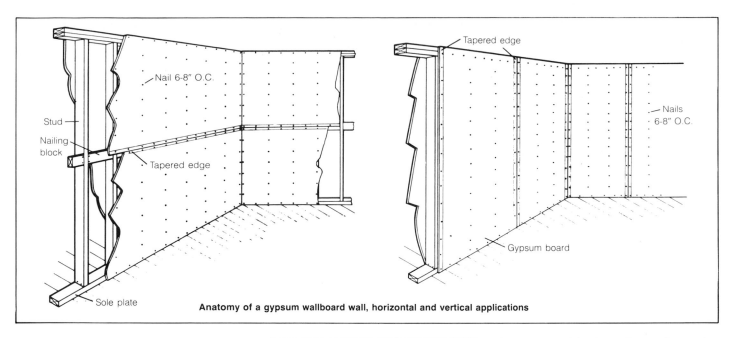

Anatomy of a gypsum wallboard wall, horizontal and vertical applications

has been removed, tap and pull out the nails and store the molding.

With a hammer, break out the damaged gypsumboard panel back to the studs to which the sides of the panel have been nailed. If you go very slowly, you can remove the entire damaged panel by removing chunks of the panel and pulling the nails as you go. Do it in small pieces rather than jerking off the whole panel at once.

When you come to the panel joints, you probably will have to cut the gypsumboard tape that spans the joints along the sides and at the ceiling line. Do this with the razor knife. Again, be careful not to rip into adjoining panels or the ceiling.

With the panel removed, you should have a neat, clean hole in the wall with the studs exposed and the "good" gypsumboard panels overlapping the side studs by about half their width.

Insert the new panel over the framing members. You will need a helper to handle the new panel so that you can mark and fit it into position. Then remove the new panel and make any necessary cuts for correct fit using the razor knife.

Nail the new panel to the framing members with gypsumboard nails. Space the nails about three inches apart. When the nailheads are flush with the panel, hit them one more time with the hammer. This creates a "dimple" in the surface of the panel and countersinks the nailheads below the surface of the panel.

When the panel is in place, check the edges to make sure that they do not project above the surface of the surrounding

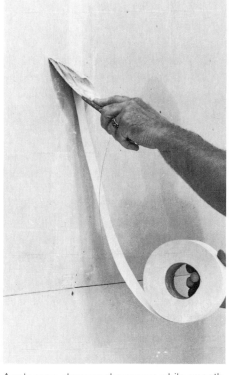

Apply even, downward pressure while smoothing the tape over the wallboard seam.

wall. If the edges do project, you may be able to trim them down slightly with the razor knife. It is likely, however, that the panel will fit perfectly.

Mix a stiff batch of spackling compound. With a putty knife or wall scraper, trowel on a thin layer of the spackling compound. Run the wall scraper over the top of the tape, pressing it into the spackling. Give the tape a downward swipe with the scraper.

With the tape embedded, fill all dimples with spackling compound, leveling

the compound in these depressions using the wall scraper to putty knife.

Let the spackling dry one day. Apply a layer of spackling over the tape; let dry another 24 hours. Add a third coat. Once dry, sand the spackling lightly and prime the new panel with paint. Once paint has dried, give the panel a light sanding and dust off the residue. Add a second coat of paint.

Replace the baseboard, nailing it to the studs with finishing nails. Countersink the nail heads using the nail set, fill the holes with wood putty or wood plastic, and touch up any spots with paint or stain.

Wallboard or Plaster Cracks

The size of the cracks we are discussing here are hairline up to about ¼ inch wide. The repair technique for cracks in gypsumboard and for plaster walls is the same. If there are large cracks and lots of them, consult a professional; there could be structural damage to the house.

Clean out the crack with the razor knife. Undercut the crack with the knife to form an inverted V. This configuration will hold in the patch.

Mix a fairly stiff batch of spackling compound. Trowel the compound into the crack, smoothing it with the tip end of the wall scraper or putty knife. Leave the patch a little high; spackling shrinks as it dries.

Let the patch set for two days. Then sand the area lightly and touch up the patch with paint. If the patch is large, you probably will have to repaint the entire wall, or room.

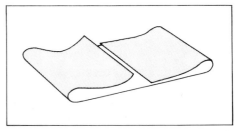

The plaid wallpaper sets the tub area apart from the rest of the bathroom floor plan, but picks up and enhances colors in the fixtures and in the other surfaces.

Wallpaper used around bathtubs or showers should be vinyl in order to avoid mildew problems and prevent moisture damage. Use the appropriate paste — usually a vinyl formula.

"Booking" the wallpaper allows you to carry it more easily to the wall. Unroll the booked paper one-half strip at a time, positioning the top half before unrolling the rest.

Hanging Wallcovering

Many of the newer types of wallcoverings are waterproof so are suitable for use in a bathroom. There are two basic types of wallcovering the do-it-yourself home-owner should consider: Prepasted and nonpasted. The former probably is the easiest to apply, as all you do is soak it in a water tray for about 30 seconds (read the instructions that come with the material you use, of course) to activate the adhesive, then you apply it to the wall. The second type of wallcovering requires application of paste to the back of the strip.

Wall Preparation. Any projecting nails should be recessed into plasterboard. Then apply patching plaster or tape compound over the recess and smooth. Widen cracks in the plaster or plasterboard, if necessary, with the pointed end of a beverage can opener; undercut so the plaster will lock into the crack. Any blemishes or scars in the wall also should be filled and smoothed. If the wall has paint on it, rough it with medium grit sandpaper.

If you have a newly built wall, with fresh plasterboard, tape and fill all joints. Recess all nails and fill with compound. When all joints and patches have dried

and are smooth, cover the walls with glue sizing, both to seal the paper on the plasterboard and to provide traction for the wallcovering paste. Even better are new products on the market (check in paint or wallcovering stores) that you apply to any wall to make any wallcovering "strippable." This means that sometime in the future, when you want to change the wallcovering, you can loosen one corner and peel off the wallcovering.

Before you begin hanging, snap a vertical chalkline onto the wall; its distance from a corner should be the width of a strip of wallcovering, less 1 inch. The first strip of wallcovering will align with the chalk mark and will run into the corner by 1 inch. The 1 inch overlap allows for a corner that is out of plumb; no corner, even in a new house, will be exactly plumb and at right angles.

It is best to apply wallcovering during the daylight hours, on a sunny day. It will be necessary to remove all switch plates and receptacle covers, and paper right over the openings. Shut off the electricity. You don't want to get an electrical shock as part of the job.

Pasting. To use nonprepasted wall-

coverings, cut a strip so that it will project below the baseboard at least 2 inches, and above the ceiling line 2 inches (some instructions call for 6 or 8 inches at each end, especially if you must match a pattern). Place the strip on a working surface for pasting. The work area can be a table with several layers of newspaper on it; when the newspaper becomes saturated with paste, you roll it up and throw it away.

Brush paste onto one half the length of the strip, then fold the paper in half again, paste surface to paste surface. Apply paste to the second half of the strip, then fold it in half. The two ends of the paper will meet in the center of the strip.

You may have trouble with some slick vinyl wallcoverings when you try to brush paste onto the covering itself. If so, take a tip from the professionals: apply the paste to the wall, then apply the wallcovering.

Not so incidentally, any paste used under a vinyl wallcovering, especially in a bathroom where high humidity is an almost constant condition, should be mildew-resistant. It will be a vinyl paste rather than an ordinary wheat paste, which is an organic material and thus readily subject to mildew attack.

Hanging the Strips. One trick used by professionals is to start in a dark or at least an unobtrusive corner. Thus, when your last strip doesn't quite match up, or the pattern doesn't line up, it will not be noticeable. Even the professionals cannot make the job perfect, but usually they manage to hide any misalignments or errors in pattern matching.

If using a prepasted wallcovering, place the tray at the base of the wall. Lift each strip out, unrolling as you go, so that the top portion can be positioned with 2 or more inches left above the ceiling line.

If using a strip you have pasted, take the folded strip to the wall and unfold the top half. Press the top half against the wall, leaving a couple of inches of runover on the ceiling. Brush to adhere the upper portion to the wall, then unfold the lower half and brush against the wall. Be sure to carefully match the pattern at the seam before applying final pressure. Bring each strip over, going back occasionally to roll the seams down after the seam has set for about five minutes. Sponge off any paste or fingerprints.

Openings. Paper over recesses for outlets or ducts, as well as windows and doors. Make an "X" over each outlet or vent opening after the paper has been applied and the adhesive has set for an hour or so. After cutting the "X" carefully, trim an opening the size of each electrical box. For windows and doors, cut diagonally to the corners and trim the material to fit against the trim (or corner in recessed windows and doors).

Faceplates. After applying a new wallcovering, you may want to change the color of the faceplates, or even install fancy switchplates to match the theme of the new decor. Receptacle covers should be unobtrusive, so their covers seldom are anything but plain brown, white or ivory color.

Another alternative is to cover the faceplates with wallcovering. You will have a lot of small scraps of wallcovering left over, and this is a good use for them. If you take the effort to match the pattern, the plates will almost disappear. If you use a vinyl or other washable wallcovering, the plates can be easily cleaned with a bit of soap and water.

Caution, No Flocks. Flocked wallcoverings should not be used in a bathroom. Although some flocked wallcoverings are water-resistant, they do stain easily and are difficult to apply without stains, resulting from glue or hands.

Extra Touch. Modern wallcoverings (and even "old fashioned" wallpaper) can be applied to furniture and decorations in bathroom. Some patterns and styles of wallcovering can be purchased with matching fabrics. The cloth then can be used as inserts in shutters and as shower curtains. In the latter case, a lining of sheet plastic prevents the material from becoming wet.

PANELING

If paneling is applied directly to studs in a bathroom, a vapor barrier and insulation are mandatory in order to prevent later

Gently smooth the wallpaper, using a large brush or sponge. This eliminates air bubbles and uneven surfaces.

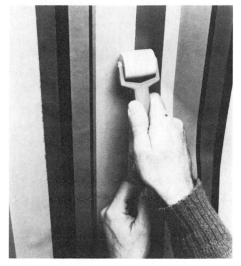

Roll wallpaper edges at seams before the paste has dried; otherwise, the edges will curl and additional paste will be necessary.

Cutting wallpaper around a medicine cabinet involves steps similar to those for a window opening. Final trims are made around unit.

Place the paper over the ceiling fixture. Cut an "X" with the razor to let the fixture emerge. Then cut final trim.

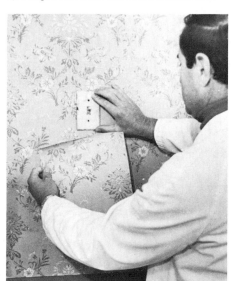

Use the switch cover as a template to cut out the paper for the switch. Then use a scrap to match up the pattern exactly.

Remove the switch cover and apply wallpaper to it, aligning the wallpaper with the pattern around it. Then re-install the cover.

moisture damage. Paneling in the bathroom is most often: (1) nailed at the studs into a plaster or wallboard wall, if the surface is even and in good condition, or (2) nailed to furring strips if the wall is not even and smooth; or (3) applied with adhesive.

Paneling With Redwood

Redwood grain can be used to create patterns and design effects. The vertical grain lumber will reveal a cross-section of the wood's annual growth rings, while the flat grain will show rippled, wavy patterns. A shipment of redwood will usually include both, although you can specify one or the other. Arrange the panels until you find the order that pleases you most; then number the backs of the panels.

Always use noncorrosive, best-quality, hot-dipped galvanized aluminum or stainless steel nails when using redwood in a bathroom.

Wall Preparation. Do any necessary painting before putting up panels. If the walls are in good condition, you can glue (use only adhesive marked for interior paneling, not contact cement) and nail

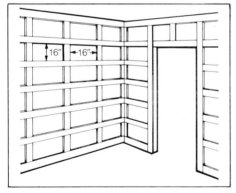

Apply horizontal and vertical furring strips to the wall to ensure a smooth surface and a longlasting paneling job. Paneling seams should always fall over the furring strips.

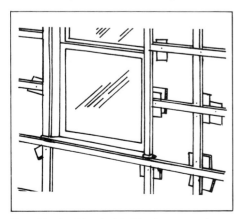

Use shingle shims behind furring to produce a smooth vertical surface.

directly to studs. Butt panels neatly against existing trim.

On uneven, badly cracked, or very rough walls, redwood lumber can be nailed to a framework of 1x4 or 1x3 furring strips of any wood species and grade, which have been kiln dried. Fit shims (ordinary wood shingles) under the strips to even out severe surface gaps.

To find furring strip requirements for vertical paneling, measure wall width to determine the length of one horizontal strip, and wall height to figure how many strips you will need, spaced about 16 or 24 inches on center; try to nail them into the studs. Furring strips must also be nailed around windows, doors, and all other openings, so add these linear measurements to the total. At windows and doors, nail strips flush with inside or wall

edges of jambs, so that build-up strips can be added later (see below).

Recessing Electrical Outlets and Ducts. To recess outlets, cut openings as individual boards go up. Measure from the adjoining board and from the floor or ceiling. Mark dimensions in the panel face, drill four large holes just inside marked corners, and saw from them with a sabre or keyhole saw. Most codes require the use of GFI in bathrooms.

Vertical Paneling. Begin at an inside corner, and work left to right if you are right-handed, and right to left if left-handed. Keep groove edges toward the starting corner, and tongue edges toward your work direction. Trial fit the first board, check for plumb (perpendicular to the floor). Nail with 5d or 6d finishing nails, even if other boards will be glued.

Redwood tongue and groove paneling can be applied diagonally or horizontally — as well as vertically — for dramatic design effects.

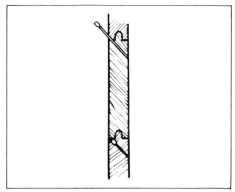

Prebore holes with bit ¾ the diameter of nail shank. Drive nails to ⅛ inch of surface; finish with nail set.

After installing each strip, use a block of wood to act as a buffer and to protect the panel as you gently tap the strip into position.

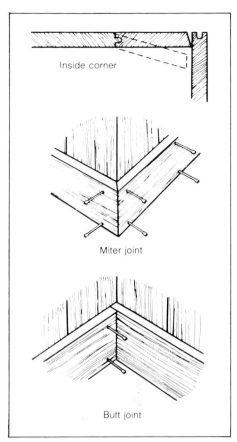

Angle-trim the last board, if needed, so it fits into the corner. Use a block plane, keeping the wide part of the angle toward the wall.

On furring strips, face nail top and bottom, and blind nail through the tongue at each strip. Without furring strips, face nail top, bottom, and every 2 feet, about ¾ inch from the corner edge, angling the nail to penetrate studs.

To avoid splitting board tongues and ends when nailing, you can pre-bore nail holes with a drill bit about three-quarters the diameter of the nail shank. To avoid hammer marks, drive nails within ⅛ inch of the board surface and finish with a nail set.

Nail Holes. Leave as is or fill in with a redwood-colored wood putty or filler. A mixture of redwood sander dust and clear cement forms a quick-drying filler. Oil-based fillers stain the adjoining wood and should not be used.

Paneling Board By Board. Measure all other boards carefully and trial fit. Tap them into place with a hammer and tapping block, a scrap with the groove edge intact to fit over board tongues. Check for plumb and, if necessary, slightly angle groove-to-groove fitting to make it square. When butt-joining short board ends together in the middle of a wall, be sure the joint falls over a stud, blocking, or furring strip.

At Outside Corner. Miter-join lumber with a table saw, making 45° cuts on board edges. Without a table saw, you can butt join, trimming off groove or tongue edges squarely, fine sanding, and covering this joint with trim or molding. With a portable circular saw, trim lumber face down. With a conventional hand saw, trim lumber face up to prevent face chip-out. On furring strips, face nail paneling top, bottom, and down the middle. Without furring, face nail top, bottom, and every 2 feet, about ¾ to 1 inch from the corner edge.

To glue instead of nail to studs, apply adhesive to panel back. Let set. Press panel to wall to coat wall and panel. Tap into place. Face nail top and bottom with 8d finishing nails.

Gluing the Panels. Generously apply adhesive, using a caulking gun to the back of a prefitted board. Let it set according to adhesive package directions, then hold the board to the wall so both are coated. Remove it, wait again, then tap the board into place and face nail top and bottom with 8d finishing nails (two nails at each end for wider boards). Because of waiting periods, you can finish one board while adhesive sets on another.

Horizontal Paneling. To even up wall surfaces for horizontal paneling, apply vertical furring strips. Measure wall height to find the length of one strip, and wall width to determine the number of strips needed, spaced on wall studs or about 24 inches apart. Nail furring strips around doors, windows, and all other openings.

Nail the baseboard first (a 1x6 or 1x8) with 6d finishing nails at each stud or furring strip. Then butt the groove edge of the first board against the baseboard, face nail the ends, and blind nail at studs. With wider lumber, face nail about ¾ inch from the baseboard, one nail per stud. Without a baseboard, place the first board tight against the floor and nail as above.

On an outside corner, miter the ends, making a cut greater than 45° in order to fit tightly. Or butt join, covering with molding or trim, if desired. Butt join inside corners also. Handle baseboards the same way, but without molding or trim. To fit the last board at the ceiling, angle trim the corner edge slightly with a block plane, with the wide part of the angle toward the wall.

Diagonal Paneling. Diagonal paneling is often used on an accent wall rather than a whole room. You need 15 percent more lumber, so that paneling 100 square feet of wall space requires 132½ board feet (115x1.15 = 132½) or 264½ linear feet (230x1.15 = 264½), plus 5 percent for errors.

If walls need them, apply furring strips vertically as for horizontal paneling (described above). Start paneling at an inside corner, working left to right if you are

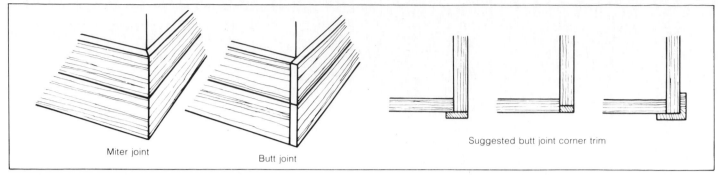

Miter joint

Butt joint

Suggested butt joint corner trim

On outside corners (shown at left) you can miter the ends at an angle greater than 45 degrees in order to fit the material tightly. If you butt-join instead of miter, cover the ends with molding or trim, as shown.

right-handed, and right to left if left-handed, as for vertical paneling. Keep the groove edge toward the starting corner, and tongue edge toward work direction.

Arrange your first three boards flat on the floor so that on the wall, tongue edges will be up. Fit tongues in grooves tightly,

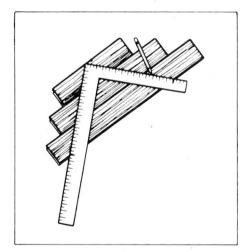

position a carpenter's square and mark for a 45° miter cut (see illustration) across all three boards. Saw and trial fit. Gently shaving the ends will assure tighter fit. Then face nail the corner piece and blind nail the rest at each end and intersecting stud or furring strip.

To butt join board ends in the middle of a wall, you can trim square or miter cut. The joint should cover a stud, blocking, of furring strip. Butt join paneling at corners, covering outside edges with trim or molding, if desired.

Window and Door Trim. Before applying furring strips or paneling, remove any window and door trim or casings that will be replaced with redwood lumber. After paneling, finish doors and windows the same, nailing build-up strips into jambs to cover board ends and/or furring strip edges (see accompanying illustrations) where necessary.

Start vertical and diagonal paneling

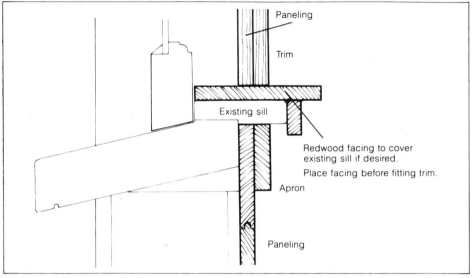

Remove window and door trim or casings before applying furring strips or paneling.

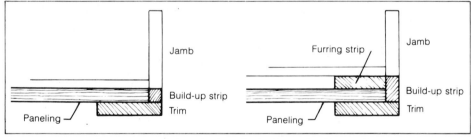

If paneling without furring strips, fit board edges flush with jambs. If using furring strips, fit board ends and edges flush with furring strips.

from an inside corner and work over to a window or door. To fit diagonal paneling at opening edges, miter cut board ends. At corners of openings, position a board diagonally as it will be in paneling, mark horizontal and vertical edges of the corner, make a cut, and finish with a wood rasp for close fit. Start horizontal paneling from the baseboard or floor and work up.

Without Furring Strips. Fit board edges flush with jambs; you do not need build-up strips. When fitting board ends around openings, leave space to nail a built-up strip into the jamb flush with paneling and the jamb.

With Furring Strips. Fit board ends and edges flush with furring strips. Nail into the jamb a build-up strip equal to the thickness of furring plus paneling.

Finishing. Apply six coats of clear polyurethane to form a tough, transparent film that will withstand hard scrubbing and resist water spots.

Hardboard or Plastic Panels
Hardboard panels covered in tough melamine plastic finish will dress up a bathroom while giving walls longlasting water resistance. The thick melamine coating is well suited for showers and tub surrounds, or for the walls in a bath

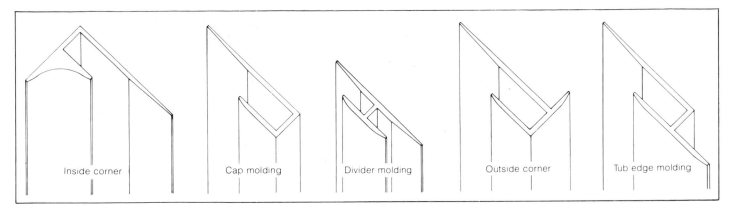

Inside corner   Cap molding   Divider molding   Outside corner   Tub edge molding

which has been badly stained due to high humidity.

Melamine-surfaced hardboard panels are installed in ways that differ from the methods used for all-wood paneling. The panels are held in place by adhesives, not nails. They should not be applied over ceramic tile, fiberboard, or furring strips. Molding strips, for butt joints, corners and the like are essential to the installation rather than just as trim. Since melamine-coated panels cannot be face or edge-nailed, the slotted moldings are what holds consecutive panels together. These specialized moldings also act as edge-finish for the panels.

It is essential the proper moldings be used according to location. Moldings can be either aluminum or plastic.

Cap Molding. This molding covers the top edges of a wainscot panel, or a vertical edge where additional panels will be installed. Use it also as a finish strip around windows and doors, at wall-ceiling junctures, at floor (or baseboard) junctures.

Outside Corner. You will use this molding to join two panels that come together at outside corners.

Inside Corner. Apply where two panels come together at inside corners.

Divider. This molding joins two panels at a vertical joint.

Tub Molding. The joint between wall panels and the bathtub will take this molding.

Panels are sold in 4x8 foot sheets; most moldings come in 8 foot lengths. Use a backsaw (and miter box) for cutting moldings. Have a keyhole saw for cutting openings within panels, such as those needed for electrical outlets, plumbing lines, faucets. Make pilot holes with an electric drill. Cut panels with a very sharp crosscut saw (8 to 12 teeth per inch) or a portable circular saw. To avoid chipping

and splitting the brittle melamine coating, here is how to cut the panel, depending upon the kind of saw you use.

Saw	Panel faces
Keyhole	UP
Crosscut	UP
Portable circular saw	DOWN
Electric drill	DOWN

In addition to saws and electric drill, the other tools and supplies you will need are: hammer, nails (for molding strips), tape measure, plane or wood rasp (for dressing panel edges, a file (for use with moldings), a pencil compass (for scribing), pencil, notched trowel, base trim, adhesive, caulk, mineral spirits or turpentine, and rags for cleanup.

Preparation. Melamine-surfaced panels must be installed over a solid backing, such as plaster that is firm and smooth, or over gypsum wallboard. The existing wall must be sound, dry, smooth, and flat. Make sure all old loose paint or wallpaper is removed, and that the wall is free of dirt, dust, and grease. If the wall is newly plastered, let it cure for at least 30 days so it will be thoroughly dry.

Caution. If you are paneling the inside of an exterior wall, install wood furring strips, and then cover with gypsum wallboard. This gives a solid backing for gluing panels on and provides the vapor barrier that must be between the paneling and the exterior wall. Use this same method of furring strips and wallboard if you plan to panel a basement bath or shower room. Basements tend to be damp and often are not well-drained, so a vapor barrier between paneling and existing wall is especially important. Have the vapor barrier contain a cover of polyethylene film. Use gypsum wallboard ⅜ inch thick or thicker.

Calculate how many 4x8 foot sheets

you will need. Be sure to include lengths and type of molding strips you will be using. On graph paper, make a scaled drawing of each wall, noting size and location of fixtures, soap dishes, towel bars, electrical outlets and so on. If you plan new locations for tissue holders, outlets and related items, include them in the sketch. Do not guess at these placements; mark them accurately now in order to save time and aggravation later. This will help you plumbers and electricians for times that best fit into your planned work schedule.

Order the material and supplies you will need. Discuss your project with your paneling dealer. He will probably be able to give you tips, help with your order, and sometimes guide you in your project.

When materials and supplies arrive, let panels and adhesive, as well as caulk, adjust to the room temperature for 48 hours. Separate the panels and stand them, on long edges, around the walls of a room while you prepare the bathroom.

Make sure all the walls are clean, patched, or have gypsum wallboard where needed. Use the waterproof wallboard for areas around tub and in showers if the walls in these locations require extensive repair. Remove all baseboards. It will make your job of cutting and fitting much easier. (Include this in your initial scale plan drawing of each wall.) Mark on the wall the location of all moldings, which should be nailed onto the wall surface at stud locations.

Wainscot Installation. Mark a level line that extends horizontally around all the walls which have panel installation. Leave the necessary gap between paneling and floor for later installation of the base trim. Measuring up from the floor, draw a line around the room that will indicate where the top of the base trim will reach.

Wainscoting is easy to install. It comes in panels or strips that can be fitted below decorative moldings or any other trim piece.

Allow for a total of ³/₁₆ inches between panels, to allow for a ¹/₁₆ inch expansion space between the panel edge and the inside of the divider molding. Never force the panels into position; always leave this small space for expansion.

To start paneling, begin at the inside corner. Nail cap molding along the line marking the top of the wainscot (use miter joints in corners). Nail an inside corner molding in the corner, extending from top of the base trim line to the bottom of the exposed flange of the cap molding. It will be necessary to cut away a little of the wall flange where it overlaps the cap molding.

Now, check the corner to see if it is straight and plumb. If not, it will be necessary to scribe the edge of the panel and trim it to conform to the corner.

Fit, but do not yet install, the divider molding for the exposed vertical edge of the panel. (If necessary, remove part of the wall flange where it overlaps the cap molding.)

Full-height panel installation. Start at an inside corner and nail a strip of inside corner molding extending from the line at top of base trim up to ceiling.

Next, install a strip of cap molding along the wall-ceiling juncture. Slip a panel into position and, if necessary, scribe and trim panel edge to fit the corner. Check with level or plumb line to be sure that the edge away from the corner is plumb. Cut and fit a divider molding, but do not nail it in place yet.

Cutting and Putting Up Panels

Panels are cut face up if you are using a crosscut saw. If you are using an electric bandsaw, the panels should be face down when cut. Handle panels carefully.

Dry-fit the first panel to the molding, which has been nailed up. Lay it face down on a padded worktable (to prevent scratching) and dust the back with lint-free cloth. Using a notched trowel and recommended adhesive, spread adhesive over the entire back of the panel. A trowel with ³/₁₆ inch notches is suggested unless otherwise specified.

For waterproof seal, put adhesive or a caulking bead (as recommended by the adhesive manufacturer) into the molding grooves.

Then slip the panel into position and press tightly against the wall. Apply adhesive into the groove of one of the divider moldings that has previously been fitted and set aside, and slip it into place along the panel edge.

Check to see that the divider is plumb, then fasten that edge of the panel to the wall by nailing through the exposed flange on the molding strip. Return to the panel and press it firmly against the wall, working from center outward toward edges. Repeat this after 20 minutes to ensure good contact. Remove excess adhesive as soon as possible, using a soft cloth and mineral spirits or turpentine. Install additional panels in a logical sequence, following the general procedures just discussed.

Note. To put a prefitted panel into place when only one side is open — that is, surrounded by moldings on two sides and across the top — set the panel on the floor and bend the panel slightly, as shown. When the two opposite edges can be slipped into molding grooves along both edges, release the curved panel, and slide the panel upward into position, in the top molding groove. Finish the job by installing base trim at the bottom of the wall.

Paneling around tubs and showers. Start by turning off the water supply. Line the existing tub with a padding of newspaper and a drop cloth or tarp to avoid scratching the tub or shower floor. Be sure no foreign material is between the padding and tub bottom.

Using heavy paper, make a template showing all locations of faucets, valves, shower arm, and the like. Remove faucets, soap dishes, or towel bars. Check for accuracy, then transfer the pattern to the back of a panel you have already edge-fitted to the wall. Make cut-outs for faucets, shower arm, and so on. Dry-fit the panel to be sure of alignment, then apply adhesive to back of panel. Fill tub molding groove and other moldings with adhesive or caulking for a watertight seal. Press the panel into position. When continuing with the installation of subsequent panels be sure that panel edges, joints and moldings are well filled with adhesives, so that the installation will be watertight.

Since no one set of instructions for installing paneling can take into account all problems, study carefully the manufacturer's instruction booklet. Variations can be adopted once you have become familiar with characteristics of the paneling material and its related molding strip-and-anchoring system.

CERAMIC TILE
Replacing Just One Tile

Score an "X" on the face of the tile, using a glass cutter. Bear down as hard as you can on the cutter, and then throw the glass cutter away; it will be ruined.

With a hammer, tap the "X'ed" spot lightly. This will break the tile into four sections. With a putty knife or scraper, pry out the broken pieces of tile. Clean the grout from the surrounding edges of tile and remove as much dried tile adhesive from the wall as you can. You can level it fairly well with a putty knife or scraper.

Chisel dried material from void left by tile. The new tile must fit flush with surrounding tiles; debris can cause misalignment.

Test the new tile for fit. Then put a walnut-sized amount of ceramic tile adhesive on all four corners of the tile. Press the tile in the void and align and space the joints to match the joints of the other tiles.

Let the job set a couple of days, and then mix up a fairly stiff batch of ceramic tile grout. Press the mixture into the joints around the tile. The best way to do this is with your index finger. When the joints are full, wash away any fresh grout on the tiles. Then, with a clean index finger, smooth the freshly grouted joints so they have a concave shape. Again, wipe away any excess grout or haze on the tiles. Let the job set for a week. Clean the area with regular ceramic tile cleaner, and spray with a silicone sealer.

Regrouting Ceramic Tile Joints

If you decide to regrout a whole counter, wall, or floor, note that the colored grout now on the market hides grime better than the white grout used in most homes.

Create a tool to dig the grout out of the joints: drive a 10d finishing nail through a piece of 1x3 near the end of the scrap. Use this to remove the grout from the joints. This takes patience; the work goes very slowly. If the nail becomes bent, remove it and drive in another nail.

To remove old grout fast, make a nail jig like this one. When the nail wears down, replace it. After regrouting, use grout sealer.

As you work, brush out the joints with the whisk broom and clean up this debris with a vacuum cleaner. It is important to keep the work clean. If you do not, you will track the grout all over the house, and then it is hard to remove.

When the joints are clean and you are satisfied with the job, mix up a small amount of grout. Spread this mixture over a small area of tile, using a damp sponge to distribute the grout and force the grout into the joints. When the joints are filled in this small area, wipe away any excess grout and move on to another small area. Repeat this process until the joints are filled.

Now go back to the first section you grouted. With a container of water, dip your index finger in the water and smooth the grout in the joints. Do not use too much water. "Damp" is good enough. Your finger will produce a concave joint, which is ideal.

Let the job set overnight. Go back with a damp sponge and wipe the haze off the tile. Keep using clean water as you go. This phase of the job will take lots of time, because tile haze is difficult to remove.

Give the grout time to harden — about a week — wetting the grout down twice a day to harden it. Then go over the tiles with tile cleaner and seal the tile with regular nonyellowing tile finish or a silicone spray.

Match existing tile and extend it up a plywood surround (aligning grout lines) to turn an existing tub into an enclosed tub.

New Ceramic Tile

In many homes a few decades old the floor — as well as one or more bathroom walls — will have tile. The job of changing the tile might seem overpowering. If you just chisel the individual tiles off the wall you will end up with a surface that is rough with the old dried-up mortar or adhesive. It is impossible to apply new tile over this rough surface. One solution would be, in cases where the house has wallboard, to tear off the wallboard back to the bare studs and then start over. In some cases that is the only thing that can be done. If you find wet plaster behind a loose tile, the odds are that most of the wall has been wet. The old tile should all be removed, the wall material taken off and new material installed. (See Chapter 5 for removal of wall surfacing material.) If the wall studs inside show signs of having been wet, let the open wall dry for a few days before you put on the new wall covering.

New Tile Over Old. An easier alternative, if possible, is to use modern materials that enable you to apply new tile over the old tile. The first step is to make sure none of the existing tiles are loose, cracked or broken. Replace any that are (as above).

Check backs of loose tiles for signs of water penetration. Even if there are loose tiles, examine the grout. Broken grout indicates water penetration behind the tiles. This weakens the bond and will damage backing. In these cases, tear out old backing and then install backer board or water-resistant gypsum board.

Applying new tile over the old will not be too difficult, because a tiled wall probably is plumb and square, and a tiled floor will be fairly level. You then will avoid the problems of leveling the wallboard or smoothing the floor with a surfacer. Additionally, the old tile can serve as a guide to laying out the new tile and assure that you make the fewest cuts.

Surface Preparation. If you have determined that the old tile is well bonded to the surface beneath, the only preparation is a thorough cleaning with a strong detergent or commercial tile cleaner, followed by sanding with carborundum paper. The abrasive action of the paper will scratch the old tile and create a better "tooth" for the adhesive used with the new tile. After sanding, wash down the tile with clear water and allow it to dry thoroughly.

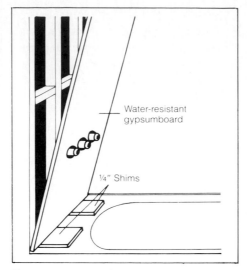

The gypsum core of water resistant wallboard has been treated so that it will be suitable for installation around bathtubs and showers.

SLOPE ALLOWED UNDER TILE

Surface	Adhesive	Must be flat within
Any wall	Any thin-sets	1/8" per 8'
Concrete floor	Epoxy or thin-set cement	1/8" per 10'
	Mastic	1/16" per 3'
Wood floor*	Epoxy	1/8" per 10'
	Mastic	1/16" per 3'

*Plywood subfloor's adjacent edges cannot be out of alignment by more than 1/32 of an inch.

Tile on Mortar Bed. This is the backing favored by most ceramic tile professionals. It is especially suited to areas that get wet.

The mortar bed is 3/4 inch to 1 1/4 inch thick on walls, counters or floors. Use the mortar to level out any surface irregularities and to help create plumb walls if they are not vertical.

We suggest, however, that the amateur use one of the less tricky methods available, listed below.

Tile on Gypsum Wallboard. This is not suitable for bathroom applications because the gypsum core will disintegrate if exposed to moisture.

Water-resistant Gypsum Wallboard. A wallboard created for areas around tub enclosures and showers, its core has been treated for water resistance. For identification, the panel's water-resistant paper face comes colored, usually in green or blue.

Tile on Plywood. If tile is laid on top of a plywood or plank subfloor in a bathroom, wood must be Exterior or underlayment grade, at least 5/8 inch thick. Place panels over the subfloor. Stagger them (the four corners should not align) with a 1/32 inch gap between each panel

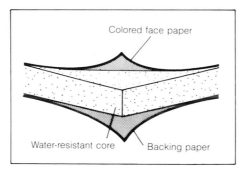

The paper face of water-resistant wallboard comes colored (usually blue or green) to help distinguish it from regular wallboard.

(1/4 inch if you will be using an epoxy adhesive). Use 6d ring shank nails placed 6 inches apart to nail panels to subfloor.

Exterior grade plywood may be nailed directly to joists if joists are spaced a maximum of every 16 inches. To fasten plywood use adhesive, or 6d ring-shank nails every 6 inches. Panels should be a 90° angles to joists. Unsupported panel joints must be backed with 2x4s.

Plywood (Exterior 3/4 inch) also can support tiled bathroom counters. Install it over a solid support, or with support braces, to keep it from flexing.

Organic adhesives or epoxies are preferred for plywood under counters and floors.

Tile on New Concrete Slab. Concrete must cure completely and be free from any cracks, films or curing compounds, before tile application. If pouring a new slab, as for an extension, place a waterproof membrane over the ground before pouring (see Chapter 12, "Expansions"). Reinforce the concrete with metal rods or mesh, because any movement of the slab will disturb the tile.

Keeping the Slab Dry. If kept dry, a concrete slab serves as a superior backing for tile. However, a damp slab will cause tile adhesives to disintegrate. Even if the builder has waterproofed the slab (covered the ground with a polyethylene barrier before pouring), test slab after a rainfall, when the ground has become saturated. Place 4 or 5 squares of polyethylene film (such as food wrap) in an irregular pattern over the slab. Attach all edges of each square to the slab for an air-tight seal, using cloth tape. Wait 24 hours and then check the squares. If they are fogged underneath, you should not lay tile on the slab.

There are several possible methods of assuring a dry slab surface. You can place drain tile into a ditch dug around the perimeter of your home, or you may lay polyethylene over the slab and then pour a second concrete slab (at least 1 inch) on top.

Tile on Old Concrete Subfloor. Before you apply tile over existing concrete, your subfloor has to be smooth, flat, clean, dry, with no cracks. Where a bathroom is built in a basement, the concrete must not only be solid and free of cracks, but have no "dusting." The latter occurs with improperly cured concrete: the surface constantly deteriorates, turning to a powder. Scrub the floor well with a strong detergent containing TSP (trisodium phosphate). To remove grease or oil stains, buy a chemical cleaner available at many auto supply dealers, officially for use on garage floors. If there is any debris, chip it off. If there is gloss, efflorescence, paint, or a sealer, roughen it by sanding. Use a floor sander with open-cut sandpaper (No. 4 or No. 5). Scour; vacuum any loose particles.

If a basement floor must be leveled for the bathroom, build 2x4 forms and pour about an inch of concrete to which an additive has been mixed to bond it to the old concrete. Then place reinforcing mesh over the concrete and pour at least 1 inch more over the mesh. Keep the new concrete wet for at least a week, then let it dry another week before applying ceramic tile with mortar or adhesive.

Fill any holes, cracks or depressions, or expansion joints with a concrete patch material if you will be using a cement-based mortar. If the adhesive will be mastic, use a mastic underlayment for these repairs. Be sure the surface is flat (see chart, earlier). If the existing floor is very rough or uneven, it may be the same amount of work to install a new film barrier and pour another slab over it, as it is to repair the old slab.

Tile on Backer Board. Concrete glass-fiber-reinforced sheets are "backer board". This material combines desirable mortar bed characteristics with easy installation. Second only to mortar beds for use in damp areas, backer board is not affected by moisture. For bonding tile to backer board, use latex-portland cement or dry-set mortar.

Fasten backer board with galvanized roofing nails (1½ inches) to wall studs or onto current wall surfaces. The big heads on the roofing nails hold better than the nails used for plasterboard. Use dry-set or portland cement mortar to seal joints around a tub or a shower receptor, as well as between panels or at other openings. Embed 2-inch-wide coated fiberglass tape into a thin mortar coat at corners.

If you install backer board over plywood, the subfloor must be at least ½ inch thick, with joists spaced no more than 16 inches o.c. Use construction adhesive to adhere backer board to the plywood subfloor, then apply mortar between the panels.

Wall Preparation. Walls must be smooth, flat and solid. As described in other sections of this book, if you are doing a bare-walls remodeling or adding a new room, the walls should have the studs spaced no more than 16 inches o.c. and the wallboard should be waterproof plasterboard, exterior grade plywood or tile backer board. If there is a difference in the surface level from one piece of wall material to another, it must not be more than $1/_{32}$ inch. Check the wall studs before you apply wall covering by using a straightedge at several points from floor to ceiling. Shim out any stud which is not flush with the others.

Use both a construction adhesive and nails to apply any wall covering and nail it well, with the nails spaced at least one third more closely than required when the wall will not be covered with ceramic tile. Use ring shank (barbed) nails that will not pop out later and push the tiles loose.

Application Over Other Surfaces. You also can apply ceramic tile over smooth marble, stone or slate.

Tools. You will need few tools for laying ceramic tile. They can be rented where tile is sold, but they are not very expensive and would always be useful for other tiling jobs or for repairing existing tiled surfaces. You will need a notched trowel for small areas, and another with a smooth edge and a notched edge for larger areas. A rubber-surfaced trowel sometimes is used for applying grout, but a regular squeegee does just about as well.

No matter what surface you are tiling, floor, wall or countertop, you will have to cut some tiles to fit somewhere. Dealers can cut tiles for you with a diamond cut-off wheel, but this takes a lot of running back and forth and you will save time, money and energy by cutting tile yourself. Tile can be cut with a glass cutter, but a regular tile cutter with a carbide tip is better; it will not dull as quickly. Tile nippers are for shaping irregular openings as for around pipes, but regular pliers can be used. The cutter and nipper can be rented from your tile dealer for a few dollars a day. Be sure to get full instructions on the use of these tools, since the devices vary. Most tile cutters are either like oversize glass cutters (for glazed wall tile) or like miniature guillotines (for heavier quarry tile as used on floors).

A tile cutter is basically a heavy duty glass cutter in a sliding frame. Clamp the tile in the device, then draw the cutter across the tile to score it. Remove the tile, place the scored line over the edge of a strong surface, or a nail or a dowel, and press both edges down to snap the tile along the scored line. The operation is similar to cutting glass.

If your tile has ridged backs, and the surface pattern permits, make your score lines parallel to the ridges. To mark the last row of tiles against a wall, when doing a floor, or the last row on a wall, place a tile over a tile in the last full row of tiles, aligning exactly. Then place an overlapping tile, butting it against the wall (or floor, if tiling a wall). Use a finetip felt pen and mark along the edge of the upper tile, the one flush to the wall, onto the loose tile underneath. Cut the marked tile along the pen line. You can mark a tile for an inside corner by repeating the previous operation twice, with the cuts at right angles.

Make a cardboard pattern (template) for places where you have to cut the tile in an irregular shape. Transfer the shape to

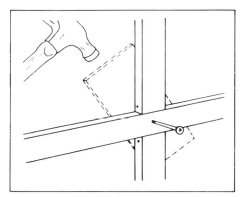

Furring strips must provide a level backing for wallboard. If original wall is uneven, use shims behind strips to make an even surface.

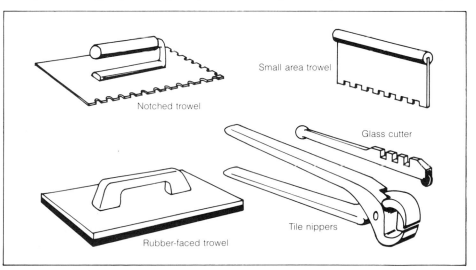

Notched trowel

Small area trowel

Glass cutter

Rubber-faced trowel

Tile nippers

Use notched trowels to apply adhesive, cutters and nippers to cut, and rubber trowel for grout.

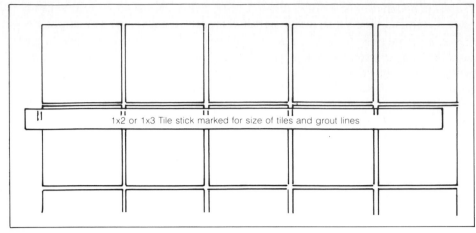

A "tile" stick is a 1x2 with tile and grout spaces marked on it. It must be straight and true.

the tile, then make what cuts you can with the tile cutter and finish up with nibbling by pliers.

When you come to projecting pipes or faucets, tile around them and fit the tiles at these places last. Remember that faucets and pipes will have escutcheons that fit around them to conceal any irregularities in cutting holes for them. For these situations, cut the tile in half on a line centered on the pipe or projection. Hold each half next to the projection and mark the half opening. Cut a V-shape with the tile cutter, then nibble the opening larger as required. Fit the tile halves tightly together so the grout will fill the small crack that is left.

If you have a fairly complete workshop, you may have a hole saw you can use in your electric drill to bore a hole from the soft side (back) of some tiles. The tile will quickly dull the hole saw unless the teeth are carbide tipped, and such a saw will be rather expensive.

Caution. When you are cutting and nibbling ceramic tile, always wear safety glasses. The bits of fired clay are glass hard and can cause serious injury.

Adhesives. Check with your local dealer regarding purchase of epoxy adhesives and mortars, mastics and sanded-latex portland cement mortars. In all cases, conventional grouting materials are used in the joints.

While dry-set or thin-set mortar is suggested for some locations, a do-it-yourselfer will do better with one of the modern mastics or adhesives which bond tile to almost anything. This is especially true of epoxy-base adhesives. The epoxy is more expensive than other types of adhesives, but it will adhere when other types will not.

Always carefully read the instructions on the container of mastic or adhesive you will use to apply ceramic tile. The instructions will tell you how to mix the tile, what sizes the notches should be on the trowel used to apply the adhesive, and how long the adhesive will remain workable after it is applied. Also, while some modern adhesives are water-based and nonflammable, others have a flammable solvent base. This means you must keep it away from all fire and flames. You must not smoke when using the material. Provide ample ventilation to keep the fumes from becoming concentrated enough to cause a health hazard.

Tile adhesives all are applied in about the same way. A notched trowel with notches along one side and one end, and the other end and side smooth, is used to scoop the adhesive out of the container and onto the wall or floor. One of the smooth edges is used to spread a thin layer of the adhesive, then the notched edge is scraped across the adhesive to create ridges, with only a thin layer of adhesive left between the ridges. Check the instructions, as the notched trowel might need to be moved at an angle or in circles, according to the manufacturer's research. Trowel on the adhesive only over an area as big as you can cover with tile before the adhesive begins to set.

Prime or Seal Coats. If the adhesive manufacturer recommends priming or sealing, use a thin coat of either your adhesive or of the material indicated by the manufacturer. The priming or sealing agent increases resistance to moisture and strengthens the adhesive bond between backing and tile.

Sizes, Shapes, Adjoining Edges, Special-Purposes. Ceramic tile comes

in a number of shapes, each shape designed for a specific location. Regular square or rectangular tiles with square edges also are called "field" tiles and they cover the major area of any floor, wall or counter. When you tile only partially up a wall, the top row will be "edging caps" that have a rounded over top edge. At the end of the top row of tiles you will need a "down corner" that has a rounded edge as well as a rounded top. Note that the down corner can be used at the right or left hand end of the top row simply by rotating it 90 degrees. Where the standard 4¼ inch ceramic tiles are used on countertops, the down corner and edging cap may be used along the edges of the countertop, with field tiles adhered to the edge of the counter under the overhanging edging cap or down corner. An alternate arrangement has field tiles flush to the edge of the counter, with shorter edging cap — just 2 inches high — applied with their top edges flush to the top edges of the field tiles. The shorter edging can also be used on a wall if the tiling is to stop shorter than the standard 4¼ inch edging cap would permit.

At the bottom of a tiled wall, or at the juncture of a countertop and backsplash a "cove base" is applied. This creates a curved transition from a surface to one at right angles. A "cove base corner" is used to make an outside corner on a wall. For an inside corner a cove base can be turned 90 degrees from its position as a cove base.

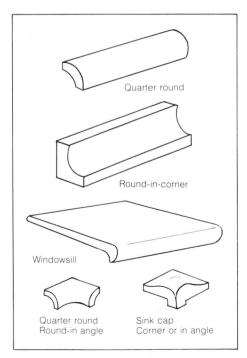

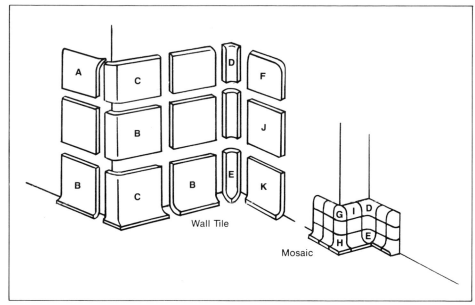

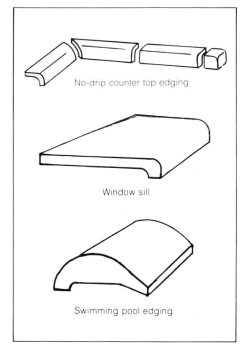

No-drip counter top edging

Window sill

Swimming pool edging

Trim tiles are shown in common usage or positions: A, Left up-angle; B, Runner; C, Right out-angle; D, Round in-corner cap; E, Round in-corner; F, Left out-angle; G, Round out-corner cap; H, Round out-corner; I, Stretcher; J, Field tile; K, Cove.

A "round top cove" is in tile installations professionally installed with a cement "mud," but is not too handy for the do-it-yourselfer. Because of the round top, it installs against the wall and on the floor, after tile has been applied so it almost meets at the wall/floor juncture. A narrow horizontal edge, which is not easily cleaned, is thus exposed along the floor. Because of this positioning the tile must be supported behind by the mud. The mastic or adhesive used for most floor and wall tiles will not provide enough adhesion or support. The round top cove also is used along the bottom of a wall when only the floor is tile, but not the wall. This shape might also be used around the edges of a shallow shower pan. (For some of these trims see pg. 78.)

Also used at the top edge of a tiled wall or the edge of a countertop is the "quarter round," which is shaped much like a wooden quarter round molding, but hollow on the back side so it resembles an L-shape. The quarter round also is used to trim around a square or rectangular vanity basin. A "quarter round in angle" is used for inside corners on such an installation.

A "sink cap" is used around the edges of a countertop, but the installation then has a raised edge which might be objectionable, although it does assure that any spilled water stays on the countertop rather than running on to the floor. Along with sink caps, "sink cap inside corners" and "sink cap outside corners" are used.

A "bullnose" or "edging tile" also is

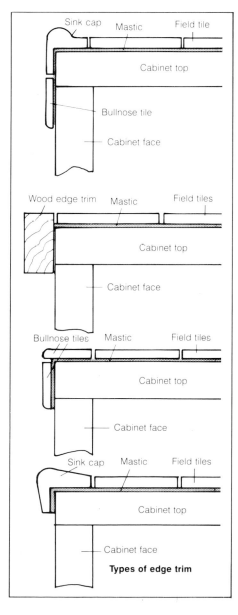

Types of edge trim

used for the top row on a wall or edge row of a countertop. Note that it differs from an "edging cap" in not having a right angle projection.

Because there are so many shapes and sizes of tile, examine typical installations at your local tile store and look over existing tile installations in homes and bathroom displays.

The tiles discussed here are the more or less standard sizes, with the field tiles 4¼ inches square. Floor tile, called "quarry tile," can be 6 inches square and ½ inch or more in thickness. These all are individual tiles and they are installed as individual pieces, along with inside and outside corners, coves, caps and the like.

Another tile comes in small hexagons, diamonds, ogees and even a mixture of small hearts interspersed with other small shapes. The tiles are held together on a backing of net, or a facing of paper. This type, with a net back, is placed right down on the adhesive, while the tile with a paper facing has the facing placed outward. When the adhesive or mortar has set, the paper lifts off after wetting it. The backing squares usually are 1 or 2 feet square, or in 1x2 foot rectangles.

Redi-Set System. One of the easier ways to add new tile is to use pregrouted panels of tile produced by American Olean Tile. They can be used over gypsum wallboard, concrete masonry, or existing tile. The sheets are suitable for walls, floors or vanity tops. Either the adhesive method or the cement mortar

Redi-Set pregrouted ceramic tile sheets contain approximately two square feet of tile. The grout joints are factory filled with a flexible silicone rubber grout. After the sheets are in place, the perimeters, corners, and tub line are grouted with the same silicone material.

Grout corners using nozzle and gun.

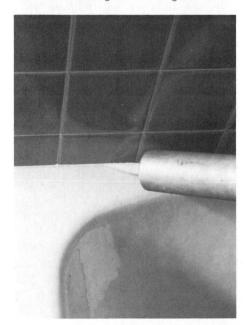

For a waterproof installation, apply caulking where the sheets meet the tub.

method of application can be chosen, using the American Olean Tile recommendations. The accompanying photographs outline the installation.

Spacing. The sheets of tiles have the spacing already determined, but the spacing between sheets must be the same as between the individual tiles. The standard 4¼ inch tiles sometimes have cast-on spacers so spacing is automatic as they are installed. If there are no spacers, then toothpicks can be used as spacers, or you sometimes can purchase spacers where tile is sold. After the adhesive has set, the spacers are removed and the grout is applied.

Tiles that do not have cast-on spacers can be aligned with thin strips of wood or other spacing material. Although a cord sometimes may be used, it is not recommended because if the adhesive has set up too much, the cord will stick and you may even loosen the tiles while you try to pull off the cord.

Another method is to use a "tile stick," which is a length of narrow 1 inch lumber marked with the proper widths and spacing of the tiles and grout lines. A good straightedge piece of lumber also helps keep a row of tiles properly aligned.

Extending Tile. If your bathroom currently has tile half-way or three-quarters of the way up, and you would like the tile to reach all the way to the ceiling, apply wallboard above the existing tile to create a flush surface. Wallboard (plasterboard, gypsumboard) comes in thicknesses of ⅜, ½ and ⅝ inches, so you should be able to match it to the necessary thickness. Should you have very thin tile, you can apply ¼-inch tempered hardboard with nails and construction adhesive from a caulking gun. Then tile over it as you did the old tile.

Grout. Although white tile is coming back in style, its antiseptic look is eliminated by using grout of a dark or bright color. Other colors gaining favor are gray and clear pastel. Epoxy-base grouts also are a good choice for floors and countertops because they resist stains more than regular grouts.

Estimating Quantities. To estimate the number of tiles you will need, or sheets of tile, measure the areas to be covered and figure out the square feet. Divide the area by the number of square feet the sheets will cover, or the other sizes of tile or have your dealer figure the

number for you. Most dealers will have a chart to determine the tile you need for your job. Allow about 10 percent over for cutting and fitting and possible breakage. The cove, edge and trim tiles are figured by the running feet, the number of inside and outside corners, and so on.

No two tiling jobs are ever alike, so work yours out carefully to suit your own situation. Draw up a grid layout to help you plan an arrangement with even rows of tiles at the edges. Allow for grout lines.

Room Preparation. Empty the room, removing even tools if they will not be used for the actual tile installation. If tiling only the floor and not the wall — which will be painted or papered — cover the wall with plastic sheeting. Remove base and shoe molding and door trims. If tiling the wall, remove all window trim. Cut a rabbet in the outside edges of door trim and window trim, just a bit thicker than the tile and about ½ inch deep. This will allow rough-cutting the edge of the last piece of tile against the trim pieces around windows and doors. The rabbet will hide the rough edges and you will avoid the cost of special edge pieces.

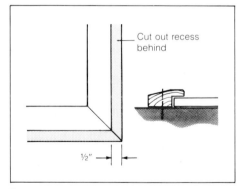

Cut out recess behind

½"

If you rough-cut tile to meet door and window trim, you can cut a rabbet in back of the trim to hide the ragged edges.

Before you start your floor or wall tile installation, have all plumbing roughed in and the toilet and vanity cabinets located. Shut off the water and remove the toilet and cabinets. You need not tile completely under cabinets, but it will be necessary to place spacers on the floor that are the same thickness as the tile to keep the cabinet level. Tile should be run under toilets close to the drain. Be sure to leave openings for the anchor bolts to drive into the floor if a cast iron soil pipe is used. If a plastic soil pipe and toilet flange are used, the bowl will bolt directly to the flange and tile can be laid close to the flange.

If you are going to tile the walls around a bathtub, remove faucet handles, as well as any grab bars, tissue holders and other fixtures. Line the tub or shower with pieces of cardboard to protect the finish and be sure drains are covered so no tile adhesive or grout drops into them.

Remember that ceramic tile is a rigid material, so any backing, whether wall or floor, must be smooth flat and fairly stiff. If a floor is springy, you will have to either double up the floor joists, or add joists between the existing joists, such as when they are spaced 24 inches on center instead of 16 inches. This removes any flex in the floor. If plywood, the subfloor should be ⅝ inch Exterior plywood (¾ inch is better) nailed every 3 inches. If the floor material is lighter, replace it (a big job, but it will pay off in a satisfactory floor) or at least add ¼ inch underlayment of Exterior plywood or hardboard, which should be nailed every 3 inches and glued with construction adhesive.

If there is more than ¹/₃₂ inch difference in level, even the surface by applying a floor surfacing putty. When dry, apply underlayment over the original floor, with the seams at right angles to any in the original floor. Be sure to allow any gaps between the underlayment panels if prescribed in the installation instructions. Just be sure that when you position the tile no grout line will fall over a seam in the floor panels.

Thresholds. The new floor will be higher than the existing floor, so doors will have to be trimmed along the bottom to allow for this, with a transitional threshold installed in doorways to match existing floors. Strips of marble sometimes are used as such thresholds, or wooden thresholds, or wooden thresholds can be added. Where there is carpeting in the adjacent room or hallway, one alternative is to shim up the carpeting at the joint and fit a metal trim strip on it to abut the tile surface. Check with your tile dealer as to what he has available for this transition area.

Order of Installation — Walls First. When ceramic tile is to be applied to both the floor and wall, tile all walls first, then the floor. Cove tiles are used at the bottom of the wall, and the floor tile then is butted up against the cove, with the proper grout line, of course. Even if you use tile with cast-on spacers, you may want to space the tiles a bit farther apart if

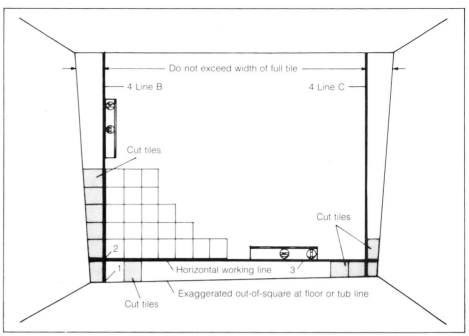

Before laying tile, square off the wall using a level and carpenter's square. Then work out numbers and locations of tiles that need to be cut to fill in out-of-square edges.

it means the elimination of a row of cut tiles.

Getting the Wall Ready. When applying ceramic tile to walls, gravity will be working against you. If the wall has no offsets, breaks or openings, the job is fairly easy. In any event, proceed carefully and plan ahead by drawing up a grid layout.

First, remove all cover plates from switches and receptacles, or any other obstructions on the wall. If part of your remodeling job will include new wiring for additional outlets or switches, or if recessed cabinets will be part of the job, add them before the tile work (see later chapters on "Storage" and "Wiring").

A wall surface must be smooth, flat and rigid. If there is any wallpaper, remove it. Wallpaper later can loosen and take the ceramic tile with it. Clean off any dirt or grease, and sand shiny areas to provide a grip for the adhesive. Where a painted surface seems to be in good condition, tile can be bonded to it. If the paint seems to be chalking, and thus porous, seal it with the proper primer according to the maker of the tile adhesive, as previously described.

Horizontal Guidelines. Lay out the job with strong vertical and horizontal lines so you can be sure the tiles are aligned precisely. Horizontal layout lines should be drawn near the bottom of a wall, because it is easier to tile up a wall than to work down from the top.

For walls in rooms without tubs, find the lowest point by using a level along the floor. When you locate the lowest point on the floor, set a tile against the floor and mark on the wall along the top edge of the tile. Where a cove tile will be used at the bottom of a wall, set a cove on the floor with a field tile above it, allowing for the grout line. Mark a level line across the wall in line with the top of the field tile. Use a level and straightedge to extend the line onto adjacent walls. The tiles will be snipped to fit in places where the floor is not at the lowest point. Now nail 1x2 battens so their upper edges reach the lines you've drawn.

Vertical Guidelines. Vertical layout lines are needed, and should be at the midpoints of the walls, crossing the horizontal working lines. Use a row of tiles or your tile stick to measure to the desired corner (or other ending point for the tile). If the end tiles will be less than half the width of a tile, move the vertical working line one way or the other by half the width of a tile. This will eliminate ending with a narrow tile, which looks odd and unprofessional. Extend the vertical working line with the aid of a level and a straightedge to the height that the tiles will be applied. If you will not be tiling all the way to the ceiling, mark this end point with your level and straightedge. Allow for a half or full bullnose tile to finish the top of the tiled area.

When making your layout, be sure to

mark in any accessories made of matching ceramic materials, such as paper holders, towel racks, and the like. If the accessories are made by the same manufacturer as the tiles, the accessories should fit into openings that are multiples of the tile sizes.

Setting the Tile. Ceramic tile can be installed in the traditional way with all horizontal and vertical grout joints aligned, or like bricks in a "running bond." The latter is not only more difficult, but requires cutting more tiles and thus wastes tiles and therefore costs more.

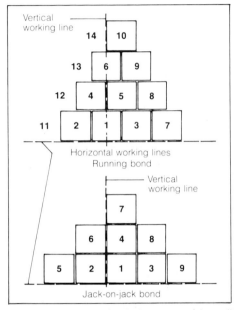

The vertical working line in the center of the wall acts as a guide for placing the first tiles. Work from the bottom up.

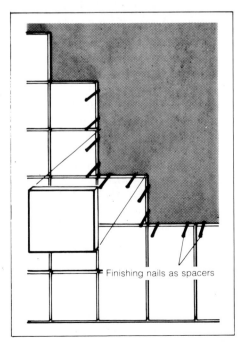

Move up the wall in stair step fashion, from the base line to the vertical working line.

To start the traditional ("jack on jack") bond, set the first tile on the batten, with one edge of the tile along the vertical layout line. Use a slight twist as you position the tile, but don't push it. Pushing will cause the adhesive to ooze up along the edge of the tile where it may prevent the proper alignment of the next tile. It also will have to be cleaned out of the joint when grout is to be applied. Continue setting tiles, using a stair-step progression. If the tiles do not have cast-on spacers, use finishing nails, cord, or other spacers to maintain a consistent grout line.

Maintain the pyramid pattern using the stair-step method, moving upward toward the corners and ceiling. Tile the entire area, with the exception of the lowest row, which is beneath the 1x2s. Every once in a while tap the tiles in with a square of plywood padded with a piece of carpeting. At the ends of the rows cut the tiles to fit (as previously described) using one of the several cutting devices. Add cap or bullnose tiles for the top row of tiles to give a finished edge.

To fit tiles around wall switches and receptacles, first shut off the power, then remove the cover plates. Loosen the screws that hold the receptacle or switch to the box and use templates to cut tile to fit the outline of the box. Apply adhesive; put tile in place. When set, position the switch or receptacle on top of the new tiles, hiding their rough edges around the

box. If the screws are not long enough, replace them with 6-32 flathead screws that are longer by the thickness of the tile and replace the switch or receptacle. Screws for the cover plates will be long enough even after the unit has been spaced out by the surface of the tiles.

Corners between adjacent walls can be handled with plain tiles for inside corners, or with one cove tile. Outside corners are handled by using a bullnose tile on one wall to cover the unfinished edge of the tile on the adjacent wall. Windows will create several corners that are handled with bullnose tiles or windowsill tiles.

Cut and fit tiles for the bottom row of each wall, then apply adhesive and push the tiles into place. Check the overall appearance of the wall, and if any tiles are not properly aligned, slowly and firmly twist and push them into alignment. The tile adhesive should still remain tacky enough to permit slight movement of the tiles. Complete curing of the adhesive will take at least 24 hours. Remove battens and spacers once adhesive has cured. Check the recommended curing time on the adhesive container. Clean off any adhesive from the faces of the tiles, and from the edges where it would interfere with grouting. Any accessories that are to be applied with adhesive should be installed now. For a faster tack and stronger grip for the accessories, use an adhesive formulated for floor tiles, rather than the wall adhesive.

When all the adhesive has set completely, including that under the bottom rows of tiles and accessories, apply grout.

Applying Grout. All grouts are applied in the same way. First spread the grout over the tiles using a float which is used to pack the grout; be sure all joints are packed full. You can shape grout lines on a tiled wall by running the handle of an old toothbrush along the joints. Let the grout set for about 15 minutes; dress the joints and clean the tiles by wiping with a damp sponge. Remove excess grout. After the grout has set for about half an hour, use a dry cloth to wipe off the film of dried grout. Let the grout cure according to the instructions on the container. Some grouts require periodic water sprayings before they will harden. Wipe the tiles again to remove any remaining film of dried grout. Give the grout several more days to cure completely, then apply a grout sealer to aid in keeping it clean.

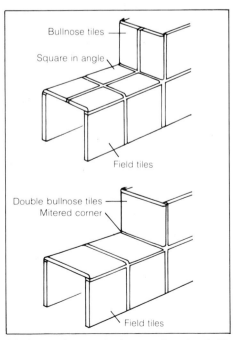

Window or shower openings can be edged with bullnose caps or double bullnose (below).

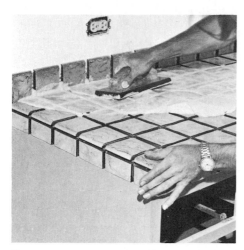

Grout can be applied with different tools. Read the manufacturer's instructions for correct tool and joint curing.

Silicone sprays are available, and easy to use. Follow any recommendations given by the manufacturer as to which type should be used with the tile and grout in your job.

Pregrouted Tiles. There is one exception to the grouting technique just given. If you use small tiles which come pregrouted, the tiles are set in a silicone rubber mat which is adhered to the floor with mastic. The sheets are spaced a grout line apart, then the joint is filled with silicone rubber grout applied from a tube or cartridge in a caulking gun.

Tiling Around the Tub. Where you will have problems, especially in an older home, is tiling around a bathtub. There almost definitely will be water damage to the tile backing, and some tiles will be loose. If this is the case, your best bet is to remove all the tile and the backing and to replace the original backing, which probably is lath and plaster but may be plasterboard. Use a waterproof plasterboard or a tile backer board as a replacement. If the studs and inside of the wall show signs of being damp and rotten, replace any lumber that has been damaged and keep the wall open a few days to be sure it has dried completely.

Although tiling around the tub is difficult, it can be done as long as the job is carefully planned. Be sure that all working lines are accurate so the tiles in the finished job will align both horizontally and vertically. The procedure when establishing working lines for a room with a tub is to first use the tub to find the horizontal lines for the tub wall; then, extend these lines onto the other walls. This enables you to align the tiles on all walls.

To locate your horizontal working line, first determine whether your tub is level. Check for level along the top lip of the tub. If the lip of the tub is within ⅛ inch of being level, locate the horizontal working line at the high point of the tub plus the height of one tile plus ⅛ inch. Then use a level and straightedge to extend this line across the back and end walls of the tub enclosure. If walls adjacent to the tub recess also are to be tiled, rather than just the recess, extend the horizontal working line around onto them also.

If the tub is not level within ⅛ inch, then work from the lowest point and plan on cutting the bottom row of tiles to fit. You cannot start from the high point of the tub because the resulting gap would be too wide to seal properly with caulking. Now create the horizontal working line just as you did for the tub that was level.

There are several ways to locate the vertical working lines. Usually you should start with the back wall that has the largest surface area and is the most visible. Measure to find the middle of the horizontal working line, and mark it. Use the tile stick or a row of loose tiles to determine how wide the end tiles will be. If the end tiles will be wider than half the width of a tile, use a level and straightedge to mark in the midpoint line.

If the end tiles will be less than half the width of a tile, move the vertical working line one half tile either way. This assures that you don't end up with very narrow tiles, which not only are unattractive, but difficult to cut.

End walls of a tub recess usually are marked off after the back wall is completely covered with tile. This assures that tiles on the end walls align with the larger back wall. When laying out the end walls, locate your vertical working line so that any narrow tiles are located in the back corners. Incidentally, newer bathtubs are exact multiples of 4⅛ inches, so if you build a recess to match the tub, no tiles will have to be cut. If the recess is deeper than the tub is wide, the tiles can be trimmed out with a bullnose tile, but there will be a strip of the wall that will have to be painted or papered. This situation occurs when only the tub recess is tiled rather than having the tile extend out onto the adjacent walls.

When working from the low end (toward the drain) of a tub that is not level, nail 1x2 battens to the wall with the upper edges on the horizontal working line (at a height equal to the width of a tile plus grout line plus chalkline, measuring from the lip of tub). The battens assure a level course of tiles and also keep the tiles from slipping down while the adhesive sets. After the tile and adhesive have set firmly, you will remove the temporarily nailed battens.

Although the same method can be used with a level tub, it is easier with a level tub to apply the tiles right above the tub. At this time, mark the locations of any accessories such as soap dishes and towel bars. If a recess in the wall is required, cut it now before you do any tiling. Omit tiles where the accessories will be located. It may be necessary to cut tiles to fit up against the accessories, but if the acces-

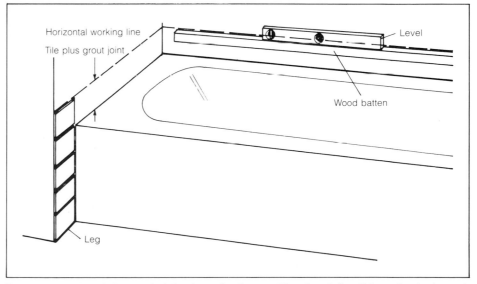

Battens above the tub (set at a height of one tile plus grout lines) are left until the adhesive has set. Then remove battens and fill in the row of tile, cutting if needed.

sories were made by the manufacturer of the tiles, they will be a standard size that fits in the space of one or two tiles.

If you will tile all the way to the ceiling, start applying the adhesive. If you will tile only partially up the wall, draw a level line at that point. Apply adhesive to within a fraction of an inch of the line, so that when tile is pressed into the adhesive it will not squeeze out above the line where it will show and have to be cleaned off. You can tile up to any height you choose, of course, but it is recommended that you plan at least one row (two or three is better) above the shower head. This will prevent moisture damage due to splashing water. When you have determined how high the last row will be, extend a horizontal line at that height.

Before you start tiling the bathtub recess, pad the bottom with cardboard and plug the drain with a cloth. With square or rectangular tiles you can use one of two tile-setting methods: jack on jack with all grout lines aligned, or a running bond such as that used when building brick or concrete block walls.

For the jack on jack, spread your adhesive and then locate the first tile at the intersection of the horizontal and vertical working lines. If battens are used, set the bottom edge of the first tile on top of the batten with one edge of the tile aligned with the vertical working line. If a batten is not used, the upper edge of the tile aligns with the horizontal working line and the vertical edge of the tile aligns with

the vertical working line. Use several shims between the bathtub top lip and the tile to keep tiles aligned and in place. To bed the tile in the adhesive, press it firmly against the wall.

Set the tiles in a pyramid arrangement, as previously described. Use nails or other means of keeping the tiles properly spaced for grout lines. If the tiles have cast on spacers you won't need the nails or other spacing devices. When you reach the end of each row cut the tiles to fit, but do not place them yet. Do an accurate cutting job or the grout line that results will be uneven.

Tile the back wall of the tub enclosure first. Mark off the end walls and work on them next. Leave openings for accessories. Every few rows, use your plywood padded with carpet to beat the tiles flat and flush. If any tiles move, adjust them, then tap them in later when the adhesive has set somewhat.

If you are not going all the way to the ceiling, the highest row of tiles will be of either half or full bullnose tiles. When you tile all the way to the ceiling the last row probably will have to be cut to fit.

With all walls finished, take a good look at the overall appearance and readjust any tiles that are out of line. Be sure all areas have been beaten into the adhesive. Once the adhesive has set (as per instructions as to time on the adhesive container) remove any battens, cut and fit tiles down against the tub, leaving a ⅛ inch space for caulking. Use only full tiles above this lip, as the bottom tile course. Seal any gap between the top lip of the tub and the first (lower) course of tiles with caulk once the tile job is done.

To ensure an adequate seal, run about 4 inches of water into the tub, then apply caulk. When the tub is drained it will adjust slightly upward due to the reduction of weight, and compress the bead of caulk. If you caulk the tub when it is empty, it can lower as much as ⅛ inch or more when filled. This movement will stretch the caulking, perhaps breaking the seal. After you have finished applying tile and it has been grouted, remove the cardboard pad, clean any adhesive or grout from inside the tub; remove the cloth from the drain.

Tiling Around Showers. The wall with the faucets and shower head will require that you cut tiles to fit. The fits must be good; a shower enclosure must be

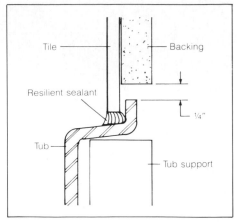

Space must be left between the tub support and the tile backing to accommodate the lip of the tub. Seal space with caulk.

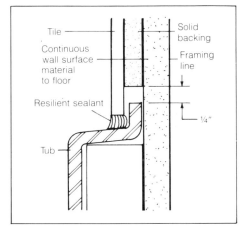

When installing a tub against an existing wall, additional tile backing is needed for the tub lip. Caulk joint to seal.

done right: the walls need to be watertight because there always is a flood of water drenching them. Even the smallest break in a grout line can mean wetting of the backing, eventual loosening of tile, and possible collapse of the wall. Allow space around all the fixtures for caulking. This allows for expansion and contraction of the various fittings and fixtures and any settling of the house. This is especially important when a new room is added, since the drying of lumber, plasterboard and concrete will cause considerable movement in the structure.

A professional can cast a concrete pan (receptor) on the job and then cover it with tiles, but this is not recommended for the beginning tile setter. Many professionals today speed the job and assure a watertight pan by using a cast iron, stamped steel or fiberglass unit. These prefabricated pans are sold in home centers, larger hardware stores with well-stocked plumbing and bath fixture departments and are available from larger

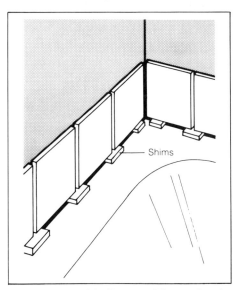

Brace the tops of the first row of tiles against the horizontal working line. Use shims of uniform size to leave the correct spacing for the caulk that will seal the tub to the tile and prevent water penetration.

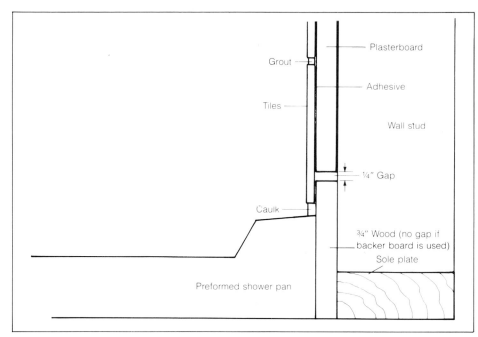

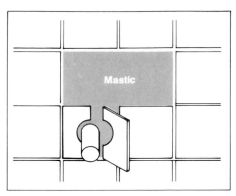

Cut tile in half and use nippers to cut space for showerhead, faucets or supply pipe. Caulk well before adding escutcheon plate.

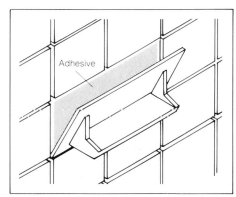

Leave spaces for soap dishes or other accessories and install after all other tile work is in place. Grout or caulk as required.

If you use a preformed shower pan, tile down to within ¼ inch of the shower pan and fill the space with caulk. Some pans have a lip that will fit behind the tile.

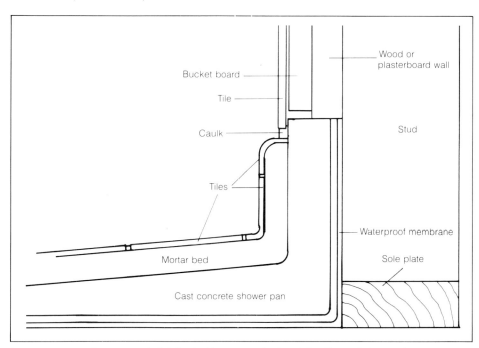

A cast concrete shower pan is finished with a mortar bed and tile. The wall tile overlaps the side of the shower pan. Joints between wall and pan are caulked.

mail order companies such as Sears, Roebuck.

Tiling a shower enclosure is done in much the same fashion as a bathtub recess, and referring to those instructions will aid in tiling the shower. Make the working lines on the back wall of the shower first, as with a tub recess. This is the wall that is most visible, as with the bathtub wall. In a situation where the shower walls project on each side of the front opening, use the back corners of the shower stall as working lines. Make sure,

first, that the corners are vertical. If they are not, make a working vertical line at the center of the back wall, work outward from it, and cut tiles to fit at the corners. Usually the out-of-plumb condition will be slight; use the grout lines in the corner to minimize the lack of an exact vertical.

Spread adhesive on the back wall first, and set the tiles as detailed for a bathtub recess. When the back is finished, tile the sides of the shower. Do the front walls last, after setting or installing any grab bars, towel bars or soap dishes.

If the shower enclosure is a new structure, or if you need to replace the existing backing because of water damage, apply materials as shown in the accompanying drawings. (Although we do not recommend a cast-in-place concrete pan, one may already be in place; therefore, details for this kind of installation are shown also.)

Some professionals will install tile on the ceiling. We don't recommend this for the beginning tile setter, and it really is not necessary. You might want to tile the walls right to the ceiling, but the ceiling itself should be regular plaster board or gypsumboard, taped if joints are included. Water resistant plasterboard is not recommended for ceilings, even if tile is applied to it.

Should you be adventuresome enough to try tiling the ceiling, do it before tiling the walls. Gravity will be against you with every tile, so use props to hold pieces of plywood up against every few tiles you apply. When the adhesive has set the proper length of time, remove the plywood and prop, apply a few more tiles, and replace the prop and board. When all tiles have been applied and have set (about 24 hours), grout all joints, completely packing every joint the full depth. Leave no gaps and no air bubbles. If you have any doubts about a particular section, scrape out the fresh grout before it sets and put in more grout. Compact it with the tip of an old toothbrush handle.

Caulk the joint between the wall tiles and the receptor with a good grade of bathtub caulk. After it has been applied, press firmly into the joint. Smooth it with a wet finger. When the grout has set, apply a sealer both to help waterproof the grout and to prevent dirt buildup.

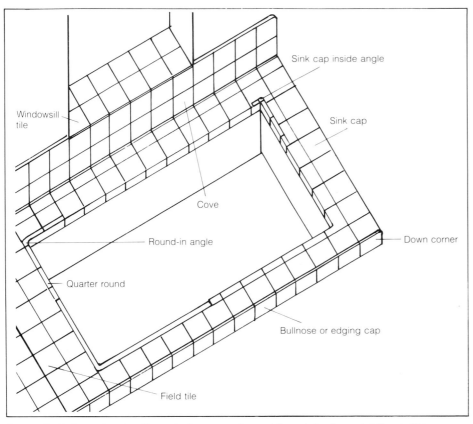

A complicated or extensive tile project may require a wide variety of special tiles to fit in corners and on edges of both inside and outside angles.

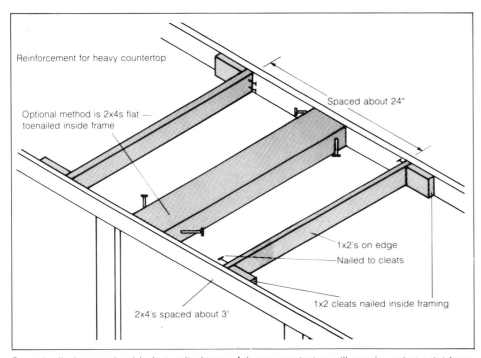

Ceramic tile is very durable but quite heavy. A large countertop will require substantial frame bracing to support the weight of the tile on the backerboard of the counter.

Tiling Countertops and Sinks

Tiling a countertop for a bathroom, whether it contains a basin or not, is handled somewhat like a scaled down version of a floor (already described). The first step is to determine how the edge of the counter will be trimmed. Several methods are possible (see illustration) as are different ways of installing a basin. A basin can be installed with the flange on top of the tile, under the tile, flush with the top of the tile, or spaced away from the tile with the space filled with caulking.

If you have bought or built a new vanity cabinet, use Exterior (waterproof) plywood or particleboard for the top, at least ¾ inch thick. Locate a cross-brace as part of the frame, every 36 inches or closer under the top, to assure a rigid surface. Read the instructions on the container of mastic you use to see if the manufacturer suggests sealing the plywood or particleboard before applying the mastic. In this case, find the specific type of sealer recommended and use as instructed.

First, find the lengthwise center of the counter and mark a line from back to front across the center. Start the first edge tile on this line and "dry lay" a row of the edge tiles toward each front corner. If the end tiles will be too small, move the center tile a bit one way or the other. If the counter is an existing one, you can apply ceramic tile right over old tile or even plastic laminate, if it is well secured.

When you have all the edge tiles positioned (still with no adhesive), place the field tiles, allowing for grout lines as required. If you will use a cove tile at the back of the counter against the backsplash, position a few of these before placing the field tile. Keep in mind that you can slightly widen or narrow grout lines to make the tiles come out to even, uncut rows. If you examine any professional job you will note that varying the width of grout lines is common practice. It can save a lot of tile cutting.

After you have figured your tile layout, remove the tiles and start application of the edge tiles. Cap tiles are fairly easy to apply, but if you use a two-piece cap, first apply the front edge tiles. If necessary, hold them in position with masking tape. When you place the second pieces (narrow edge tiles), position outside edges flush with the outside surfaces of the first edge tiles. This creates a horizontal joint that resists moisture penetration.

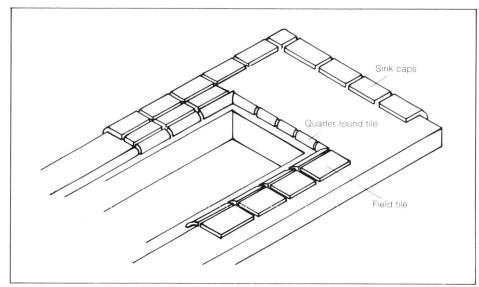

To tile a countertop with a recessed lavatory, you will need field tiles for the flat surface, quarter-round to edge the sink, and sink caps to cover the outside counter edges.

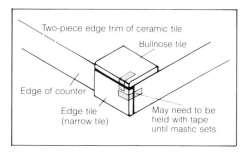

To finish the edge of a counter, combine edge tiles along the edge face and bullnose tiles along the edge of the counter surface.

If the basin fits down below the surface of the countertop, install it now, with caulking under the rim. Tighten clamps firmly, spacing them as detailed in the instructions for the sink.

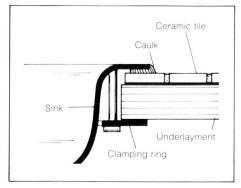

A self-rimming sink fits over the tiled countertop surface on a bed of caulk to prevent water leakage that would damage underlayment.

Place the field tiles until you come to the basin, then cut the tiles to fit, allowing for the quarter round or other trim tile to be fitted around the basin. Every few rows of tiles use the beater (as described for use on floors and walls) to firmly contact all the tiles into the adhesive and

make all surfaces flush. If the tiles are square or rectangular, use a 2-foot square to check alignment.

When you reach the back of the countertop, install the cove tile (if one is used), then apply tile up to the height you wish. If the tiles do not reach the wall cabinets, use bullnose tile for the last row. If a cove tile is not used, butt the last row of field tile against the plywood backsplash. Now apply field tiles to the backsplash, allowing for a grout line between the tiles on the countertop and those on the backsplash.

Allow the adhesive to set for the required time, usually 24 hours, then apply epoxy grout as in the instructions on the container. As with other types of grout, the epoxy kind can be obtained in attractive contrasting or compatible colors.

Because counters are relatively small areas, you can eliminate spacers if the tiles do not have them. When you tile the backsplash, however, spacers are a must — or the tiles will slide down.

Setting Floor Tile. Some types of floor tile, especially quarry tile, tend to be dusty. If you have dusty tile, rinse them in water to remove the dust, then let dry thoroughly. Dust keeps the adhesive from sticking to the tile, as does moisture, so make sure the tile is both dust-free and dry before you apply adhesive to the surfaces.

We have already discussed the need for a transitional strip in doorways because the tile may be higher than an adjacent floor. If the floor outside the bathroom is not carpeted, you probably can use bullnose tiles to make the transition, as the rounded edge will look good.

Ceramic floor tile can be laid in one of two methods. The first method is to start at the center of the room, after marking center lines at right angles in the center of the room. Tiles are then laid in four directions, along the lines, toward the walls. In most situations this means that you will have to cut tiles along all four walls. This involves more work, but for tile patterns where a symmetrical design will be in the center of the floor, start in the center.

Centered Layout. Snap chalklines to intersect in the center of the room. Lay out the tile without adhesive to adjust for spacing and minimize tile cutting. Then begin at the chalkline intersection: lay the four central tiles. Run a row of tiles along one side of one chalkline, from one of the center tiles to the wall. Then lay another now at right angles to the first, from the same first tile to the facing wall. Repeat for the other side of the chalkline. You will have four arms of tile from the center to the walls. If you have correctly located the midpoint and if all your walls are true, the number and spacing of tiles will be the same in each row. Now fill in each room quarter, working from the center outward.

Although not absolutely necessary, it will help if you tack nail very thin, straight wood strips along your layout lines to ensure the tiles will be properly aligned.

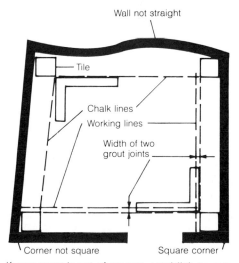

If your room is out-of-square, establish square working lines from the most square corner of the room. Cut tile to fit uneven edges of the room.

Working From Corner. The second layout for tile is to start at one end of the room and work to the other. This method originated with tile layers who used a mortar bed into which the tiles were set. It was necessary to work from one end of the room to the other to avoid kneeling or walking in the carefully leveled bed of mortar. It is recommended that you do not use this method unless at least two walls meet at right angles. In this case, tiles will be set so they butt along the two adjacent walls, then out across the floor to the other two walls. To determine which two walls, if any, are at right angles to each other, fit a tile snugly into each corner of the room. Have someone help you by stretching a chalkline alongside two of the tiles, from corner to corner. Pull it taut and snap a mark on the floor. Any curves or irregularities in the walls can be seen by comparing the straight chalk mark to the wall. If there is any doubt in your mind, measure between the chalk mark and the wall at several points. If there is only minor variation, enough to be handled by a grout line or a base cove set on top of the floor tile, it can be ignored.

Check the corner meetings of the four chalklines with a 2-foot square. Use the corner that is square, or nearly so, for a starting point. Dry lay out a line of tiles across the floor to determine if full tiles only can be used, or if some will have to be cut at the wall. If the last tile next to the wall will have to be cut shorter by just a bit, go back and make the grout lines just a fraction narrower. This trick often will eliminate the need for tile cutting. If the opposite happens — that is, the last tile doesn't quite reach the wall by the width of several grout lines — then go back and slightly widen the grout lines. All this arranging is "dry," with no adhesive. If you have to cut tiles, try to make all four rows that meet the wall the same width.

Use your chalked lines on the floor as guides to make your layout. Start with the walls that are at right angles, then mark another line beside your original chalkline, on the side toward the center of the room, spaced the width of two grout lines away from your first chalkline. This allows for the grout line against the wall, and the grout line between the first and second row of tiles. Make a similar line on the floor alongside the adjacent wall at right angles.

Tack nail a straight 1x2 along each of the two working lines. Make sure the lumber is straight. Hand-select the lumber; modern 1x2s are not usually very straight. Use the 2-foot square to check that the two 1x2s are at right angles.

To lay the tile, trowel a strip of tile adhesive onto the floor alongside one of the 1x2s. Use the trowel recommended by the maker of the adhesive. Apply an area about 3x3 feet for the first several times, then increase the area as you become more experienced at laying tile.

Position the first floor tile in the corner

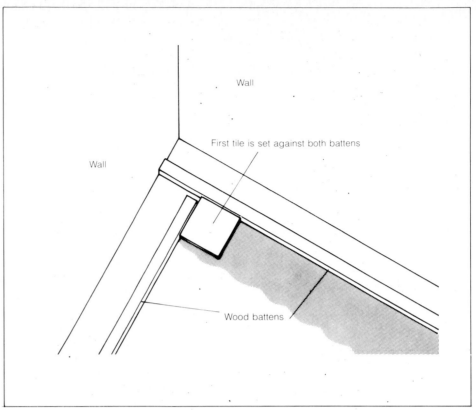

Nail battens to floor along chalkline guides so that you will have a permanent squared edge as a guide for laying your tiles. Install the first tile in the corner.

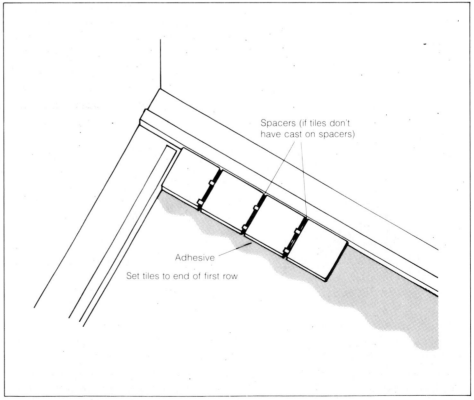

Use identical sized spacers to establish even spaces for grout lines. Many tiles come with spacers molded on. Set entire first row, keeping spaces even.

formed by the 1x2s, setting it with a slight twisting motion. The tile should be snug against both wood strips; this is the starting tile and the key to a straight row. If the tiles do not have cast-on spacers, use spacers or a strip of wood that is the right thickness to create grout lines.

When the adhesive has begun to set up (in about 15 or 20 minutes), gently remove any spacers. At this time also remove any adhesive on the faces of the tiles. A solvent may be required. Most epoxies can be removed with a damp cloth, but be sure to remove all of it. Epoxy will not come off once it has set, although other types usually can be scraped off. Do not leave any adhesive on the tile faces because it could stain the tile even if later removed.

Continue troweling on adhesive with the notched trowel, placing the row of tiles until you get to the other end of the room. Cut the last tile as required, then go back to the wood strip at the other end of the room — where you started — and lay the second row of tiles. If you prefer a "running bond" (staggered pattern, one tile offset against the next) rather than having all the grout lines align, start every other row with a half tile.

Once the second row is set, slide a block (wood about 2 feet square that you have faced with a scrap of carpet) along the tiles. Firmly tap the block over several tiles at once to "beat in" the tiles. This puts the tile in firm contact with the adhesive and levels all the tiles.

Occasionally stand back and check that you are keeping the tile straight. If you have any doubt, use the long blade of a 2-foot square, or a straightedge board, to check alignment. If any tiles are out of line, firmly push them into place. The adhesive will permit this for about an hour after being applied. Cut, fit and adhere the last rows, then embed them with your block. Gently pry up the 1x2 starting strips.

Check the instructions on the adhesive container to see how long you should stay off the tile. This will be at least overnight, and possibly longer. Don't let anyone walk on the tile until after you have grouted the floor. Without the support of grout, tiles can break easily. Once the adhesive has set, apply grout and sealer as for walls.

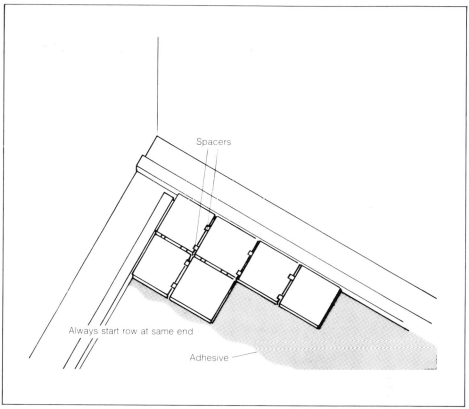

Begin second row where you began the first. Always work in the same direction. Use the spacers between each tile so that grout lines are identical in all directions.

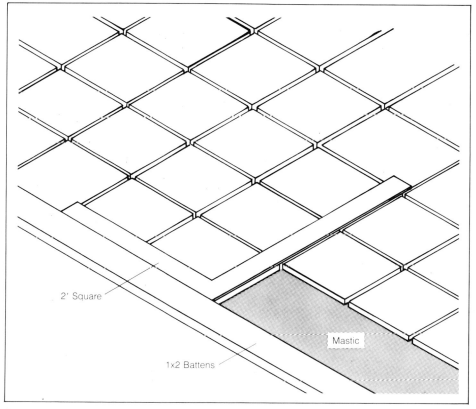

Check the square of your layout regularly and adjust before mastic can set. A two-foot square has arms long enough to check several rows of tile at a time.

6 Skylights and Windows

SKYLIGHTS

No-cost illumination is understandably welcome in an age of constantly rising electricity costs. A skylight offers a practical and attractive means of flooding a room with natural light without loss of privacy. This is especially true of a bathroom, where a skylight can serve as a window that combines privacy with sunlight.

On the negative side, a skylight can be a security problem; it can leak; it may cause great loss of heat in winter and promote heat buildup inside the room in summer. It can be difficult to clean and maintain. Local security and building codes may restrict their use. Be sure you know and understand the local regulations governing size, placement, material, safety, and shape before you make a final decision.

Selection

Before the advent of glazing plastics, skylights consisted of flat panels of tempered sheet glass, either clear or frosted, often reinforced with wire mesh, and supported in metal or wood frames. Today, skylights made of plastic in dome and bubble shapes come from the factory complete with metal frame, anchoring flanges, and watertight seals. Installation is relatively easy, and how-to instructions are provided. Installation does require you to cut into your ceiling and/or roof, so you may wish to leave this to an experienced carpenter if you have not previously done this type of work.

Ready-to-install plastic domes can be placed flat over a lightwell, or situated on a sloping roof. In either case, domes are easier to keep clean than flat sheets of glazing because rainfall tends to wash away accumulations of dirt and grime.

Whether your skylight is of dome-shaped plastic or flat sheets of glazing, try to situate it to face east or north so hot afternoon sunlight cannot overheat the bathroom. Choose skylights with double glazing to cut down on condensation. Depending upon how much privacy and light you want, select clear, reflective, tinted, or textured plastic or glass glazing material.

If local codes permit, and you feel there would be no security problem, select a skylight that can be vented. Some varieties of plastic domes are made to be opened from the inside. This design is ideal for proper ventilation, and for control of humidity and condensation. Flat skylights can be made to open and close by a system of pulleys, pivots, and/or sliding mechanisms. These are harder to find today, since most were designed and made for city apartment buildings and townhouses of the past. Venting skylight systems are used by commercial greenhouses; these the most common users of these models, which were once widely mass produced. An architect or professional builder may be able to guide you to a source for a greenhouse system for your skylight.

The accompanying illustrations (pages 83-85) detail the installation of a skylight in an existing structure. Installing one in a room addition involves similar proce-

To aid in heat loss prevention, specially designed shades slide in grooves in the casements of this skylight. The shades are covered with wallpaper that matches the rest of the room.

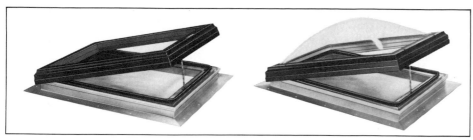

This skylight is available with either safety glass or an acrylic dome.

dures. In the latter case, you frame in an opening in the roof (and the ceiling if there is one) during construction, rather than cutting out the opening.

Step One: Cutting the Roof Opening

Carefully read all instructions, which will call out the size of the opening necessary for that particular model. If the opening goes directly through the roof, as in a ceiling which is also the underside of the rafters, both the ceiling and roof openings are the same size. If the skylight will require a shaft to direct the light from the skylight in the roof to an opening in ceiling — where there is an attic — then the ceiling opening will be a different size. The chart lists the required openings for the various sizes of skylights, in both the roofs and in the ceilings.

Finding the Slope. To use the chart on page 85, find the slope of your roof. Use a level to measure one foot along the roof, horizontally, from a point where the level intersects the sloping roof. Mark the roof at the intersection and the one-foot point. At the latter mark, use the level (or a ruler) to find the vertical distance between the one-foot mark and the point on the roof slope directly above it. You will have created a right triangle which intersects the roof slope at two points, and which gives you the rise-to-run ratio. For example, if the vertical distance is 4 inches, the slope is 4 in 12 (4 inches rise in 12 inches run).

Measuring for Ceiling Cut. Try to avoid cutting into joists or rafters, although it is likely you will have to cut through at least one. To minimize the problem, and to avoid having to cut two joists or rafters, determine roughly where you want to locate the skylight and then bore a ⅛ inch hole through the ceiling near the center of the skylight location. Push a length of wire through the hole, then go upstairs and check where the wire is in relation to the floor joists. (If the

ceiling is against the underside of the roof rafters, you will have to use the time-honored method of tapping on the plasterboard to locate the rafters.) Measure from the projecting wire, down against the plasterboard, to the joists on either side. Then go downstairs and repeat the measurement on the ceiling. If it is possible to keep the skylight opening between joists by moving it an inch or so either way, then do so; you will save time and labor, and avoid structural complications.

Cutting the Ceiling. Mark the opening on the ceiling and cut along the lines with a keyhole saw or handsaw. Hold up the plasterboard as you cut the last side, to keep the saw from binding as the board starts to tilt down. Wear safety glasses, and mask, or a face shield, to keep plaster dust out of your eyes and lungs. Even if you cut away from yourself so that the dust does not fall on your face during cutting, you can expect the plasterboard to drop afterward and create a shower of dust and debris.

The Roof Cut. At this point, measure up from the opening you have cut, using a plumbed straightedge, at each corner; mark the underside of the roof. Drive a nail through the roof at each marked corner, then go up onto the roof. Leaving the nails in place, remove the roof shingles inside and about 6 inches to a foot around the opening marked by the nails. Now snap a chalkline from nail to nail, or mark along a straightedge from nail to nail.

Remove the nails and cut along the lines. A portable electric saw will work well for this job, but stop just short of the corners and finish the cuts with a handsaw to avoid cutting beyond the corners. Even the largest of portable electric saws will not cut completely through a rafter; it will have to be cut loose with a handsaw. Make sure, of course, that no one is standing under the opening to be hit by the falling lumber. Check also that there is no furniture or any other item below which can be damaged. One safety procedure would be to nail a stout piece of rope or light chain to the roof at one side and to the section of roofing being cut loose. When the final cut has been made the piece will fall in, but will be held by the chain or rope. A helper then could lower the piece after prying up the nail on the roof, and there would be no danger. To work safely, think several steps ahead and realize the possible consequences of each operation.

Mark the opening from below. Then remove roof covering and saw over lines extended from the nails or wires. If you cut through a rafter, save for reframing later. A portable electric saw doesn't cut through full depth of a 2x6 or heavier rafter; use a handsaw to finish the cuts.

Frame in the opening with lumber that is the same size as the existing rafters or joists, using doubled lengths.

Apply roofing compound around opening. Don't let the compound run over edges of the skylight well, especially if it will be painted.

Step Two: Framing The Opening

Frame in the opening you have created, using lumber of the same size as the rafters or joists. Double up the framing at right angles to the joists. This may require cutting another 1½ inches from the ends of the joist or rafter that was cut. The additional 1½ inches will allow for 2-inch joists at each end. If a light shaft is required down through an attic, build it from the 2-inch framing down. It probably (almost certainly) will be necessary to cut a ceiling joist and box in the opening as in the drawing.

Step Three: Positioning The Skylight

Now spread roofing mastic or compound around the opening on the roof. Keep it away from the opening so none will run down inside. Position the skylight over the opening so its corners are aligned with the corners of the opening. It will be hard to keep your knees out of the mastic, so ask a friend to help with this step.

Once the skylight is in position, press it firmly into the mastic. Nail through the flange into the roof. Use large-headed shingle nails that will not easily drive through the aluminum flange.

Step Four: Finishing Off

Replace the shingles and apply roofing compound between the shingles and the curb of the skylight. Cover the flange completely with mastic before applying the shingles, and cover all of the nail heads with dabs of mastic. The last step can be the application of a bead of roofing compound between the edges of the shingles and the skylight from a cartridge of the compound, using a caulking gun. This is quick and easy, and is less messy than scooping out the black liquid tar from a container.

If the skylight has been installed in a roof with a ceiling on the underside, finish off the inside of the opening with plasterboard, paneling or other material.

No matter how plasterboard is used, it should be finished off in the usual manner with paper tape and joint compound. For outside corners we suggest using metal corners, especially if a hinged drop-down window is used at the bottom of the light shaft. The drop-down window gives the ceiling a more finished look, and avoids the sometimes objectionable appearance of a "hole in the ceiling" which a light shaft can produce. The ceiling window can be replaceable, to change with the seasons, so that a tinted glass can be used to reduce the glare when the sun is directly overhead in the summer. As an alternative, a translucent sheet of plastic, or plastic sun film, can be placed on the clear or translucent glass of the drop-down window.

Once your plasterboard has been taped, and the two coats of compound applied, dried, and sanded smooth (per instructions in Chapter 5), then brush on a sealer. Paint the taped joints and edges. If the ceiling has been painted recently with latex paint, you will have no problem

Position skylight over opening, aligning skylight corners with all four corners. Press skylight firmly into compound. Nail skylight flange to roof deck, using large-head roofing nails. Cover nail heads and edge of flange with roofing compound. Replace shingles as necessary to fit against edges of built-in skylight curbing.

With the skylight in place finish the inside of the framing and the ceiling around the opening. Paint or cover the surface with plasterboard or paneling.

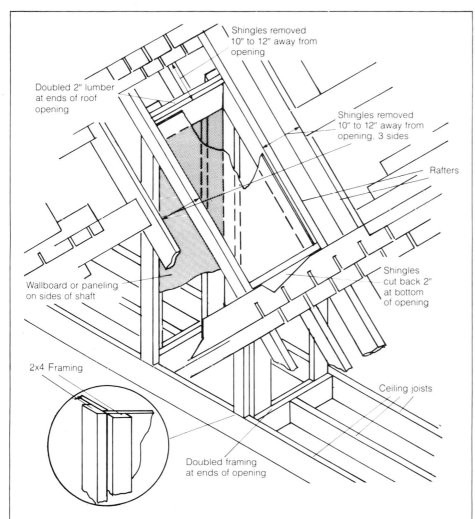

Shingles removed 10" to 12" away from opening

Doubled 2" lumber at ends of roof opening

Shingles removed 10" to 12" away from opening, 3 sides

Rafters

Shingles cut back 2" at bottom of opening

Wallboard or paneling on sides of shaft

2x4 Framing

Ceiling joists

Doubled framing at ends of opening

For an attic, build a light shaft between roof and ceiling. The ceiling opening is shorter (in line with roof slope) than the roof opening. Drop a plumb line from the corners of the roof opening to locate the ceiling opening, or project a straightedge board up from each ceiling-opening corner to find the roof opening. Plumb the straightedges 2 ways with a level to align the 2 openings. Frame the light shaft as for a wall, using 2x4 studs. In unheated attics, install insulation on outside of the light shaft.

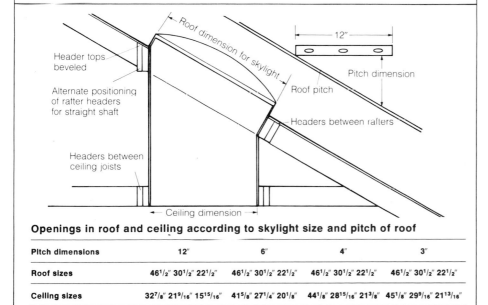

Roof dimension for skylight

12"

Header tops beveled

Pitch dimension

Alternate positioning of rafter headers for straight shaft

Roof pitch

Headers between rafters

Headers between ceiling joists

Ceiling dimension

Openings in roof and ceiling according to skylight size and pitch of roof

Pitch dimensions	12"			6"			4"			3"		
Roof sizes	46½"	30½"	22½"	46½"	30½"	22½"	46½"	30½"	22½"	46½"	30½"	22½"
Ceiling sizes	32⅞"	21⁹⁄₁₆"	15¹⁵⁄₁₆"	41⅝"	27¼"	20⅛"	44⅛"	28¹⁵⁄₁₆"	21⅜"	45⅛"	29⁹⁄₁₆"	21¹³⁄₁₆"

Chart gives the sizes of openings in roof and ceiling according to the skylight size and the pitch of the roof.

matching the surfaces. But if the paint is several years old the new paint will be a different shade, which means the entire ceiling should be repainted. However, if you are remodeling extensively, redecorating will be in order and you would probably already have planned on repainting the entire ceiling.

WINDOWS

The ideal bathroom window should be weathertight, reduce glare, resist heat transfer and condensation, provide privacy, not take up too much wall space, be easy to open, close, clean, and be shatterproof.

As with most things in life, such perfection does not exist in a single unit suitable for all conditions. Your best option is to use whichever available window designs and materials come closest to solving your particular and most pressing problems, such as heat loss, glare or privacy.

To have a window that functions best for your bath, consider three components: (1) the frame construction and the design of the window; (2) the glazing; (3) the window's decorative treatment.

Size, Shape, Style

Each type of window offers a different advantage or best fits a particular use. Sliding windows set high in the wall will increase privacy, allow more usable wall space, and open and close easily. A small double-hung window, adequate for most baths, will be easier to insulate (using weatherstripping, storm window or glazing) than will a larger one.

Light, air, and privacy can be controlled by folding shutters with movable louvers.

Outward-opening casement and awning windows are suitable for use in cold-weather regions provided they are well insulated. Jalousie windows are often preferred by homeowners, but are best used only where the climate is warm.

Makers of top quality (brand name) windows have realized the need for better window construction to help control drafts, heat loss, and condensation. As a result, you can find well-made windows at your building supply dealer's or home center. Quality windows consist of double — or even triple — glazing with a thermal barrier already built in. Frames of metal or vinyl clad wood have all-weather seals and resist swelling caused by humidity. Some windows can incorporate extra weatherstripping, but on an optional special-order basis. If you plan to install a window yourself, ask your dealer for information and specification sheets on prefinished, ready-to-install windows that come with frame and hardware.

Glazing

Window glazing can be made of glass or plastics, or a combination of both. The glazing controls heat loss, glare, condensation and creates privacy.

Certain types of glazing help block heat loss from the bath on cold days, and also reduce the amount of heat coming inside on hot days. Other types of glazing reduce glare, sun-fading, solar radiation or heat-buildup inside the room.

Inadequate glazing causes as much, if not more, heat loss as poor weatherstripping. If the window contains only a thin sheet of glass or plastic, the glazing will stay as hot or cold as the outside air. Your home heating and cooling system can work overtime and still not be able to compensate for the heat or cold transferring through the thin glazing material. The primary way to control heat transfer and condensation is with storm windows and with insulating glass. Condensation occurs when hot humid air inside the bathroom strikes the cool, inside glazing surface.

Tough, shatter-resistant plastics for window glazing are now free of distortion, permit good light transmission, and resist abrasion. The glazing plastics are easy to install and in general are lighter in weight than most glass of the same size.

Clear Glass. This is the most common and inexpensive kind of window glazing. It allows the highest amount of natural light to come through. However, a single layer of glass does not block heat loss. Condensation will form quickly on cold days when humidity rises inside the bathroom.

Insulating Glass. This type of glazing will block the transfer of heat and cold, and is best able to prevent condensation. Its double-glazing consists of a sealed-in layer of gas or dry air between two sheets of glass. It can also be given a reflective surface coating to further reduce heat transfer. Tints can reduce glare and sunfading.

One-way Glass. With a reflective mirrorlike finish, you can see through it from the inside but those on the outside cannot see in. Reflective coatings cut down on the amount of heat transfer and act as a form of insulation. However, the amount of natural light coming through will be reduced by one-half or more. Select this kind of glazing where glare, intense sunlight and fabric-fading have to be controlled, and privacy is important.

Tinted Glass. The advantages include lowered glare and a certain amount of privacy during the day. When interior lights go on at night, window curtains or shades will still be necessary.

Safety Glazing. This will often be required by local safety codes. Usually such regulations deal with tub and shower enclosures, skylights, sliding glass doors, and fixed-pane window walls. You should be aware of this kind of glazing, especially for windows situated near or over bathtubs.

Tempered Glass. This glass is four times stronger than plain ordinary glass. The tempering process makes it less likely to break when struck, so is often required for windows and doors that need an extra safety factor. It is not much more expensive than untempered glass and is available tinted, patterned, or clear. Tempering only makes the glass stronger; it has nothing to do insulation or condensation control.

Safety Glass. A sandwich composed of two sheets of glass laminated to a vinyl plastic core, the plastic liner keeps fragments of shattered glass from flying loose. The vinyl core can be clear or tinted.

Wire Glazing. Thin strands of metal mesh embedded in the material help control shattering if the window is broken. The glazing material can be clear, frosted, or textured.

Thick Plastic Glazing. With high impact strength and shatter resistance, loose shards of this glazing are less likely to cause cut injuries than will glass fragments. It offers many benefits, and is

This privacy-controlling window treatment made of plastics has diamond-shaped panes with an assemblage of colors and textures.

often required for doors, windows, skylights.

Sound-control Glazing. Specially made to muffle the transmission of noise through windows, doors, or window-walls, this material is expensive but can be worthwhile if sound-proofing is important to you and for your home. The material consists of two sheets of glass laminated to a core of thick layers of plastic.

Privacy. If you want windows that provide privacy yet need little or no extra covering like shades or curtains, choose one of these: stained glass, frosted glazing, textured glazing, reflective glazing. They can be made of glass or plastic. Textured glazing may have surfaces that are pebbled, rippled, stippled, or ridged. This material is available in strong colors, pale tints, or no-color. It helps diffuse light and also reduces glare.

Placement Makes a Difference

Experts in the field of heating and cooling, in bath design, and in home construction all seem to agree on two things: bathroom windows should be as weathertight as possible; bathtubs should not be placed under a window. Yet few such windows are well insulated, and a high percentage of tubs and windows are situated near each other. There may be several reasons

for the latter: dramatic effect; construction fashion trends; or, because there is just no other place to install one or the other.

In new construction the tub-versus-window controversy can be settled by homeowner and builder-designer in the planning stages. In warm climates, tub-and-window combinations, particularly with garden areas, are feasible. In cold climates, the tub should not be placed beneath or next to the window.

Decorative Treatments

Primarily, window treatments are used to carry forward your decorative theme. The materials you use can express your feelings about color, texture, atmosphere and mood. But window dressing also does even more. Shades, blinds, curtains, interior shutters, stained glass panels help control heat transfer and drafts to some extent; they control light and privacy to a large extent.

If drafts, heat and cold concern you, use these guidelines in deciding upon your window treatment (courtesy of the Kirsch Company).

The more layers of fabrics and material there are, the more trapped air there will be; air pockets create better insulation. Tightly woven, bulky fabrics are better than thin, sheer open-weaves. If window

fabrics have thermal, foam, or millium lining, they will work even better to control heat loss.

Window treatments must be kept away from heat sources. If fabrics cannot be below the sill or floor-length because of floor registers, baseboard heating, or radiators, then install the material inside the window frame, keeping it in contact with the window sill, as well as top and sides of the recess.

If using shades or louvered blinds, use an outside mount. Mounts placed inside the frame can cause air leaks along the edges.

When it is warm outside, you can turn back the sun's rays by reflection. The best reflection is provided by a white or light-colored nonporous surface. A sheer white curtain will turn away some sunlight, but even more will bounce off a tightly closed, white metal, louvered blind.

Shutters and Blinds. Folding shutters with movable louvers have the practical advantage of being single-unit window coverings that let you control light, air, and privacy. You can paint them any color to highlight a particular wall, or to help an oddly sized or poorly placed window blend in with the surroundings.

Window Repair or Replacement

When you remodel an old bathroom you

Woven-woods are thick, bulky and warm-looking, can be rolled up and down, or raised in folds. Here, the woven wood shade and valance are treated as a unit.

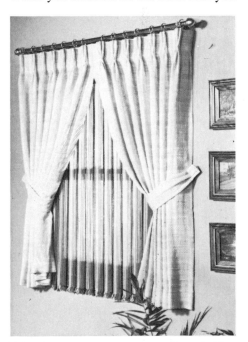

This window treatment uses ordinary knitting yarn tied around sash rods at top and bottom. Short draperies go over the striped yarn covering. If window has no sill, use sash rods. If it has a sill, use small diameter cafe rods. Extend so yarn clears sill and trim.

almost certainly will find that the window(s) need repair or replacement. The high humidity in a bathroom is a guarantee that there will be moisture damage due to condensation in the outside wall (or walls, if in a corner room). One option is to completely remove the wallcovering and the wallboard on the inside of the exterior wall so you can check for moisture damage.

Rot and Repair. When you strip off the wallcovering you probably will find little insulation, if any, and no real vapor barrier. What insulation there is may be damp. Even the sheathing and/or siding will be damp from condensation and it is likely there will be some rotted spots. The windows are a structural part of the outside wall and they take more punishment from moisture than is even the case with walls.

If the siding or sheathing (in some older homes the siding was applied directly to the studs, with no sheathing) is simply damp, leave the wall open for about a week until the wood dries out completely. If there is any rot damage, now is the time to replace any studs, sills and top plates which show any effects of the damage. Remember that rot is an organism that

thrives in the presence of moisture and heat. Any wood that has been damaged by rot should be replaced. Simply letting it dry might just temporarily stop the rot, which would immediately be reactivated when you closed in the wall, and the heat and humidity were restored in the bathroom.

Removing Wallboard Panel. To remove the wallboard, first gently pry off the base molding. Use a pry bar and hammer for this but take it easy when you pry; you want to save the trim and reinstall it.

When the molding has been removed, tap and pull out the nails and store the molding out of your way.

With a hammer, break out the gypsum-board panel back to the studs to which the sides of the panel have been nailed. If you go very slowly, you can remove the entire damaged panel by removing chunks of the panel and pulling the nails as you go. Do it in small pieces rather than jerking off the whole panel at once.

When you come to the panel joints, you probably will have to cut the gypsum-

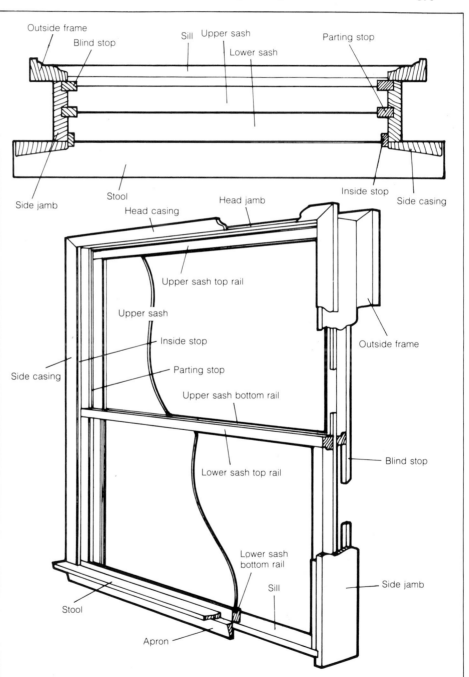

Pull end sections of cut sill out of dadoes

Saw windowsill in two places (inside stool already removed)

To remove existing window, first cut twice across stool (inside sill) and remove section. Pull out side pieces, which usually are in dadoes in side frames. If window was made on the job, the stool may butt to sides. In most cases you cannot tell this just by looking.

Nomenclature of standard double-hung window shows that some parts have odd names; the "windowsill", for example, is the outside bottom of the window, but the "stool" is the inside sill. Modern double-hung sash will be spring-loaded; weights will not be used to counter-balance the separate sash as in old-fashioned windows.

board tape that spans the joints along the sides and at the ceiling line. Do this with the razor knife. Again, be careful not to rip into the adjoining panels or the ceiling.

With the panel removed, you should have a neat, clean hole in the wall with the studs exposed and gypsumboard panels overlapping the side studs by about half the width.

Cutting Inside Sill. To replace a window with one of the same size, or one of another size, start by cutting a section of the stool (the inside sill) so it can be removed. We are assuming that the inside surface of the wall has been stripped of covering, including the trim around the window. With the section of the stool removed, pull out the ends of the stool, which will be in dadoes in the side frames.

Now, pry out the nails in the sides of the window frame. These have been nailed to the wall framing with casing nails. The nails look like oversize finishing nails. Next, pry out and take down the top (head) jamb. Finally you will have an opening in the studding that should have a double header at the top, above which there are cripples, and a single header below with cripples under it, as in the accompanying drawing.

Nonstock Sizes. If your house is quite old, the windows probably are a size for which you no longer can purchase a stock size of window. For this reason, *before* you tear out the window, measure the "rough opening." That is the vertical and horizontal dimensions of the opening inside the 2x4 framing in which the window is held. Check with your local lumberyard or home center to see what windows they have that are close to that dimension, remembering that the window should be about ¾ inch smaller in each dimension than the rough opening. You will note that the old window has shims at the sides to make it plumb and square. Similar shims will be required for the new window.

Larger Sizes. Because windows in the bathrooms of older homes often were quite small, you might want to install a larger unit. In this case, you will have to frame in a larger opening. The first step is to purchase the window and bring it home (or have it delivered if it is too large for your car). Instructions with the window will specify the required rough opening. Now determine how high you want the

stool (inside sill) to be. Try to keep it higher than the top of the bathtub. However, if you are considerably remodeling a bathroom you will want to try to move the tub from any outside wall for the best positioning.

Next, determine where the sides of the window will be. You can decide to move a window so it is offset even though it previously was centered; or conversely, you can center a window that previously was off center. Remove the wallboard panel as previously described. Locate the four corners of the desired opening and drive nails through the sheathing and/or siding at these points, from the inside. Now, go outside and mark between the four nails to outline the opening. Doublecheck that the bottom and top of the opening are level, and that the sides of the opening are plumb.

Cutting the Opening. Use a portable circular saw and a carbide-tipped blade or a flooring blade. These blades will withstand cutting through a few nails, which you are bound to do. The saw will notch some 2x4s, and you will have to finish cutting through them with a handsaw. Go back inside and frame in the opening with a double header at the top, a single at the bottom and a filler stud (trimmer) at each side. Note that the studs at the top and bottom of the opening will have to be shortened with a handsaw to allow for the headers: 3 inches at the top, 1½ inches at the bottom. If a stud is too close to either side of the opening, it will have to be removed and replaced with another stud and filler stud to come flush with the side

of the opening. Cripple studs are installed above and below the opening to support the lower header and the ceiling. Double cripples are aligned directly above and below the filler studs at the sides of the opening.

Ceiling Supports. If the rough opening is less than about 5 feet, you may not have to provide support for the ceiling while you frame in the opening. Most windows are less than 5 feet wide in a bathroom. However, if the bathroom is on a first floor, with a second floor above it, discretion dictates that you support the ceiling before you start knocking out studs in an exterior (load-bearing) wall. To do this, cut a couple of lengths of 2x8 or 2x10 about 6 or 8 feet long. Place one on the floor about 3 feet away from the wall — you will need room to work. Fasten the other length of lumber on top of it, then measure the distance from the top of the second piece up to the ceiling. Cut two supports to equal this distance, minus 1¾ to 2 inches.

Cut a length of 2x10 or 2x12 that at least equals that of the horizontal props on the floor. This sandwiches between the supports and the ceiling, protecting the ceiling from gouges caused by the supports and evenly distributing the ceiling weight between them. Lay the face of the ceiling support against the tops of the vertical supports. Place each support about a foot in from each end of the protector and nail all three pieces together. Put the open end of the vertical supports against the floor prop. Tilt the shoring structure up to the ceiling itself. The vertical legs

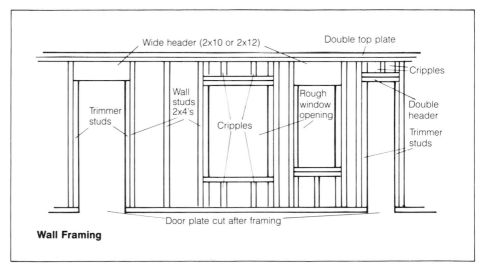

Wall Framing

Window rough opening (and door opening) have double header at top, single at bottom, with filler (trimmer) studs at sides for double side studs. Cripples at top and bottom of opening are short support studs. If a wide window is installed, the header can be of doubled 2x10s or 2x12s. When a door opening also is made, the last step is to cut out the sole plate.

should rest on top of the floor prop. Drive two shingle wedges or pieces of ¼ or ½ inch plywood under each of the vertical pieces — one driven from each side —

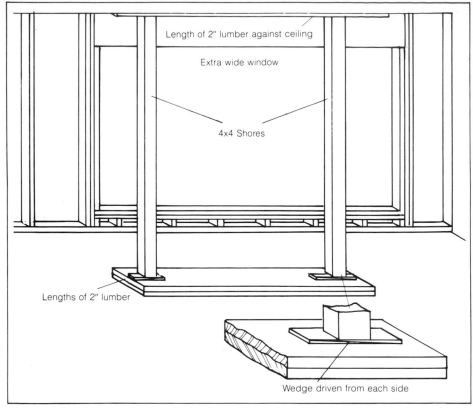

Where a ceiling must be supported, as for an extra-wide window or door — or where there is a second floor above — shore up the ceiling with 2-inch lumber. Vertical shores are jammed against ceiling piece with shingle shims under them. Occasionally tap in the shims, as they may loosen from hammer blows during work on the wall framing.

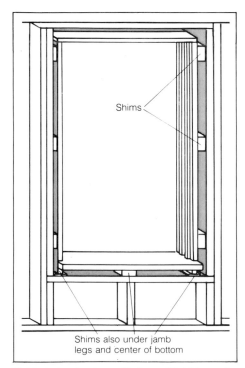

Hold window in place with 2 small finishing nails; go inside and drive shims around frame to level and plumb window. Check corners for square. Don't bow in sides, top or bottom with shims. Nail through frame and shims into 2x4 studs using casing nails.

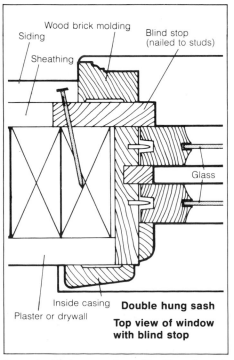

Some double hung sash are fitted from the outside of the opening, and are attached by driving nails through the blind stop into wall studs. For this application, space the sheathing 1½ inches away from the edges of the rough opening, all the way around.

until the vertical unit is held solidly in place, wedged between the floor and the ceiling. Periodically while you are working on cutting the window opening, tap the shingle shims lightly to make sure the support posts have not loosened due to your hammering on the wall. As soon as you have finished framing in the opening, you can remove your ceiling shores. You don't want any more obstructions in the room than necessary.

Checking for Plumb and Square. Many of the windows available come already assembled, and are designed to be slipped into the opening from outside. Some will be "self-trimming." That is, they require no outside trim, and the siding butts against the self-trim. Other types of windows will require brick molding around them. If you want the new window to match existing windows in appearance you may even decide to apply trim around a self-trimming window.

Slip your new window into the rough opening and drive a couple of small finishing nails into the side frames to hold it lightly in place. Go inside and check the window for level and plumb. Drive shingle wedges (buy a few second-course shingles at a lumberyard or home center) under the window and at the sides between the window and framing to level and plumb the window. Be careful not to bow the side frames in which you drive the wedges. Check this by sliding a two-foot (or longer) level up and down the side frames. Check also at the corners of the window for square. Take your time and be absolutely sure the window is level, plumb and square. This will assure that the window operates properly, whether it's a double-hung sash, a casement or a sideways sliding unit. Then nail.

Insulation. Stuff scraps of insulation in the spaces alongside, above and below the window beside the wedges. Any too-thin insulation you pulled out of the wall can be used for this. Now staple up roll or batt insulation, at least 3½ inches thick, between the wall studs. Over the entire wall staple sheets of polyethylene at least 4 mils thick. Do not use thin plastic dropcloths; they are not thick enough and will not be impermeable to moisture. Make sure the edges of all plastic sheets end up on studs, and overlap the sheets at the studs.

Plasterboard or paneling now can be glued and nailed to the wall. Use a good grade of construction adhesive in a cartridge gun and apply a bead of the adhesive the full length of each stud. Fewer nails then can be used. Tape the plasterboard as you would for any application.

The window should have insulated glazing (double pane), as should the sliding glass door.

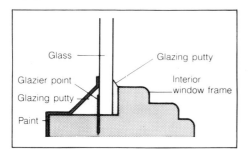

Sliding Glass Door. It might seem a bit outrageous to consider a large sliding glass door for a bathroom, where privacy is a must. First, there must be a high privacy fence around the small patio outside the bathroom door and, absolutely, there should be a drape that can be closed across the door to assure privacy and keep out the cold in winter, and the heat in summer. But it is very pleasant to look out at a sunny garden while you shave or put on makeup, or take a leisurely bath, with only birds and perhaps an occasional squirrel looking in.

The opening for a sliding glass door is framed much like that for a window. The bottom of the door, however, must be positioned so its sill is flush with — or a fraction of an inch above — the floor. In the example given, one end of the room was used for growing plants, taking advantage of the usual high humidity. The two fairly high windows were removed and the rest of the wall was opened to make an opening as dimensioned in the instructions packed in with the door. The header above the pair of windows was long enough to handle the door opening, so it was only necessary to install double 2x4s on each side of the door opening. There was some flex in the double 2x4s, so the homeowner spiked in a couple of horizontal lengths of 2x4, across, to stiffen them. The horizontal braces also assured that the latch on the sliding door would close solidly and prevented flexing of the framing of the door when it was closed. A horizontal length of 2x4 was nailed in place above the top of the door, up against the header, to hold the door snugly in place.

Note that there was a wall register under the windows. When the wall was torn down, the register was removed and the ductwork cut flush with the floor. A floor register then was slipped into the opening. To create a sill for the door, the homeowner had a piece of hardwood planed down to $5/16$ inch thick. The edge toward the room then was beveled with a plain and it was stained to match the door, which was stained to match the old-fashioned wainscoting on the walls.

Incidentally (or not so) the reason the window header went across the full length of the wall is that the windows were set in a "hanging closet," the construction of which will be described along with bay windows, in a later chapter.

Plaster-Wall Variation. If you wish not to remove a whole wall section in a plaster wall, you would cut only the out window areas and the extra space needed to frame in around it. You would have to choose your window size carefully so that you would plan your cut-out to fit within studs — if your studs are every 16 inches, then a multiple of 16 inches would always have to be the horizontal dimension of the new window. Otherwise, when you cut the rough opening for the new window, you will probably end up with a section where the lath and plaster have no support. This will happen because you cut between wall studs. In this case it will be essential to install a stud to provide the necessary support.

Start by nailing short pieces of 2x4 to the bottom plate and the top plate inside the wall, the same thickness as that of the stud inside the wall. Now you will have a support when you insert the 2x4 and toe-

nail it to the top and bottom plates. Additionally, because the 2x4 studs in older homes were sometimes a full 2 inches by 4 inches, you will have to shim one face of the new stud to make it as wide as the old ones. Carefully nail into the plaster and lath to keep damage to a minimum, although you definitely will cause some cracks that will require spackling and sanding. Nail also from the outside through the sheathing and/or siding into the new stud.

Install the new window and check for level and plumb; fill in the area between it and the old plaster. This may require inserting pieces of plasterboard between the window and the old plaster to fill in the space. More than one board layer will probably be required to shim it out so it is flush with the old plaster. Tape the joint and apply joint compound as you would with modern plasterboard.

If you are logical enough to want insulation in the wall, cut holes near the ceiling between each set of wall studs and blow or pour vermiculite into the holes. Patch the holes with plasterboard, then paint the wall with a product such as "Insul-Aid" (made by the Glidden Company) to provide a vapor barrier. You then can apply paint over it.

If the old plaster is in poor condition, nail up sheets of foil-back plasterboard to provide both a vapor barrier and a new wall surface. Because old walls are thicker due to wider studs and the plaster, it is possible you will have to nail strips of wood onto the window frame to bring it flush with the inside surface of the wall. It then can be trimmed with molding in the usual manner.

The end of this room was used as indoor "greenhouse" to take advantage of high humidity. Windows were loose-fitting and drafty, so were removed in favor of sliding glass door. Windows are in a "hanging closet".

After door was installed, insulation was jammed into wall cavities; scraps were stuffed into every crack. Wallboard was added and the room was redecorated. Wainscoting was removed; new wallcovering was applied.

7 Storage Needs and Projects

There never seems to be enough storage in a bathroom. A single person may have only two sets of towels, one toothbrush and tube of toothpaste, but most homeowners find that they do not have enough storage for all the articles and accessories they use.

This chapter offers many ideas and several projects to help the homeowner plan the type, the size and the location of bathroom storage. As you prepare your final bathroom remodeling or addition plan, evaluate your obvious needs as well as the conveniences you would like in your bath. Examine the room closely with your eyes and a measuring tape. Fill those empty vertical spaces with tall cabinets and shelves. They need not be deep.

Folded towels, paper supplies, bath appliances do not need the big storage places that blankets or kitchen appliances do. What is more, not all bath storage units need to have doors. Attractive open displays of linens and toiletries can enhance a color scheme as well as wallcoverings and curtains. Among your other major considerations will be: lockable storage for medicines (if you have small children); storage for hairdryers or other electrical equipment used in the room; a rack for hand laundry; soaps, bathoils, sponges; cleaning materials such as scouring powder and brushes and, of course, towels.

Surprisingly, more storage potential exists than you might think. Look closely and you will see where wasted space can be put to work. Most of it is above eye level. True, fixtures are immovable and fill up most of the space. However, since they are only 30 inches high or less, plenty of under-utilized space lies between them and the ceiling. Furthermore, there is space between fixtures that often goes unused. Creative cabinetry and shelving will fit these oddly shaped nooks, and crannies provide storage.

This book offers several projects that a homeowner may build to meet storage needs, plus information on medicine cabinets and storage units available commercially. From this information, you should be able to pinpoint your needs and then find answers to your bathroom storage problems.

STORAGE OPTIONS

Often a bathroom has structural imperfections you would like to hide, perhaps behind a false wall, but the space can be put to better use if you fill it with storage built-ins, as one homeowner did for a large bathroom in an old house. Extra storage space was "found" at the end of a boxed-in tub. A shallow closet and open-shelf recess disguise protruding beams and pipes which marred the symmetry of

A mini-version of the standard medicine cabinet hides behind sliding mirror doors. Above could be a fixed mirror or an in-wall bath cabinet with matching sliding mirrored doors.

the stately high-ceiling room. A slender closet holds tissues, cleansers, small appliances. Shelves are filled with towels and live plants.

Even a large bathroom will be more convenient when needed supplies are close at hand. A tall divider of open shelves is one good solution; you can adapt the arrangement for smaller baths by placing the shelves against an end wall.

What law says a medicine cabinet has to be set into a wall? When there is horizontal space to spare, make the most of it in unique ways. In one dressing-room-bath combination, the walls were needed for closets, so a medicine cabinet was set flat into one end of the cantilevered vanity top.

One of the most neglected spaces for storage is the wall around the toilet. An open-shelf built in of 1x8s can hold an enormous amount of towels, toiletries, books, magazines. The unit can be as high and wide as you care to make it, though the shelf over the tank should be removable so fixture repairs and maintenance can be handled easily. See the storage projects later in this chapter for more ideas you can adapt to your own use.

Storage You Can Buy

With the proliferation of bath accessories and appliances, makers of kitchen and other utility cabinets realized the need for storage units scaled for bathrooms. Now modular units come in a wide range of sizes to fit almost any space available.

The vanity base cabinet represents the first major breakthrough. It brought decorative focus to the bath, as well as extra storage space. Most manufacturers offer optional components you can add to the cabinet interior — shelves, drawers, bins, or hampers enable you to arrange storables any way you want.

Medicine cabinets are now redesigned to hold more, add style and color to decorative schemes. Most are finished so they can be surface-mounted wherever you want them— singly or in rows.

If towels and tissues are now stored in an out-of-the-way hall linen closet, bring them inside the bath where they belong. Tall, narrow free-standing cabinets fit nearly any extra floor space. These linen cabinets generally are 84 inches high, 18 inches wide, and 12 or 24 inches deep. They are a dressed up version of the old

utility broom closet (made for kitchens).

Some models have adjustable shelves. Others are fitted with one or two full-depth shelves, for towels and linens, and also with half-depth shelves for toiletries.

Still others feature doors with attached shelves.

All sorts of extra components are available for linen closets — slide out drawers, shelves, hampers, for example.

If you are willing to sacrifice some counter space, vertical storage can be gained by adding a divider and installing shelves between the divider and the wall.

Manufactured storage units come in assorted shapes and sizes to help you handle specialized living areas and storage needs.

A large mirror combined with 2 medicine cabinets handles various storage situations. These cabinets are surface-mounted.

Flexible Arrangements

You can restyle an existing bathroom in such a way that the modular cabinets look like built-ins. A twin-bowl vanity is flanked by tall matching linen cabinets that create the look of a custom-built vanity alcove. Filling the expanse with mirror and lighting will give the grouping decorative impact and unity.

Another possible arrangement places two linen cabinets side by side to create an alcove effect for a vanity which fits against the shower wall partition.

Where a hall closet and bathroom share the same wall you might be able to make the closet work twice. Open the wall (see "Shelves Inside Walls" later in this chapter) and recess one or two linen cabinets into the space beyond. Linen storage then becomes accessible from inside the bath.

Styling and Finishes

Modular bathroom storage units cover every decorative scheme from Early American to French Provincial to ultra modern. Hardware such as handles, knobs, and pulls are compatible in styling, too. Colors range from natural wood tones to vibrant hues and gleaming white. To assure durability, bathroom modulars are final-coated in clear thermoset acrylic and resin finishes that are moisture resistant.

Shelves Inside Walls

Much space exists inside studded walls for installing display cases for toiletries, perfume, lotions, or even a door cabinet for cleansers, brushes, soap. You will have to locate the studs, break through the wall, and install the type of storage arrangement you want.

However, be careful not to chop into a wall where there may be plumbing and electrical lines. Notice the positions of wall switches, outlets and lighting fixtures. Check the wall on its opposite side, and the walls above and below the room if possible. Note where pipes and drains enter and leave walls and floors.

Next, locate the studs. Most studs are centered 16 inches apart. You will cut your opening between them, about 16 inches wide. To judge where they might be in the wall, measure from a doorway or corner. If double studs were used in these locations, your calculations may be off. Test by driving a long, thin nail where you think the studs might be after first testing

— tapping — for a solid rather than a hollow sound. Such small exploratory holes can easily be filled later.

Stud finders may help. Some people have great luck with them. Also, if wallboard was used, the nails at their seams may be revealed by subtle shadows or dents when exposed to a downlight or a sidelight.

Cutting the Opening, Wallboard. If the wall is of wallboard, mark size of the rough opening on the wall with pencil or scribe. At one corner, drill a hole large enough to insert keyhole or saber saw blade. Keeping inside the guideline mark, cut out the section of wallboard. When you get to within two or three inches of a corner, make a curved cut rather than a square one. After the main section has been lifted out, you will find it easy to cut the corners squarely.

Plaster. If the wall is plaster over wood or metal lath, follow these steps: Mark the rough opening as above. At a top corner, chip out all the plaster down to the lath, using hammer and chisel. With saber saw and a blade appropriate for wood or metal, insert the saw blade into the opening and cut away the entire section. Curve-cut the corners, as above, and square-cut the corners once the big section has been removed.

Creating the Box. With opening made, dust debris out of the area using a stiff brush. Measure the opening to determine the size of shallow box you will

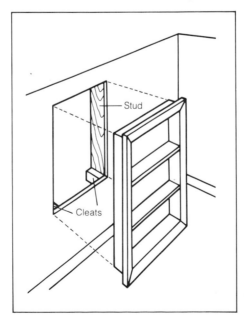

Recessed shelves can be built as a box unit that fits between studs and is supported by cleats. A wide facing molding used to trim the box will hide cut wall edges.

make to fit inside it. The depth of the box will be size of studs (usually 3½ inches) plus the thickness of the wall material. The width of the box will be the distance between the studs; the height will be your choice.

Build the box using ¼ inch plywood for backing, and ½ inch stock lumber for top, sides, and bottom. Glue-nail together, then clamp and set aside.

Next, make support cleats inside the opening for the box. Use scrap or ¾ inch molding strips. Nail cleats directly to exposed wall studs, placing them at the bottom of the opening with their top edges flush with the edge of the opening.

Before you fit the box into the wall opening, prepare its sides for the kind of shelf supports you will be using — peg holes, L-brackets, adjustable shelf standards, or your choice. Shelves can be of wood, glass, or plastic. Also, give the interior of the box a decorative finish — paint, paper, stain, fabric, or mirror, for instance.

Tilt the box into the opening and bring it to rest on the bottom cleats and back of inner wall. Fasten into place with nails driven into the studs.

Measure and cut face trim molding, mitering the corners. The purpose of the trim is to cover both the raw edges of the opening and the exposed edges of the wooden box. Nail trim molding into place around the opening. Final-finish the face trim with paint, paper, stain or fabric; set shelves into place on their supports.

Your in-wall storage recess can be open, partially or fully covered by swing-out, drop-down, or sliding doors, or even lightweight louvered shutters.

MEDICINE CABINETS

The tradition that once dictated placing recessed medicine cabinets over the washbasin has given way to freedom of style and placement. Medicine cabinets are likely to be anywhere, in any form — small, large, triple and double, recessed or wall-hung, set high or low. In fact, many bathrooms have no medicine cabinet at all in the accepted sense. Supplies and medicines are kept in drawers, on open shelves, or on shelves inside vanity base cabinets.

In planning your budget for a new bathroom project, consider the medicine cabinet as a unit of storage which is flexible in style, size, and location. After all, if you want an extra-large expanse of mirror with superior grooming lighting over the lavatory, the conventional mirrored medicine cabinet would be insufficient. Small bottles, boxes, and grooming aids can be handily stored in decorative boxes or baskets on the vanity countertop, in an open-shelf divider, in decorative corner cabinets or wall-mounted cabinets on the end walls. In some arrangements the medicine cabinet becomes part of a nearby linen closet.

Styles and Sizes

Medicine cabinets come in styles ranging from classic traditional to ultra-modern, in fine woods, polished metals, or thickly curved plastics in vibrant colors. Some are made for recessed in-wall installation, but cabinets today are fully finished on the outside so they can be surface-mounted. Wall-hung medicine cabinets came to the fore when standard bathroom sinks gave way to new sizes and shapes, as countertop and vanity cabinets became popular. You no longer have to settle for a too-small cabinet firmly entrenched in a wall. If an extra big cabinet is needed, you can remove the old one and surface-mount a grand new one over the old location. Extra-wide cabinets are especially convenient, since their mirrored doors can be used for three-way viewing when shaving, applying makeup, grooming hair. Some designs combine a recessed storage cavity with an extra-large over-lapping door. These help bring a skimpy medicine cabinet into better harmony with the scale of the wall area and base cabinet below it. Big mirrors are often preferred today because they are more convenient for grooming than are small ones.

Not all medicine cabinets are mirrored, nor do they need to be. If you prefer to hang an unusual or uniquely framed mirror over the lavatory, team it with one or two cabinets with solid doors. Buy a mirror that is well-crafted, ample in size, and proportioned to be wall-hung over the lavatory area.

Installation

There are two basic types of medicine cabinets used in bathrooms: surface-mounted and recessed models.

Surface-mounted. There will be screw holes in the back of this cabinet, through which the screws are driven. The

This recessed medicine cabinet has an extra-large mirrored door that is framed in solid oak. The larger mirror and door add balance and focus to the room.

A medicine cabinet need not be located only over the vanity, especially if you want a large mirror there. The cabinet shown is positioned above a toilet tank that has a wood finish.

A bank of three slender cabinets hung together over a vanity gives more storage space and better viewing since the doors can be opened outward for three-way inspection.

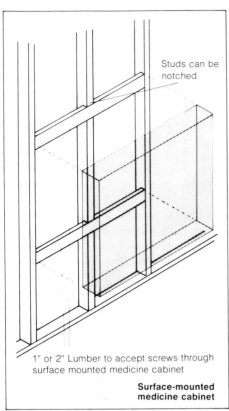

Studs can be notched

1" or 2" Lumber to accept screws through surface mounted medicine cabinet

Surface-mounted medicine cabinet

To surface-mount medicine cabinets, provide attachment surfaces in wall framing, using 1- or 2-inch lumber set on edge. The width of the pieces will allow for cabinet movement up or down, or from side to side.

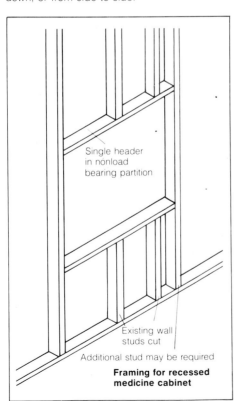

Single header in nonload bearing partition

Existing wall studs cut

Additional stud may be required

Framing for recessed medicine cabinet

For a recessed medicine cabinet, frame the opening as for window. In a non-loadbearing partition, the header can be a single 2x4, or 2x6 if wall is thicker to accept plumbing. If more than one existing stud is cut for the rough opening, add an additional stud.

best method is to drive them into wall studs, but this is not always possible, in which case screw anchors or Molly bolts can be used. If the cabinet is quite large and the family will place a lot of heavy items in the cabinet, we suggest you drill a couple of extra holes midway between the existing prepunched holes to take a couple of extra screws, if screw anchors or Molly bolts are employed.

Surface-mounted medicine cabinets cannot be as deep as the recessed type because they will project too far. If the cabinet is placed over the vanity basin there is a good chance that someone will bump a head on a projecting cabinet.

Where you add a bathroom or do extensive remodeling, include extra bracing in the wall on which the cabinet will be hung. Use 2x4s or 2x6s on edge in the wall to give some tolerance in the positioning of the screws. This also enables you to move the cabinet to the right or left, up or down, of your original cabinet location.

Recessed. If you purchase a medicine cabinet that must be recessed, then the wall framing will have to be assembled to allow for it. Instructions with the cabinet may specify a rough opening, which you build as you would an opening for a door or window. Because the medicine cabinet will be installed in an inside partition wall you usually don't need a doubled header. An exception to this would be if the partition was a load-bearing wall. This might happen if the partition was the center one down the length of the house, and the ceiling joists rested on it. In this case, it must be handled as a load-bearing wall. If you build your own medicine cabinet or pick one up second hand and there are no instructions with it, then make the opening for it about 1½ inches larger in both dimensions than the size of the cabinet. This can vary if the cabinet is "self trimming"; that is, if the face of the cabinet is larger than the cabinet itself. If so, it will cover the edges of the opening into which the cabinet fits. In this case create the opening so there will be at least ⅛ inch face overlap all around; ¼ inch would be better, for the face of the cabinet to completely conceal the opening.

Some tolerance in the size of the opening is required, because it is necessary to shim the cabinet level and plumb after it is in place. With a self-trimming cabinet,

Recessed display areas can be created following steps similar to those for medicine cabinets or shelves. Finish off the surfaces with paneling, wallboard or tile.

pull the cabinet out of the opening far enough to permit slipping wood shims under the bottom and along one side for level and plumb. Where possible, drive screws through the cabinet, through the shims and into the wall framing. With some cabinets this might require drilling additional holes, and not using the existing prepunched holes.

On the other hand, recessed cabinets are usually only a bit deeper than the width of a 2x4. Modern 2x4s are 3½ inches wide, so a cabinet will be that depth plus the thickness of the wall covering, which could be plain plasterboard, or plasterboard with tile adhered to it, or thin paneling.

A recessed cabinet can project from the wall an inch or two to increase its usable depth. In this installation, it is necessary to apply trim around the cabinet on the wall, or to run plasterboard or tile right up to it. If you are building a wall of 2x6 studs to handle the plumbing, then the medicine cabinet can be deeper. When you buy the cabinet, know the depth of the wall and the size for which you will have room.

Placement. Determine the location of the cabinet and mark this position, including the holes for the mounting screws. If you are very lucky, you will drill pilot holes at these locations and find the studs. However, if the mounting holes and the studs do not line up, you will have to change the location of the cabinet. Some cabinets have a row of mounting holes that allow you to drive screws directly into the studs from any of several positions in the back of the cabinet.

Lighting

Medicine cabinets with built-in lighting fixtures are available, as well as cabinets with separate but matching fixtures. There are, for example, medicine cabinets with matching fixture panels for mounting across the top of the cabinet and down both sides of it. Extra-long fixture panels can be mounted along the sides of a cabinet which, for whatever reason, cannot have a lighting strip across the top of the mirror.

Homemade Version

Just as there is practically no limit to the kind and style of medicine cabinet you can buy, there is equally no restriction on the style of medicine cabinet you can

build yourself. If you are handy with tools, you can create your own in just the style and size you want, for whatever location is handiest for you and your family.

Medicine Cabinet Shelving. A shallow box with molding strip shelf supports will hold your store of boxes, bottles, and brushes. Or, if you prefer glass shelves, choose tempered safety glass with rounded outer edge. Strips of ¼ inch plastic in clear or bright colors also make good shelving material, as do strips of prefinished paneling or ¼ inch plywood sanded and painted — or even covered in bright vinyl wallcovering. Use shelf supports in holes spaced equidistant in the sides for adjustable shelf spacing.

Doors. The door hinges to the cabinet, or to the wall, and can be a piece of plywood. A framed or unframed mirror then can be adhered to the plywood with construction adhesive formulated to hold glass. Use a molding for a finished edge. As an alternative you can make a frame for the mirror, much as for a picture, to hold it to the plywood door. Beveled-edged mirrors can be held in place with clips. If the cabinet is quite wide, make two doors. Sliding doors can be used also; the doors are simply pieces of mirror cut to size at your local glass shop. The charge is usually minimal.

Lighting. If you plan to include built-in lighting, see Chapter 10 for the basics of good illumination for grooming. When building wall framing to accept a cabinet, run an electric line adjacent to the cabinet for lights that will be above or on one or both sides of the cabinet. There must be a receptacle to power shavers, hair dryers and so on. Plan for your medicine cabinet when you begin your remodeling. Frame the wall or partition so an opening can be made to accept the cabinet. If you don't, you may have to cut and remove studs, or even install additional studs, to create the framing for the cabinet opening. This can be time-consuming, since you have to allow also for plumbing lines that might be in the same wall. Unless you are very experienced in wiring, have a qualified electrician handle the final installation and hookup. Consider using color-corrected fluorescent fixtures with acrylic diffusers; such lighting is cooler and less expensive to operate than incandescent.

Locate the studs by driving a nail through the wall behind the proposed cabinet location. Adjust the position of the cabinet and drill new pilot holes. Support the cabinet in position with a box, several props or with the help of a few strong friends. Drive the screws through the holes into the studs. Test the stability of the cabinet before use.

This medicine cabinet is easy to build and, because it is surface-mounted, it does not require cutting into the wall. Arrangement of the partition and shelves can be varied.

The decorative trim found on (or added to) a vanity can be repeated on the surround of an enclosed tub (also see Chapter 4) to unify and enhance the design.

BASIC VANITY

Basic carpentry skills are all that are needed to build this practical plywood vanity out of ¾ inch Exterior plywood. Using the Materials List as a guide and following the diagram, cut out pieces. Notch the sides, cutting out a piece 4½ inches by 3½ inches from each side for the kickplate. Notch the back for the back brace. Rabbet the back to fit into the sides. The front framing members will butt against the sides. Dado the sides to accept the bottom.

Join the sides, back, bottom, center partition and front framing pieces with butt joints, using 6d finishing nails and white glue. Add shelves inside as needed. Use ¾ inch cleats as shelf supports.

Drawers

To build an overlay drawer, construct the back, sides and front from pieces that are ½ inch narrower than the height of the opening. Cut the sides 1½ inches shorter than the interior depth. Cut back and front pieces 1½ inches shorter than the width of the cabinet. This will allow space for side mounted roller hardware. Rout rabbets in the front edges of the sides for the front piece, and dadoes to hold the back piece. Check the fit for square. Dado all pieces for the bottom and cut the bottom to fit.

Check the fit again and trim or sand bottom edges and/or dadoes to achieve a good, square fit. Assemble with glue and 3d finishing nails. Then attach the overlay front to box. The overlay front should overlap the opening by ¼ inch all the way around. Attach with No. 8 flathead screws from the inside. Space screws equally in two rows. Add hardware and drawer pull(s).

Doors

The simplest door for this project is an overlay door. Cut a piece of plywood one inch wider and one inch higher than the door opening. Sand the edges so they are smooth and slightly rounded. Use concealed hinges to attach doors to the base. Add magnetic catches and suitable door knobs. You may prefer to cut the door 1¼ inches larger in each direction and rout a cove recess all the way around the back edges to give you a recess for a finger pull all the way around. In this case, you will not need a door knob.

Finishing

If you intend to cover the vanity with plastic laminate, it is easiest if added at this point. First, nail on 1x1 edge facing strips. Apply cement to base and laminate and let dry. Use either strips of lath or

overlapping sections of kraft paper to keep glued surfaces apart. Square the base and laminate. When they line up perfectly, remove one strip of lath or a section of paper. Press the laminate surface to secure, and smooth it with a roller. Cut openings with a router and laminate bit. Cover the sides first, then the back and front. Laminate the doors and drawer prior to installation.

Cut the sink opening in the top, using a saber saw. Instructions for sink installation will come with the unit.

Laminate top and backsplash pieces. Attach the top and backsplash pieces to the base with No. 8 flathead screws, 1¼ inches long. Add hinges, hardware and pulls. For economy, you may enamel the base and laminate only the top.

BUILT-IN VANITY

This vanity adapts easily to various spaces because it is merely a frame covered with paneling. The standard height is 30 inches; the usual depth is 2 feet.

Begin by cutting parts as required to fit. Build your base from 2x4s or 2x6s. Assemble with screws. Build a second, larger base framework of 2x4s as shown, using dowel and glue joints. Attach the frame to the base with nails, creating a toespace.

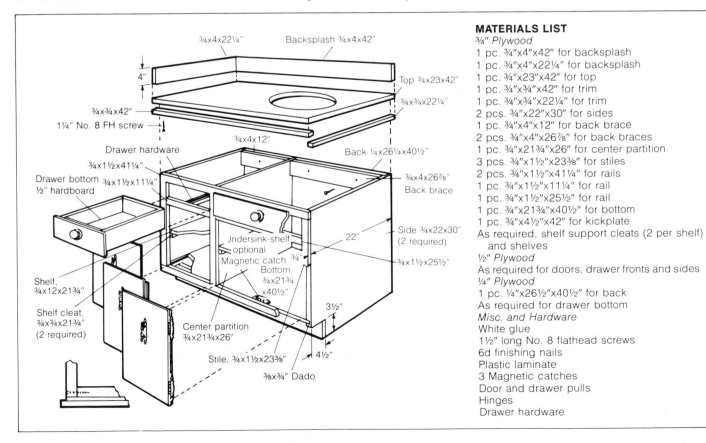

MATERIALS LIST

¾" Plywood
1 pc. ¾"x4"x42" for backsplash
1 pc. ¾"x4"x22¼" for backsplash
1 pc. ¾"x23"x42" for top
1 pc. ¾"x¾"x42" for trim
1 pc. ¾"x¾"x22¼" for trim
2 pcs. ¾"x22"x30" for sides
1 pc. ¾"x4"x12" for back brace
2 pcs. ¾"x4"x26⅞" for back braces
1 pc. ¾"x21¾"x26" for center partition
3 pcs. ¾"x1½"x23⅜" for stiles
2 pcs. ¾"x1½"x41¼" for rails
1 pc. ¾"x1½"x11¼" for rail
1 pc. ¾"x1½"x25½" for rail
1 pc. ¾"x21¾"x40½" for bottom
1 pc. ¾"x4½"x42" for kickplate
As required, shelf support cleats (2 per shelf) and shelves

½" Plywood
As required for doors, drawer fronts and sides

¼" Plywood
1 pc. ¼"x26½"x40½" for back
As required for drawer bottom

Misc. and Hardware
White glue
1½" long No. 8 flathead screws
6d finishing nails
Plastic laminate
3 Magnetic catches
Door and drawer pulls
Hinges
Drawer hardware

Labels on diagram:
¾x4x22¼" Backsplash ¾x4x42" Top ¾x23x42"
4" ¾x¾x22¼"
¾x¾x42"
1¼" No. 8 FH screw
¾x4x12"
Drawer hardware
¾x1½x41¼" Back ¼x26¼x40½"
Drawer bottom ¾x1½x11¼" ¾x4x26⅞"
½" hardboard Back brace
Undersink-shelf optional 22" Side ¾x22x30" (2 required)
Magnetic catch ¾" ¾x1½x25½"
Bottom ¾x21¾ x40½"
Shelf, ¾x12x21¾"
Shelf cleat, ¾x¾x21¾" (2 required) Center partition ¾x21¾x26" 3½"
Stile, ¾x1½x23⅜" 4½"
⅜x¾" Dado

Build the cabinet framework from 1x2s. Adjust the plan shown in the drawing to conform to your specific requirements. Join the pieces with finishing nails and glue. Secure with screws to the base.

Cut the top 24⅝ inches wide to the length you need. Attach a reinforcing strip of 1x2 faced with a ¾ inch plywood lip below the front edge on the top (see detail). Cut sink opening in proper location. Face the cabinet with paneling.

Construct overlay drawers (as in the "Basic Vanity" above) and install.

It is not difficult to construct the translucent light box shown (see drawing for details). The light box is made of a 2x2 nailed framework. The bottom is covered

MATERIALS LIST
2x4s or 2x6s for base cut to size for your requirements
2x4s for frame assembly on base cut to size
1x4s for cabinet framework. Draw plan and calculate needs
¾" plywood for top
1x2 reinforcing strips for tops
Resawn redwood paneling for vanity front and drawer fronts
Plastic laminate for vanity top
Stock for drawers plan and calculate needs
Drawer hardware

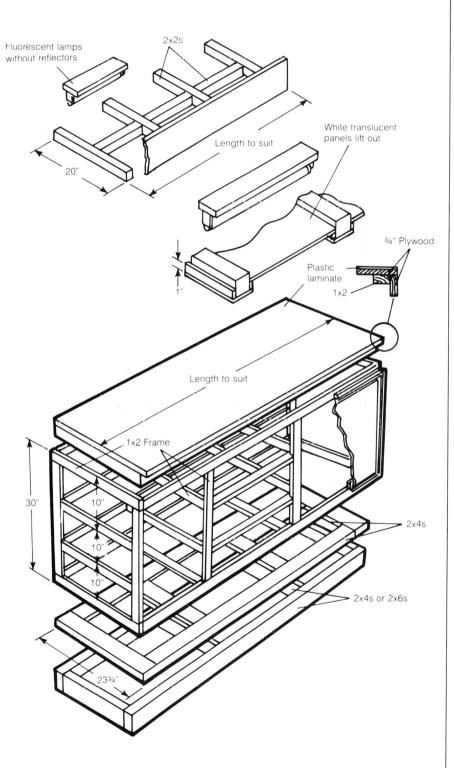

with strips of paneling that create rabbets on which translucent plastic sections rest.

BUILDING UPWARD

Often, the only space available for new storage in a bathroom is a narrow area or the space above a toilet. Here is a plan for a sturdy, narrow cabinet to fit.

Using the Materials List as a guide, cut all lumber to size. Lightly sand cut edges.

To construct the lower cabinet support box, join two 28½-inch long 1x4s with two 2½-inch 1x4s. For the upper box, join two 28½-inch 1x4s with a 5-inch 1x4. Use noncorrosive 6d finishing nails, such as aluminum, stainless steel, or hot-dipped galvanized.

Build two doors, using four 36-inch long 1x4s for each door. Choose 1x4s with the best grain if you plan to use a clear finish. Glue and clamp four 1x4s firmly. Attach 1x2x13 bracing pieces, each 1 inch from the top and the bottom to the back of each door panel. Fasten braces with No. 8 1¼ inch brass screws. Recess the ends of the bracing pieces approximately ½ inch from the door panel sides.

Draw a 1½-inch diameter circle in the center of each side panel, 3 feet, 7¼ inches down from each top edge (Detail B). With a 1½-inch bit, drill half way through each side panel. These recesses will hold a towel rod or pole.

Place the rod or pole between the side pieces and attach the top and bottom cabinet support boxes with 6d finishing nails and glue. Nails should be countersunk and holes filled with wood putty. The back of the upper box should be flush with the back edges of the side support panels. The bottom box is slightly recessed from the back to allow the box and side panel to fit around any molding or tile at the floor.

All open shelves measure 1x8x28½ inches long. Glue a shelf to the lower box. Other open shelves can be attached at needed heights with shelf hangers. Allow at least 24 inches between the towel rod and the shelf below.

Shelves in the closed cabinet are 1x6x28½ inches. Attach the shelves so the bottom shelf will be 3 feet, 1½ inches below the top of the cabinet. If you need more shelves in the cabinet, attach them as required.

Cabinet doors are attached to the sides with two 1½-inch hinges per panel. Use self-closing hinges for convenience. Add a pull or knob to each door. Use one magnetic catch for each door.

The cabinet may be given a finish of polyurethane varnish that then is sanded lightly between three coats. Fasten the unit to the wall with screws, through the support box backs.

MATERIALS LIST

1x2:
4 pcs.   13″ door bracing pieces
1x4s:
2 pcs.   5″ for cabinet support boxes
2 pcs.   3½″ for cabinet support boxes
4 pcs.   28½″ for cabinet support boxes
8 pcs.   36″ for doors
1x6s:
1 or 2 pcs.   28½″ for enclosed shelves
1x8s:
3 pcs.   28½″ for exposed shelves
2 pcs.   7½″ for side panels* (or to the length necessary for height of bathroom)

Hardware
6d finishing nails
#8x1¼″ brass screws
#10x2½″ screws with washers
Hinges
Magnetic catch
Wood towel rod 29⅜″ long
*(Side panel lengths depend on height of bath ceiling; see Detail A.)

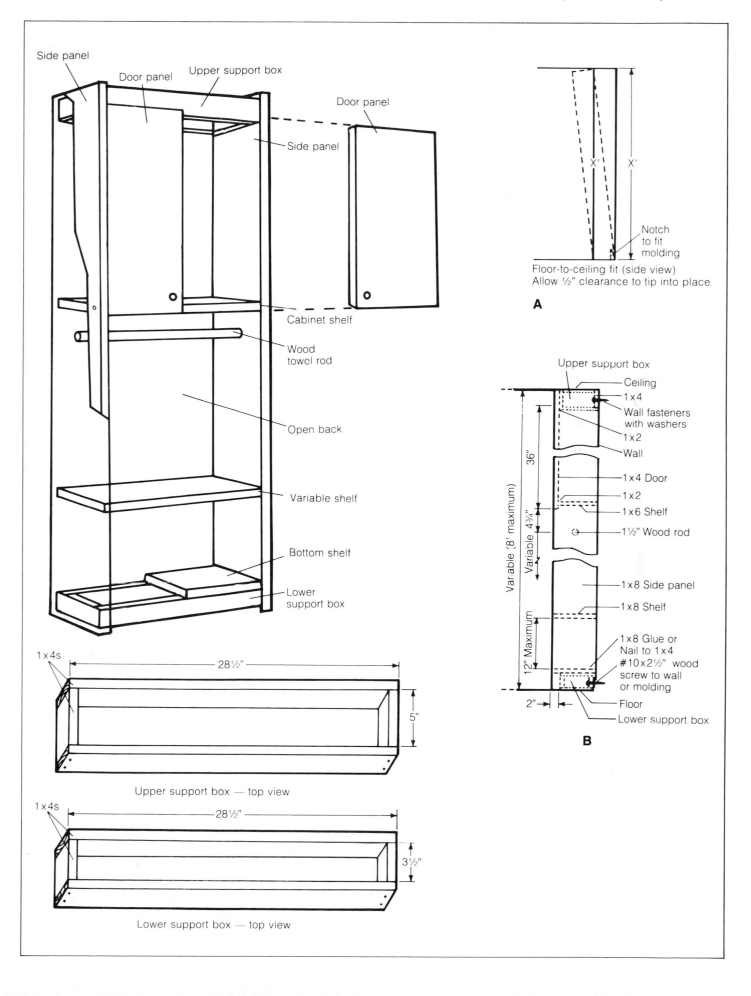

Side panel

Door panel

Upper support box

Door panel

Side panel

Cabinet shelf

Wood towel rod

Open back

Variable shelf

Bottom shelf

Lower support box

1 x 4s

28½"

5"

Upper support box — top view

1 x 4s

28½"

3½"

Lower support box — top view

Notch to fit molding

Floor-to-ceiling fit (side view)
Allow ½" clearance to tip into place.

X'   X'

A

Upper support box

Ceiling

1 x 4

Wall fasteners with washers

1 x 2

Wall

1 x 4 Door

1 x 2

1 x 6 Shelf

1½" Wood rod

1 x 8 Side panel

1 x 8 Shelf

1 x 8 Glue or Nail to 1 x 4
#10 x 2½" wood screw to wall or molding

Floor

Lower support box

36"

Variable 4¾"

12" Maximum

Variable ('8' maximum)

2"

B

FAUCET BASICS

Any room in the house that has plumbing and associated fixtures — kitchen, bathroom, laundry room or bar — has faucets. These are devices that require more consistent maintenance and repair than any other plumbing item.

No matter what type, faucets are designed to do just one thing: control the flow of water. Mixing faucets, including a number of the newer one-control types, regulate a mixture of hot and cold water to create the desired temperature.

All faucets have a valve (or valves) of some kind, plus other moving parts that must be sealed to prevent water leaking. Except for cleaning out mineral deposits (usually referred to as "lime") and cleaning out foreign matter, the major part of faucet maintenance is replacement of seals and valve components that have become worn or lost their resiliency.

There are four basic types of faucets: stem, disc, ball, and cartridge. Stem faucets are the most common. They also need more frequent repair because the washers wear out, and cause leaks. The other faucets, if they leak, simply require an exchange of the washer or cartridge.

Replacements

If you install new faucets in your home, by all means save the installation and maintenance sheets that come with them. Some of the newer types of faucets are quite complex, and the instruction sheets are absolutely necessary if you intend to do your own maintenance and repairs.

These instruction sheets usually have "pull-apart" drawings to show how they are assembled, plus information on obtaining special replacement parts. Sometimes the dealer from whom you purchased the faucets will have the information and special parts. Most well-stocked hardware stores with good plumbing departments will have O-rings, washers, spray hoses and even complete repair kits and replacement "cartridges."

Decorative faucets add decorative focus to bathroom remodeling. All faucets serve the same function, but a distinctively designed set can change the impression of an entire room.

A self-rimming lavatory simplifies installation and cleaning. The unit fits into the rough opening and hides any uneven cutting. Clamps on underside complete secure installation.

If you have mislaid the instruction sheets, or never had them, take the defective parts to the hardware store and find a knowledgeable clerk to help you find the correct replacement parts. Even without the knowledgeable clerk (a rarity in this day and age) faucet parts are packaged in see-through containers that let you match the old part with a new one.

Faucets are available in many styles and materials, such as metal and crystal or porcelain.

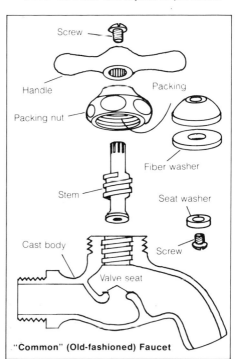

"Common" (Old-fashioned) Faucet

The old-fashioned, or common, faucet has a cast body with coarse threads into which the threaded stem is screwed. The washer at stem bottom bears again valve seat to shut water off. At upper end of faucet, packing is squeezed around the stem for a watertight seal.

Even replacement faucet knobs can be purchased, should you have one that is broken or worn. You may, however, have to buy a pair of knobs for a two-knob fixture to get one that matches. It is not probable that you will find a knob to duplicate a knob you own if it is 30 or 40 years old. Even if you could, age changes the color and look of a knob, so that a new pair is the best answer.

A faucet that is damaged or badly worn may require replacement. Measure the center-to-center spacing on the old faucet to make sure the new one will fit. Older faucets may have a different spacing between the holes than do modern faucets. There are faucets that have adjustable spacing on the supply pipes. Make sure the adjustment is such that it will fit the spacing of the holes in your sink or basin.

Components

Common faucets have a cast body with a removable stem that has coarse threads. There is a washer on one end of the stem and packing fits around the upper portion of the stem to prevent water leaking out around it. The latest types of washer faucets have O-rings that replace the packing around the stem.

One of the modern "metal-to-metal" faucets has a special alloy valve cartridge that is simply replaced when the faucet starts to leak. The cartridge cannot be repaired, it must be replaced as a unit. Another type of modern faucet has a neoprene diaphragm that seals across the seat and also the valve stem.

One-lever mixing faucets may have a lever, turn knob or T-handle that controls both the volume of water and the temperature. There are three general types: (1) a model that has either a ball that swivels in a cup-shape seat, or a cup-shape cap that swivels over a ball-shape seat — spring-loaded cup-like seals are utilized in both types to control water flow; (2) a cam system that is moved by a lever, which contacts the stems of spring-loaded valves; (3) a version with a spool that is sealed by an O-ring — the spool moves laterally and rotates to control the volume of water and the mixture of hot and cold. The usual repair for this faucet is replacement of the spool with its O-ring.

If a swing spout leaks around the faucet body, it usually means the O-ring around the spout needs replacing. The O-rings are sold in the plumbing departments of hardware stores. Take along both the O-ring and the spout; the O-ring may have stretched with age. The new one should fit snugly, yet project enough to create a watertight seal.

DISASSEMBLING A FAUCET

Disassembly is similar for all faucets. You first remove the knob or handle. The bonnet, packing or gland nut is removed next. Then the stem is unscrewed to get at the valve seat. Some faucets have removable valve seats, with a square or hexagon

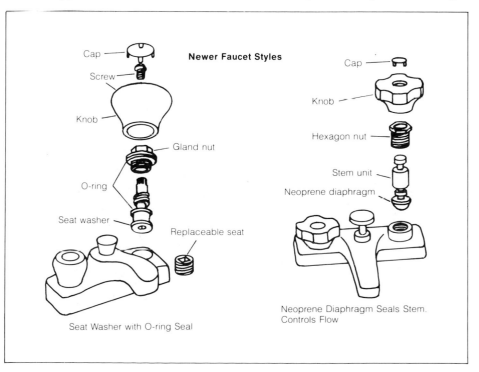

Newer Faucet Styles

Seat Washer with O-ring Seal

Neoprene Diaphragm Seals Stem. Controls Flow

opening at the center. An Allen wrench or special square wrench is inserted in the opening and the seat is unscrewed. This generally takes considerable effort, as the seat will be "frozen" in the threads due to corrosion.

Use caution when disassembling faucets (and be sure the water is shut off first) because you will be removing highly polished parts and hidden screws, and some pieces are delicate. The screws that hold handles on faucets usually are hidden under friction-fit caps that can be pried off with a knife blade. Some faucets may have an Allen setscrew near the base of the handle. Before using force to disassemble a faucet, examine it to see if there is a hidden setscrew, or if there is any other reason the part will not come free easily. Avoid damage to polished, chromeplated fixtures by wrapping wrenches and pliers with rubber or plastic tape.

O-rings and rubber seals will leak if chafed by rough metal surfaces; always smooth metal surfaces with crocus cloth if the seals show abrasion.

REPAIRS FOR FAUCETS

Packing and sealants are handy to seal some faucet leaks. For example, if a new dome packing is not immediately available, a temporary repair can be made by wrapping packing around the stem. Joint compound or sealant can be used to prevent leakage on fittings that are removed or replaced.

Replacing Stem Washers

After turning off the water, remove the handle with a screwdriver — use a Phillips head or standard blade. The screw may be under a decorative cap. The handle lifts straight up and off. You may need to encourage it by prying up lightly on the handle.

When the handle is off you will see a hex nut. This nut holds the stem assembly in place. Loosen and remove the nut, using an adjustable wrench or channel lock pliers. If you don't have channel locks, cover the jaws of regular pliers with adhesive bandages. This will protect the metal valve from the serrations of the regular pliers.

Now slip the handle back on the stem and turn the handle. You don't need to screw the handle in position; the handle will loosen the stem in its assembly. Then back out the stem — which is threaded —

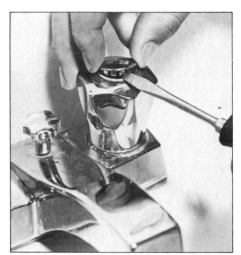

To disassemble most faucets, first remove the decorative cap that hides the faucet handle screw. Pry the cap off of the handle using a screwdriver or pick.

Remove the faucet handle held by a standard or Phillips head screw. If the screw does not come out, coat it with WD-40 penetrating oil; let it set an hour, then try again.

Once screw is out, pry off the handle. Pad the chrome or china parts with an old towel, which also acts as a leverage block. If the handle has no screw, just pry it off.

Take off the packing or cap nut. Loosen the stem, as shown, with a wrench. You may also place the handle back on the stem, without the screw, and then loosen the stem.

The stem will now lift out. The stem is a threaded unit. It has a packing washer at the top and a small, rubber faucet washer at the bottom of the stem.

To avoid scratches on the chrome plating or damage to the delicate parts during disassembly, use pieces of rubber (or tape) on the tools, and work carefully.

with your fingers, or with the pliers or adjustable wrench. You may be able to lift the entire stem assembly after loosening the bonnet nut.

At the bottom of the stem is the washer. It is held in place with a screw. Remove the screw and remove the old washer. Be careful not to damage the thin-walled housing that some washers set in. For best results, replace the old washer with the one recommended by the faucet manufacturer.

Fit a new washer on the stem and fasten it in place with the screw. If the screw is damaged, replace it. Most washer assortments contain extra screws in the package. If there is any corrosion on the stem, clean off the corrosion with fine steel wool. Just buff the metal; don't try to remove any.

Re-assemble the faucet — stem, cap, handle. Tighten the assembly carefully, using the wrench or pliers; too much pressure can strip the threads and cause the faucet to start leaking again.

Replacing Cap Washers

With a screwdriver, remove the faucet handle, exposing the cap that holds the faucet stem in place. Remove this cap. Under the cap, you will find a flat washer or the remains of a stringlike material.

The string is packing and serves as a washer between the stem and the cap. With the screwdriver, pry out the washer or packing, replace it with new, and re-assemble the faucet. The string is wound around the stem so it forms a seal between the stem and the cap.

Replacing O-Rings

O-ring washers look like tiny rings of rubberlike material. They can be found almost anywhere in faucet assembly: on the stem, around the cap nut, under the handle, where two different parts are screwed together.

The first step is to remove the handle from the faucet with a screwdriver, then the cap nut with an adjustable wrench or channel lock pliers. Twist or pull out the stem of the faucet to expose the entire assembly.

To replace the washer, remove the old one, clean the stem, and slip on the new one, making sure it is properly seated. We suggest applying a lubricant before you re-assemble the faucet.

Regrinding Valve Seats

When a washer becomes worn, you probably try to turn the handle of the faucet tighter to shut off the water. This causes the stem of the faucet to grind into the washer seat at the bottom of the stem. Sometimes a new washer will seal the resulting damage. If not, you will have to regrind the valve seat so the washer seats properly when the faucet handle is closed.

Remove the faucet handle, cap nut, and stem assembly (see "Replacing Washers," this chapter).

Insert the grinding tool into the faucet housing and adjust the guide nut (it moves up and down) of the grinding tool to match the depth of the opening of the faucet housing. This aligns the grinding tool in the faucet housing and provides a turning base.

Now turn the grinding tool with its handle or pliers. Be careful; the metal is soft. You don't need much grinding to smooth the seat in the faucet.

Repairing Tipping Valve Faucets

Remove the handle, the faucet spout, and the metal escutcheon covering. This will expose the diverter assembly, bottom cage of the faucet, and the valve stem assembly.

You will see a plug at one side of this assembly. Remove this plug with the screwdriver. Inside will be a gasket and a water strainer. If these parts are clogged with sediment or damaged either clean or replace them.

Leaking can be caused by a worn O-ring that fits between the faucet spout and the diverter assembly. Replace the

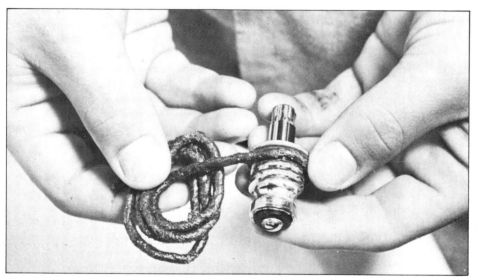

Wrap new string packing around the stem of the faucet just below the packing nut. The rubber washer is visible at the base of the stem. The packing keeps the faucet itself from leaking.

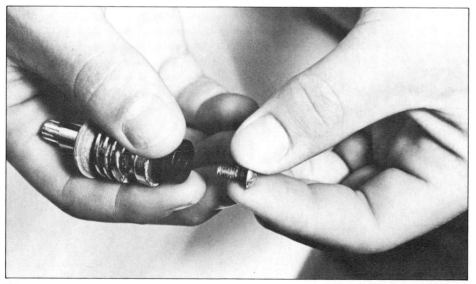

If the water drips from the spout, the rubber washer is worn. Remove the screw in the base of the stem and replace the washer. Stop dripping temporarily by reversing old washer.

O-ring with a new one. Also replace any worn gaskets or O-rings in the cam valve assembly. The handle attaches to this unit. If the unit goes bad, which is unlikely, you may be able to buy a replacement. Take the old unit to the store for matching purposes.

Repairing Disc Faucets

Some disc faucets have O-ring seals at the top of the stem; others don't. Remove the handle and the escutcheon covering, which will expose the faucet assembly. The assembly is held together with two

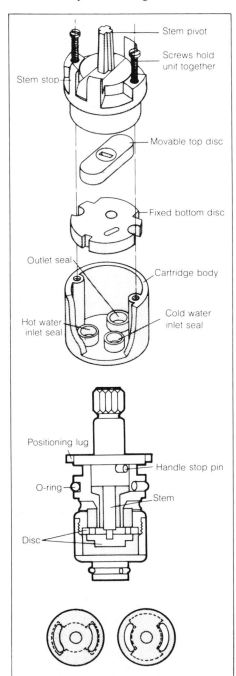

In a disc valve faucet with O-ring, water flows through when holes in the disc align as at right. Water flow stops when discs align as at left.

screws. Remove these. Below will be the O-ring (if there is one), a top disc, a bottom disc, and inlet and outlet seals.

O-rings and the inlet and outlet seals do need maintenance, and sometimes replacement. Clean the assembly, make any replacements necessary, and re-assemble the faucet. If the discs are worn, you may be able to replace them. Take the worn parts to the store to match them. If not, you will have to install a new faucet.

Repairing Cartridge Faucets

Remove the screw on top of the faucet assembly. This screw may be hidden by the decorative cap; pry it up and off. Push the tip of the screwdriver in the screw hole and press down on the screwdriver. At the same time, lift off the faucet handle and housing or sleeve. The screwdriver holds the cartridge in position while you lift off the handle and housing (sleeve, which also may be separate).

If the faucet is dripping, the problem may be the faucet lever. Check that it is properly seated under the lip of the sleeve, so it fully engages the stem of the faucet and the handle that turns off

the water. If you suspect this is the trouble, reseat the handle or lever, reassemble the faucet.

To remove the cartridge, pull out a little metal clip that holds the cartridge in the faucet stem. You may be able to slip the tip of the screwdriver into the slot in the clip. Pry out the clip, but keep it square to the assembly. If the screwdriver doesn't work, use pliers. You now can lift out — and replace — the cartridge.

Take the old cartridge to the store so you can match it with a replacement cartridge; not all are alike.

Replacing Bathtub Spout Diverters

Remove the old spout with a strap wrench; another way is to stick the handle of the wrench in the opening of the spout and turn the spout counterclockwise. However, this could damage the spout.

Replace the old spout with the new spout, applying plumbing joint tape to the threads of the pipe to prevent leaking between the pipe and spout connection. A different nipple length may be required. Use the strap wrench to install the new spout.

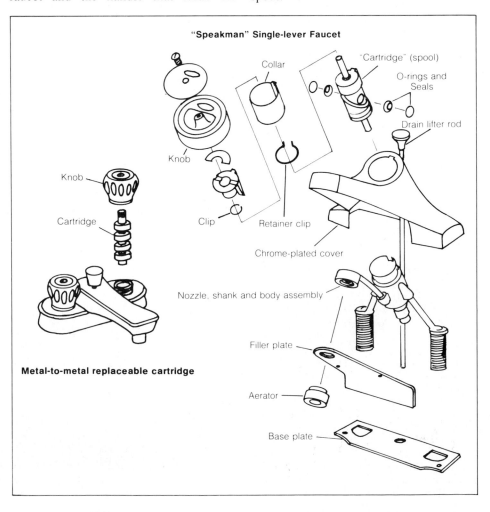

Newer, single-lever faucets come with many different mechanisms. This unit has a swivel-ball that fits into a cup-shape seat. Handle has a round base that fits over the ball.

This style faucet has a decorative cap that fits over the set screw. Pry off cap to reach the screw for faucet removal. Wrap tape around screwdriver tip to avoid scratching faucet.

The holding screw will be a Phillips head. Use Phillips head screwdriver to remove the screw to lift off cover so you can reach the interior of the faucet for repair.

Conversion of Separate Hot-Cold Faucets

Many older homes — particularly those with attractive pedestal sinks that are again fashionable — have separate hot

Knurled cap covers the ball-shaped mechanism that controls water flow. Pad the jaws of your wrench to prevent damage to this cap. Turn counterclockwise.

Ball control unit lifts right out to reveal water seals. Polish interior with steel wool to remove corrosion. Use a very light touch to buff. Do not scratch.

and cold water faucets. This is not only inconvenient, but the undiluted hot water can be dangerous. Conversion of these types of faucets to a type that mixes the hot and cold water can pose problems, because the distance between the faucets sometimes exceeds the distance allowed for by new faucets. However, there are some models that will handle such a situation. The example shown here is the Delex by Delta. The only problem that was encountered when we installed it was that the copper tubing that had been provided to connect the faucets to the hot and cold water lines were not long enough. It was an easy enough matter to buy two pieces of copper tubing, each about 5 or 6 inches long and of the same diameter. We cut the pieces to the necessary length, using couplings to add them on.

TOILETS

This is probably the plumbing fixture that causes the most concern to the average homeowner. Most toilets bolt directly to the floor flange with the aid of T-bolts (closet bolts). The bolts also may have a wood screw thread on one end and a machine screw thread on the other. Most toilets have two bolts. The wood thread end is turned through the base toilet flange; then a nut is turned onto the machine screw end to pull the toilet bowl down against the floor. This causes the bowl to press down on a ring of plumber's putty, a gasket (or the modern counterpart, a ring of wax), which creates a waterproof seal between the bowl and the floor.

A toilet fits over the cast iron drain line and is sealed with plumber's putty. The base is held with hanger bolts turned into the flooring. Bolts are covered with porcelain caps.

Leaks at the Floor Connection

A toilet that leaks at the floor line is usually one of the easiest problems to fix. If you note water around the bowl on the floor, it means that the seal should be replaced with a new one. In most cases you need not remove the tank from the bowl. But you do have to remove the tank and bowl from the floor or wall and then replace it again. You do have to be careful, and a helper is handy. First, remember to shut off the water, which is no problem if you have installed a shutoff valve in the supply line to the tank.

Next, flush the toilet so the tank is emptied. It will be necessary to hold open the ballcock to drain as much water as possible. There will still be some water in the tank, which will have to be cleaned out with a sponge. A sponge also will be required to mop up any water in the toilet bowl.

Now, remove the porcelain caps (if there are any) over the nuts on the closet bolts. Remove the nuts, then gently rock the toilet to loosen the seal. With the help of a friend, lift the toilet up off the closet bolts and place it on a stack of newspapers, or an old blanket or a rug. Remember that both the toilet bowl and tank are of vitreous china, and are quite fragile. The toilet can chip or crack if not handled gently.

Turn the bowl upside down and remove the old wax ring or plumbers' putty; install a new wax ring or gasket. The ring is available at any well stocked hardware store, and should be used in preference to the plumbers' putty. Position the toilet back over the hanger bolts and gently press it down so it is about level. Replace the nuts on the hanger bolts and turn them gently but firmly, so the toilet bowl is pulled down flush with the floor. Remove any putty that may have been squeezed out from under the base.

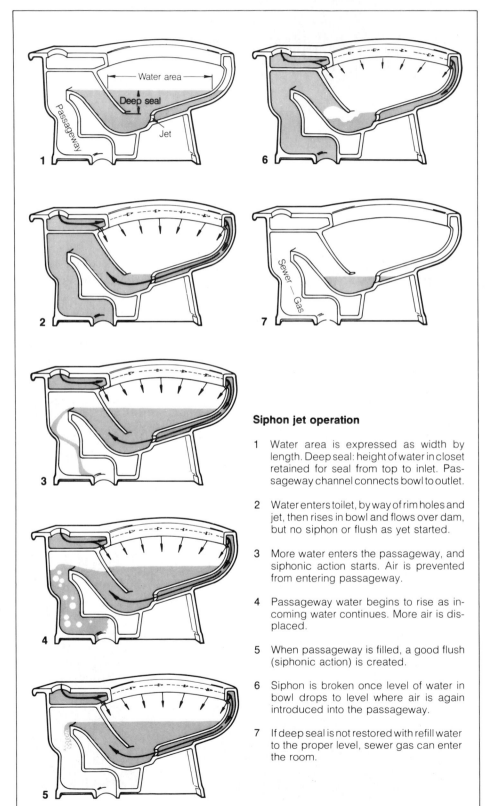

Siphon jet operation

1 Water area is expressed as width by length. Deep seal: height of water in closet retained for seal from top to inlet. Passageway channel connects bowl to outlet.

2 Water enters toilet, by way of rim holes and jet, then rises in bowl and flows over dam, but no siphon or flush as yet started.

3 More water enters the passageway, and siphonic action starts. Air is prevented from entering passageway.

4 Passageway water begins to rise as incoming water continues. More air is displaced.

5 When passageway is filled, a good flush (siphonic action) is created.

6 Siphon is broken once level of water in bowl drops to level where air is again introduced into the passageway.

7 If deep seal is not restored with refill water to the proper level, sewer gas can enter the room.

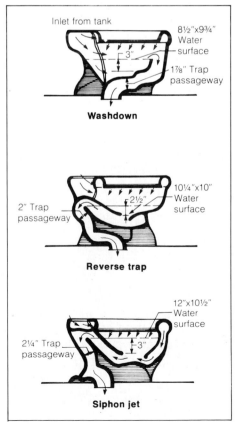

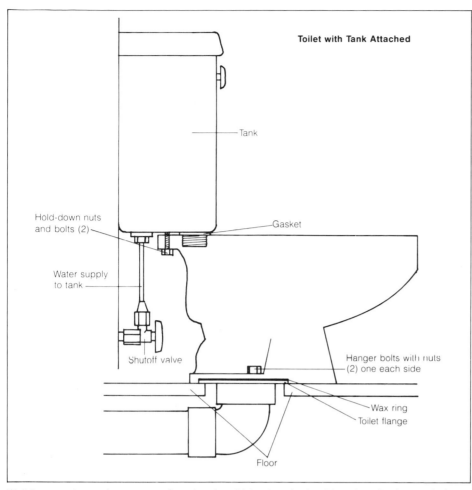

Toilet with Tank Attached

Tank

Hold-down nuts and bolts (2)

Gasket

Water supply to tank

Shutoff valve

Hanger bolts with nuts (2) one each side

Wax ring
Toilet flange

Floor

Wall-hung tank may be separate from bowl and joined to the bowl by a length of curved pipe.

The previous description is for working with a toilet that sets on cast iron pipe. For cast-iron and plastic drain lines, the toilet will be fastened with bolts that fit into slots in the flange at the top of the drain. The plastic flange is fastened to the floor (wooden) with wood screws. The square-head T-bolts fit in curved slots in the flange and thus are prevented from turning when you install or remove the nuts that hold down the bowl. The same wax ring is used for a toilet set on plastic pipe as for one on cast iron or copper pipe. The hold-down nuts are turned gently but firmly to pull the stool down flush with the floor; however, do not turn too strongly because you can crack the fragile porcelain of the bowl.

While you have the toilet/tank off the floor, check for water stains between the tank and toilet that would indicate a water leak. If there are such stains, unbolt the tank and replace the gaskets between the tank and toilet. It is much easier to do while the toilet is inverted, since the nuts that hold the tank to the toilet are under the back flange of the toilet. This means you will not have to stand on your head to remove and replace them. Again, use caution when tightening the nuts, as the tank and bowl are both fragile procelain.

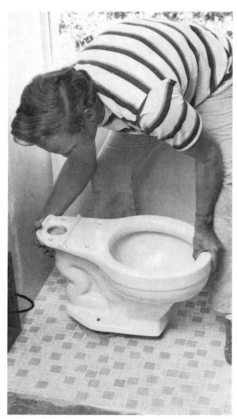

Although heavy, a toilet is procelain and fragile. Handle a toilet gently to avoid damage.

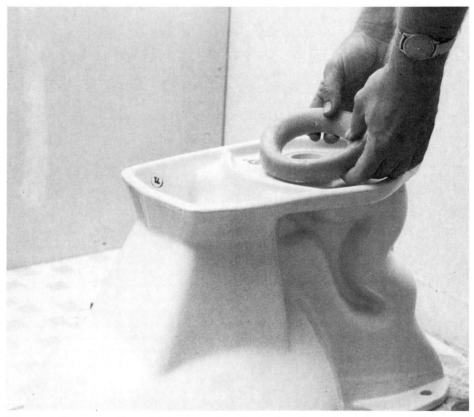

When installing or repairing a toilet, replace the plumber's putty seal to ensure a good base seal against leakage where toilet joins the drain.

If your toilet tank connects to the wall rather than to the bowl, it will fasten to the wall and be connected to the bowl by either a straight or curved pipe. To take the bowl off the floor, you must first disconnect the section of pipe between the tank and bowl. If it is badly corroded, cut it free with a hacksaw and plan to replace it. Have a pan handy to catch any water left in the pipe. Buy a new section of pipe to replace the one you cut, then carefully remove the pipe sections from the tank and bowl. If you are replacing a toilet bowl and/or tank, simply discard the units

and then use a new section of pipe. You might also decide to install a new toilet with the tank fastened to the bowl. All gaskets and parts will be provided with the new unit.

Installing a New Toilet
The steps given above are also those for replacing an old toilet with a new one. The only difference is that replacement calls for a complete collection of new parts.

Practicality is the most important feature in bathroom fixtures, but you can find units styled to compliment any decor.

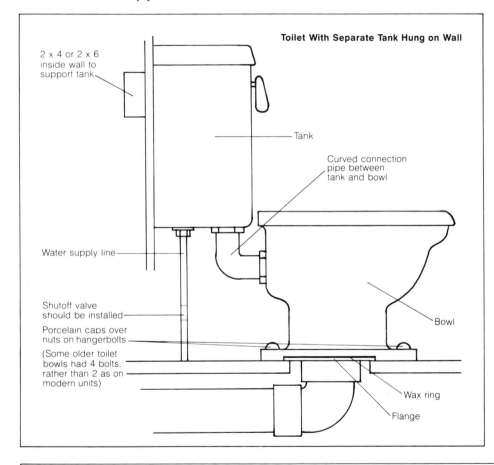

Toilet With Separate Tank Hung on Wall

2 x 4 or 2 x 6 inside wall to support tank

Tank

Curved connection pipe between tank and bowl

Water supply line

Shutoff valve should be installed

Porcelain caps over nuts on hangerbolts

(Some older toilet bowls had 4 bolts, rather than 2 as on modern units)

Bowl

Wax ring

Flange

Water-saving shower heads come in many designs. Side handle controls spray on this model.

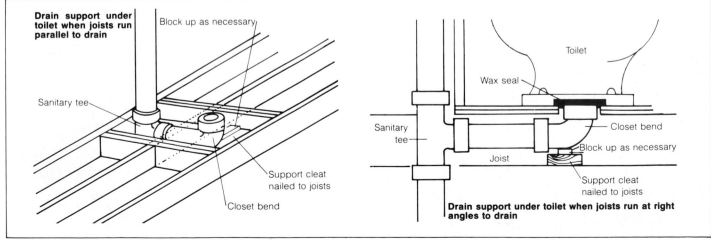

Drain support under toilet when joists run parallel to drain

Block up as necessary

Sanitary tee

Support cleat nailed to joists

Closet bend

Toilet

Wax seal

Sanitary tee

Closet bend

Block up as necessary

Joist

Support cleat nailed to joists

Drain support under toilet when joists run at right angles to drain

Drain pipe for toilets is cast iron. If you cut a floor joist, add doubled headers to reinforce joists and give support for pipe blocking.

Aquamizer™ fits in showerhead and cuts water flow by 60% while retaining water pressure.

NOVA showerhead is designed to provide very high pressure/low water consumption showers.

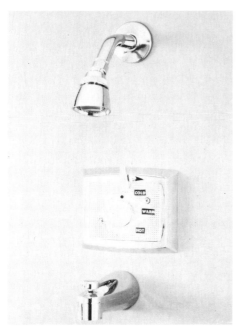

This anti-scald faucet protects the user from sudden changes of water temperature.

Holders keep tissue boxes in place and in sight. Decorative holders may sit on any surface available, but if surface room in your bath is limited, you can install a recessed wall unit.

A fold-down bathroom scale is one device that will help eliminate bathroom clutter.

If window ventilation is eliminated from your plans, install a vent fan. This unit fits through exterior wall and has a shield to prevent drafts in bathroom.

9 Pipe, Old and New

Pipe is the transportation system for your hot and cold water supply. You will probably have threaded steel and copper pipe in your house; if installations are recent you may also find plastic pipe. The following sections deal with pipe repair and replacement, as well as problem areas that can result in noisy pipes or inconvenient supply.

CODE REQUIREMENTS

Many cities specify what types of piping can be used, according to usage. For example, only copper or steel may be specified for hot water supply, even though plastic PB will handle pressures up to 200 lb. and temperatures up to 180 degrees. Most codes permit plastic pipe for cold water supply or for waste systems. Carefully check the code requirements in your area so that you will not have later difficulties and expenses because you failed to meet local code.

COPPER

Copper tubing is relatively expensive, but it has become the material most used in homes today for both the water supply and drain, waste and vent systems. It offers several advantages: it is lightweight, readily available and easily fabricated. It is also quite strong, noncorrosive and resistant to high temperatures.

Types of Tubing

Copper tubing comes in 10- and 20-foot lengths and in three weights: Type M has a thin wall, Type L has a medium wall and Type K has a thick wall. Unless otherwise specified by local code, Type M is considered sufficiently strong for the water supply system in a home. Copper tubing is always ⅛ inch larger than the nominal size, meaning that, for example, ½ inch copper tubing measures ⅝ inch in outside diameter. The actual inside diameter varies with the thickness of the pipe wall; the thicker the wall, the smaller the inside diameter.

In the 10 and 20-foot lengths Types K, L and M are available in "drawn temper," which is a rigid form of tubing. In the piping trades this is usually referred to as "hard" tubing because it is rigid. The three types of tubing are also made in soft tubing, and in the same lengths. However, the soft tubing comes packaged in rolls rather than being in straight lengths as is hard tubing.

Another class of copper tubing, called DWV (drain, waste and vent), is available only as rigid tubing in larger sizes. As the name implies, this tubing is used for waste, drain and vent lines in the drainage system of a home. Because the tubing is quite large, it may be necessary to use an extra large tip on your propane torch.

Tubing in sizes of ⅜, ½, ¾ and 1 inch are suitable for home water supply systems, while 1¼, 1½, 3 and 4 inch sizes are for drain, waste and vent.

Tools and Flared Joints

An ordinary propane torch will handle pipe and tubing up to about 1 or 1¼ inches in diameter. Above that size you would better work with a "Mapp" gas torch or an oxy-acetylene torch. You can buy or rent the latter in a modified type, with small tanks of oxygen that are the size of standard propane tanks. The torch uses a tank of oxygen and a tank of propane to create an extremely hot flame.

When you are working with copper tubing smaller than ½ inch, as for connecting faucets under sinks and basins, flexible soft tempered tubing is easiest to handle. It can be bent and shaped to go around obstacles and up into tight places. The soft tubing is not usually soldered, but is joined with flare fittings. Flared fittings are mechanical connections created with a special tool that grips the tubing in a sort of vise. An anvil then is forced into the end of the tubing by turning a screw, to spread the end of the tubing out to form a flare or flange. The main thing to re-member when using this flaring tool is to always slip the connector onto the tubing before making the flare. If you don't, you will have to cut off the flare with a tubing cutter, slip on the connector, and then remake the flare.

Do not overtighten the flaring tool, as this will make the flare thin at the edges and will cause splits. It then is necessary to cut off the flare and remake it. Examine the flare after you make it to be sure there are no burrs or scratches. The flare must be smooth to mate snugly with the connector and to create a watertight joint.

Soft temper tubing could be used for a full run in a water supply system because it can be bent around corners, eliminating the need for elbows or other connectors. The drawback is that flare fittings are quite expensive as compared to solder fittings. The same is true of compression fittings, which are made by slipping a ball-shape ferrule onto the tubing — after first slipping on the connector nut — then tightening the connection. The tightening action causes the ferrule to bite into the tubing to create a watertight joint between it and the tubing. The fitting then bears tightly on the ferrule so that connection is watertight.

The ferrule compression joint is quick and easy to make, but again it is quite expensive. If the joint for some reason must be remade, the tubing must be cut off behind the ferrule and that part of the tubing and the ferrule discarded.

There are tubing-to-pipe adapters available, with one end of the fitting designed to be soldered to copper tubing, and the other end threaded to turn onto steel pipe.

It is not recommended that copper pipe or tubing and steel pipe be used in the same system because of galvanic action. There are "dielectric" fittings with an insulator in them to minimize galvanic action, but the fittings simply cannot prevent the slight but constant flow of electricity between the unlike metals; the

Cut tubing cleanly, quickly, and squarely using a tubing cutter. The compact unit can be carried in a pocket or small tool box. A reamer in back pivots out for use.

Use flare fitting to join soft-temper small-sized copper tubing. Tubing ends clamp into flaring tool and cone-shaped "anvil" turns into end of tubing to flare it out. Put the nut onto tubing before making flare.

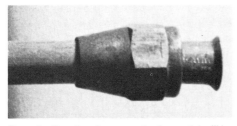

Once the flare has been made, the metal will be nearly as thick as it was originally. If you overtighten the tool, the edge of the metal will be too thin and may crack. If this happens, cut off the flare and remake it.

The flare surface must be smooth to perfectly match polished surface of fitting to which it is mated. The fitting shown is an adapter from copper tubing to steel pipe fitting.

copper gradually will be deposited on the steel, and leaks will occur in the copper. This is especially true at fittings, where brass or copper threads offer a knife edge that deteriorates rapidly.

Solder and Flux

Rigid copper tubing in a home plumbing system is assembled with sweat-soldered fittings, using "soft" solder. This solder is a combination of tin and lead; "50-50" (half tin, half lead) solder is most commonly used, but 60-40 is sometimes used. The higher percentage of tin causes the 60-40 to melt at a lower temperature; however this also makes it more difficult to use than the 50-50.

Solder generally is used in wire form, but paste-type solders also are available (do not use acid-core solder with copper pipes). They consist of finely ground solder in a suspension of paste flux. You must follow four rules when using paste-type solders:

1. Wire solder must be applied in addition to the paste. The wire helps fill voids and aids in displacing the flux, and if it is not used you may have nicely tinned surfaces with a poor joint resulting from a lack of continuous solder bond.

2. The paste solder must be thoroughly mixed if it has been standing in the container for more than a short time. The heavy solder has a tendency to settle to the bottom of the container, and taking material from the upper portion of the container will result in a mixture that is mostly flux.

3. Do not depend on the flux to clean the end of the tubing — clean the tubing manually with steel wool or fine sandpaper. Emery cloth is sometimes used but is more expensive than sandpaper, and metal particles can become deposited in the joint; steel wool actually is best as it readily conforms to the shape of the tubing or the inside of a fitting.

4. Remove any excess flux — only enough flux should be used to lightly coat the areas to be joined with solder.

The functions of flux are to remove any residue of oxide from the surfaces of the tubing and fittings, to promote "wetting" of the solder so it flows easily, and to prevent the heated surfaces from becoming oxidized. Because copper is an "active" metal, and oxide will quickly re-form on its surface after it has been cleaned, a flux should be applied to the metal as soon as possible after cleaning.

If using solder/flux in paste form, you must add wire solder to the joint. This guarantees that the band, which shows completely around the edge of the fitting, will be packed full with solder.

Always remove any corrosion, oxidation or oil from the end of rigid copper tubing. Emery cloth or sandpaper may be used, but steel wool leaves a smoother surface.

The fluxes that are best suited for 50-50 and 60-40 solders are mildly corrosive liquids, or petroleum-based pastes containing chlorides of zinc and ammonium. Some liquid fluxes are claimed to be "self-cleaning," as are some paste-type fluxes; while no one doubts that a corrosive flux does remove some oxides and dirt films, it is uncertain whether or not it provides a uniform cleaning of the surfaces. Also, if the flux is not completely dissipated by the heat of the torch, it may continue its corrosive action after the soldering has been completed and at some future time cause a leak.

Remove excess flux. Shown is solder flux applied to illustrate the excess that would be forced out by the fitting.

When soldering, always heat the metal and then apply solder. Fully pack joint between pipe or tube and fitting with solder.

When heat from a propane torch is applied (shown for demonstration purposes) flux bubbles up; solder migrates to copper surface.

As heat is continued, the flux melts and drops off tubing (or out of fitting if in use) leaving only clean, shiny solder. Shown is the activity that would take place inside the fitting.

How to Solder

Solder joints on copper tubing are made with the following simple steps.

1. Measure the length of the tube, figuring the distance between fittings plus the necessary lengths to fit into the fittings.

2. Cut the tubing square; because copper is quite soft, even a "pocket-size" cutter can be used.

3. Ream the cut end; a smaller tubing cutter will have a reamer on the handle that pivots out for use.

4. Clean the end of the tubing.

5. Clean the inside of the fitting.

6. Apply flux to the end of the tube.

7. Apply flux inside the fitting; be sparing.

8. Slip the tubing into the fitting until it contacts the shoulder inside; some tubing does not have the shoulder, and the tubing is simply inserted approximately ½ inch.

9. Use a cloth to wipe away any flux that squeezes out, or is on the tubing outside the fitting.

10. Apply heat with a propane torch, playing the flame first on the fitting, which is the thicker metal, then on the tubing.

11. Apply wire solder to the joint between tubing and fitting; do not play the flame on the solder — the heat of the tubing should melt the solder, and capillary action will pull the solder into the small opening between tubing and fitting.

12. Keep applying solder until a small fillet (band) of solder shows all around the fitting.

13. Allow the joint to cool completely before you move the assembly; any movement can fracture the cooling solder.

When you first start making solder joints in copper tubing, you may have a couple that leak just a little after the tubing has been installed and the water turned on. To correct this, shut off the water and open a connection near the joint. This can be a union, or a valve. Loosen the union or valve and, in the case of the valve, unscrew the bonnet. The point is to provide an escape for the steam that will be created when you heat the joint to melt the solder; the water in the line boils. If there is not an escape route for the steam, it will blow the solder out at you when it liquifies. Use caution!

Heat the leaking joint and pull it apart after the solder has melted. Heat the tubing and wipe off the molten solder with a clean cloth until there is just a thin, shiny coating of solder. Also heat and wipe out the inside of the fitting. Apply fresh flux, slip the tubing into the fittings and heat the joint. You will need a little less solder this time because both the tubing and fitting have been "tinned" with solder from the first attempt.

If you are making up new tubing and fittings that will be installed in the system and you are working at a vise in the shop, separate flux and solder are fine. However, we have found that when making joints in copper tubing, especially with tubing and fitting already installed, using paste-solder/flux is a time saver. The problem with working on joints in an installed system seems to be that the mass of tubing (with some water in it) pulls away the heat of the torch. It therefore takes a long time to heat the tubing and fitting sufficiently so the solder is pulled into the joint by capillary action. The flux/solder material heats up as you heat the tubing and fitting, and flows more quickly.

This is strictly a personal observation, of course, and some do-it-yourself homeowners have used the separate solder and flux without any problems. Also, the paste flux/solder is relatively expensive, costing several dollars for a small jar. In a matter of several years, and only making a few joints or repairs each year, my jar of solder/flux still is half full. I will say that if you are having problems making joints in copper tubing, the flux/solder might be your answer.

While soldering of copper tubing and fittings is done with a relatively low temperature — and the metal never changes color — there still is enough heat to burn you severely if you put a bare hand on the metal soon after a joint has been made. It is good practice, therefore, to wear gloves when soldering joints. It is not good practice to pour cold water on a newly soldered joint; this could cause too rapid shrinking of the solder which could cause a leak or, in extreme cases, could cause a fitting to crack. Let the joint cool normally.

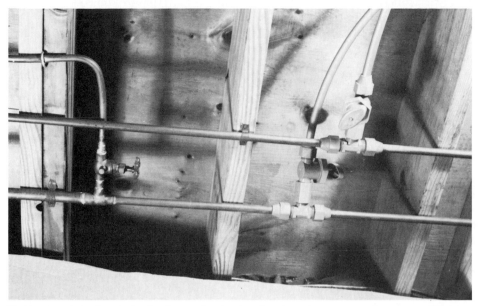

Rigid copper pipe is attached at the top to plastic valves by using compression nuts on T-fittings. The valve at the bottom is soldered to a reducing tee.

Copper Plus Plastic

Copper tubing can be connected to plastic pipe. Because plastic is inert and does not react with any metal, no problems occur when mixing plastic and copper in a water supply or drain system.

Fittings are attached to plastic pipe with cement. One end of the plastic fitting is threaded and it is turned into a threaded fitting that has been soldered to the copper.

Valves and other plastic fittings that have compression nuts at the ends can also be used on copper tubing (and sometimes steel pipe). Just cut out a section of the pipe to allow insertion of the fitting, then put it on the line and tighten the nuts. You will usually need to retighten the nuts about three times over a matter of several days in order to prevent any leaks and still not stress and break the plastic fittings.

Leak in Copper Pipe

If you note a leak in copper tubing at a fitting, it might be that the joint was subject to vibration, possibly from an automatic clothes washer — or water hammer may have battered the joint often enough to break the solder.

Shut off the water and drain the line. Open the nearest connection, a union or a valve. Remove the valve stem by unscrewing the packing nut and turning out the stem so the washer — if there is one — will not be damaged by the heat. The line must be dry and free of water before the solder will melt and fresh solder can be applied to be pulled into the joint by capil-

lary action. Never try to solder a joint without an opening nearby where the water can drain. This way if the water turns to steam, the pressure can be dissipated. If you heat a solder joint with no place for the steam pressure to escape, you are likely to get a splash of hot solder blasted out by the steam pressure.

Treat the joint as you would a new joint, heating both the copper tubing and fitting until the solder will melt when it contacts the surface of the tubing.

If the joint shows signs of having leaked for some time, you should heat the joint until the solder is molten and then pull the joint apart. There will be a streak of dirt and corrosion in the solder, and you will have to heat the tubing and wipe off the solder all the way around. It may be necessary to apply flux to the dirty spot. Then heat it and apply solder. Wipe it off immediately so a clean, shiny "tinned" surface is left. Do the same with the inside of the fitting.

If you find that the tinned surfaces of the inside of the fitting and the outside of the copper tubing will not slide together because of the added thickness of tinning solder, then heat both the fitting and tubing until the solder is molten (wear gloves for this operation). Slide the tubing into the fitting, being careful not to burn yourself with the excess solder that will be forced out of the joint. Keep the heat on the joint as you slide it together. After the tubing has bottomed in the fitting, apply more solder to create a fillet all around the edge of the fitting.

Let the solder cool, then retighten the nearby joint, or reassemble the valve. Turn on the water. Check the joint for any leakage. If you have been thorough, there should be no leak.

As described earlier, you will need an ordinary propane torch and wire solder, plus flux, to remake the solder joint. Or, after heating and wiping the old solder off the pipe and from inside the fitting, you can apply the flux/solder mixture as described previously. If the leak is in a drain or vent of copper pipe, the same rules apply. You will have to heat the joint to make the solder molten, then add flux and solder. Because the joints in most main drains and vents are horizontal, you might be able to "cook" out the foreign material in the solder that is causing the leak. It is best, of course, to melt the solder and disassemble the joint to clean it. This is difficult with a large drain line, and there are no unions to make it easy to remove a section.

Where a copper drain line does spring a leak in the pipe itself, you can, in some cases, repair it by soldering. It would be best, however, to replace the section. Cut the leaking length out and install a fresh piece. You can use a straight coupling that will slide up on one pipe, then slide down over the joint so it can be soldered. For an even quicker repair, use neoprene rubber sleeves with stainless steel clamps. While basically made to join plastic drain and vent lines, the sleeves can be used to repair copper tubing and to join plastic and cast iron.

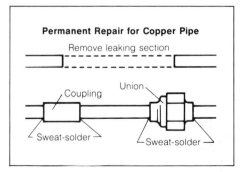

Soldering a leak is only a temporary repair; the damaged section should be cut out and a new piece of tubing soldered into the fitting.

Emergency repair. You can make an emergency repair to a hole by soldering the pipe — but the hole cannot be too big. It is also necessary to grind off the chrome plating, because solder will not adhere to chrome. This requires a grinder, because a file will not touch the very hard chrome.

After grinding, heat the metal, apply flux, then the solder. Use a propane torch and play the flame lightly around the repair spot. You want to puddle the solder and build it up. If you apply too much heat, the molten solder will fall through the opening. It will take a little practice, and perhaps a lot of solder, but you can make a temporary repair in this manner. The minute you can get to the hardware store, buy a new section of the drain and install it. Once a leak has developed, it will spread and your solder job will last only a short time.

STEEL PIPE

The piping system in any home ten years old or older (and in a few newer homes where cost is a major factor, or in areas where copper tubing is in short supply) will have threaded steel pipe and fittings. Repairs to this type of pipe, which is also called "iron", call for more tools and somewhat more skill than when dealing with either copper tubing or plastic pipe.

One of the main problems with steel pipe is the lack of flexibility in making up a system. You must be quite accurate with your measurements. If the made-up length is too short, you have to replace it with a longer one; if it is too long, you have to cut if off and rethread it. The second problem is that after many years, steel pipe tends to become plugged with mineral deposits.

On the plus side, steel pipe has a lifespan of 20 to 25 or more years, as proven by the piping in homes built at the turn of the century and now being restored. Some of the piping has to be replaced, of course, but much of it is still serviceable.

One note of caution for a house that has steel pipe: if your system has shown few if any leaks, but you install a watersoftening system, there is a good chance leaks will

appear. The softened water appears to remove the deposits which over a number of years not only plug the pipes somewhat but also seal slight leaks in threaded joints. Luckily, the leaks seem to occur in horizontal runs in the basement or crawl space, rather than in risers.

To sum up about steel pipe: it has been used in more homes than any other kind of pipe, and unless your home is brand new it is likely there will be threaded steel pipe in the system.

Pipe Threads

Steel pipe requires the use of dies in order to cut threads on the ends. Although not free, a set of standard pipe dies is not too expensive and the dies are a must to work with steel pipe.

The basic instrument is a round or square block of steel in which there is an opening with hardened teeth that cut threads into the relatively soft steel of the pipe. Most such dies come in sets with

pipe sizes of ⅜, ½, ¾, and 1 inch. The latter size generally is the largest size that will be used in the water-supply line of a home. Larger pipes would, of course, be used in commercial and industrial applications, but the homeowner seldom has need for tools to handle the larger sizes of 1¼, 1½, 2, 2½ or 3 inches.

Steel pipe in sizes of 1¼ and 1½ inches are used for drain lines from sinks and some vents, but when you get to this kind of a job, it's best to go to a local hardware store and have them thread the larger sizes of pipe with their threading machine. A hardware store often can cut and thread pipe to the lengths you want, and also will have bins full of pipe "nipples," which are short lengths of pipe threaded at both ends and ready for use. The nipples vary in length from 1½ inches (called a "close nipple," which is so short that the threads at each end meet in the middle) to 6 inches. The lengths are in ½-inch increments: 1½, 2, 2½, 3 inches and so on. While the 6-inch nipple is the longest "standard" size, you can often find nipples that are 8, 10 and 12 inches long to suit the requirements of do-it-yourself homeowners. Professional plumbers also find these "overlong" nipples very handy too, and sometimes make them up while on the job if they are not readily available.

Once pipe has been threaded, oil must be applied to the die to lubricate the cutters. Quite a bit of metal is removed by the cutters. After making one turn with the die, you must then back up about a half turn to clear out the metal shavings. Repeat this until the thread is completely cut. In most cases a full length of thread is completed when the pipe just starts to project from the edge of the die. Be careful when handling steel pipe that has just been threaded; the threads will not only be knife sharp, but there may be some small shavings still in the threads that can cut your hands quite badly.

When buying new lengths of steel pipe, the threads will be protected by straight couplings that are put on at the factory. To prevent damage to the threads, and to your hands, leave the couplings on until you are ready to work with the pipe. Also, if you are in a situation where you need to run consecutive lengths of pipe that must be joined by a straight coupling, be sure to remove the coupling and apply joint compound. The coupling then is snugly turned onto the pipe with a pipe wrench.

For a watertight seal, wrap strip of Teflon™ around threads of the male connection. The tape substitutes for pipe-joint compound.

A die is used to cut threads on steel pipe. The tool can have a fixed die, or a ratchet handle that enables its use in tight areas.

Fittings

A complete hardware store will have bins full of fittings, such as elbows, tees, couplings and unions. These fittings come in one size, as well as in a "reducing" size. That is, while a fitting will have one size to accommodate the pipe you are using, there will be one or more connections that are smaller. An example would be a ½-inch tee fitting that has a "straight-through" size of ¾ inch, while the connection at right angles would be ½ or ⅜ inch for the connection that supplies water to a sink or basin.

Another way to "reduce" pipe size is with "reducing bushings" and "reducing couplings" (sometimes called "reducing bells" after their shape). The bushings have "male" threads that twist into the "female" threads, with a smaller opening that has female threads into which a smaller pipe is turned. The term "male"

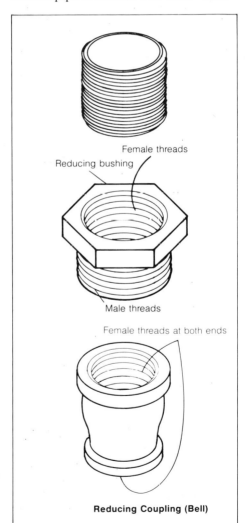

A close nipple (above) is used with female threads; it adds only ½ inch to the length. Reducing bushings and couplings are a common way of going from one pipe size to another in a pipe run (as opposed to a turn in the pipe).

means that threads are on the outside of a pipe or fitting, while "female" refers to interior threads.

One fitting that has both male and female threads is a "street elbow," commonly called a "street ell." All elbows, whether 90 degree, 45 degree, or street (which comes as both 90 and 45 degree fittings) are commonly called "ells."

Fittings in steel pipe provide right-angle or 45 degree changes of direction, but you can create a "swing joint" by using two street ells. These fittings come in either a 90- or a 45-degree angle. They can be angled in a combination of two (or more), sometimes along with a standard 90- or 45-degree elbow which has female threads in both ends, rather than the combination of male and female found in a street ell.

Tool Use For Steel Pipe

Tools needed for working with steel pipe include a pipe vise, which has jaws with teeth that grip the pipe. Some machinists' (bench) vises can be fitted with removable jaws for pipe work. Pipe wrenches also have gripping teeth in their jaws. A pipe wrench is designed with one jaw that is spring-loaded; as you apply turning force to the wrench, the movable spring-loaded jaw tends to bite or tighten on the pipe. The more you turn the wrench, the tighter the jaw will clamp.

Most steel pipe is galvanized. The zinc plating that helps prevent rusting also can cause a pipe wrench to slip and to scrape off the plating. When working with galvanized pipe, avoid putting tremendous strain on a pipe wrench or it will slip as the

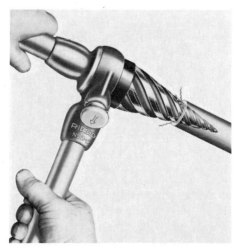

Even when a pipe cutter is used, a burr is left inside the steel pipe that must be removed with a reamer. The burr causes restriction in the pipe and encourages mineral buildup.

Steel water pipe usually is galvanized inside and out. This coating can cause a pipe wrench to slip, especially if the wrench is a cheap model whose jaws have dull teeth.

Use a pipe vise, or pipe jaws in a machinist's vise, to hold pipe during threading or when pipe and joints are being "made up."

galvanizing peels away under the pressure of the jaws. Since you cut through galvanizing when threading pipe, the threads are usually the first place to rust on steel pipe.

After steel pipe has been cut with a cutter, or even a hacksaw, there will be a burr inside. This must be removed to prevent its creating resistance to water flow and becoming a place where mineral deposits can collect and build up. A reamer is used to remove it; and most pipe cutters will have one as part of the tool. As an alternative, you can purchase a pipe reamer as a separate tool.

A pipe thread is tapered, rather than being straight as on a bolt. This taper creates a wedging action that produces tremendous pressure as the threads turn into a fitting. When working with steel pipe, always use two wrenches. One wrench holds the fitting, while the other turns the pipe into it. Conversely, a wrench can hold pipe while a fitting is turned onto it. The use of two wrenches is especially important when working on

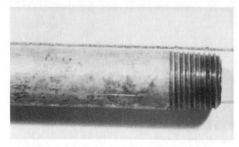

Threads on pipe end taper, as opposed to the threads on a bolt, which are straight. The taper creates wedging effect for watertight joint, but can split fitting if overtightened.

Always use two wrenches when working with steel pipe. One wrench holds the pipe as the fitting is turned onto it. A pipe vise can take the place of one wrench when used for making up pipe and fittings.

pipe that is already installed. If you do not hold the existing pipe against turning pressure, you could turn a fitting somewhere inside a wall and cause a leak — and a lot of trouble.

For most work in a home, a pipe wrench need not be larger than the 14-inch size, and an 18-inch size will handle almost everything you will ever need turned. Be cautious when working with a pipe wrench on smaller sizes of pipe; you can overtighten a fitting. This causes the fitting to expand, and not only will the threads probably leak but the fitting may crack.

Once again, the importance of the quality of your tools cannot be overemphasized. Using a pipe wrench with dull or soft teeth in the jaws could easily cause muscle strain.

Steel Pipe Replacement
One common repair of steel pipe is replacement of a section that has rusted or corroded and has begun to leak. The first step, as with any kind of repair on any kind of pipe, is to shut off the water supply. The next step is to measure the length

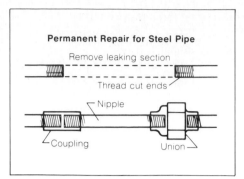

Repairs to steel pipe require cutting out the leaking section and cutting threads on the ends of the new pipe and the remaining pipe.

of the pipe between the fittings — the "exposed" length. Write that length down somewhere; it is too easy to forget it.

Next, locate the leaking section. Water can run a considerable distance down a pipe before it drops off. Run your hand along the pipe in either direction from where the water is dropping and you will be able to pinpoint the direction from which the water is coming. Cut out the damaged section, making the cut several inches away from the leak. This is to assure that you leave only good pipe. You can use a hacksaw, which almost every homeowner has, or a pipe cutter. The latter is easier to use and makes a clean cut that is exactly at right angles to the length of the pipe. Few of us can make a right-angle cut with a hacksaw. If you are going to do any amount of plumbing, or work on various types of piping, a pipe cutter will quickly pay for itself. You can buy quality cutters that will handle steel pipe, copper tubing (rigid or flexible) and plastic pipe.

Then look at the end of the piece of pipe still in place. If it looks rusted or corroded inside, or is plugged with "lime", you would do well to remove it and replace the complete length. If you don't, it will leak in the near future and/or slow the flow of water to the fixture it supplies.

If the remaining pipe does look good, it still must be unscrewed from its fitting in order to be threaded. Thread it yourself, or take it to the hardware store where you will be buying the new piece of pipe. If you are replacing only the cut-out section, measure it. You must then subtract the length that will be taken up by the unions. The result is the length you need. In any instance it is better for the pipe/union assembly to be just a fraction too long than too short. You can almost always turn the pipe into a fitting one additional turn, which will shorten the overall length.

If replacing the complete length of pipe, the damaged piece of pipe plus the length of the good pipe will tell the hardware man (or you) how long the replacement piece must be.

If the leak is at a fitting, it might be that turning the pipe a partial turn to tighten it in the fitting will stop the leak. However, it really is best to unscrew the pipe (after first shutting off the water, of course) from the fitting. Examine the threads inside the fitting and at the end of the pipe. If they look all right, then apply pipe-joint compound or Teflon tape and (using two wrenches) tighten the pipe in the fitting.

Union. A union consists of three parts: there is a piece at each end that turns onto the pipe, and there is a large "nut" at the center that draws the two end pieces together. The mating surfaces of the two end pieces are polished concave and convex surfaces that create a kind of "ball joint." Be careful when making up a joint with a union not to drag one polished surface over another. This could cause a scratch or gouge that would make the joint leak. Because of the ball-joint effect, a union can even make up for some misalignment in the pipe. The misalignment should be very slight, however; too much could cause a leak.

No joint compound is applied to the meeting faces of a union. Compound is used, however, on the threads at the ends

A union allows replacement of a pipe section. Leave the union mating faces clean, but coat each end of the union, and the large nut that joins the halves, with pipe-joint compound.

Shown is an assembled union, to which pipe-joint compound or Teflon™ tape is applied.

of the fitting that turn onto pipe, and also to the nut that pulls the two halves of the union together. A substitute for pipe-joint compound is Teflon™ applied as a tape around the threads of the male connection. The plastic provides a lubrication that eases tightening of the threads and also makes the joint watertight.

Leaks Inside Walls

A really desperate situation is when you find a leak inside a wall. This will occur mostly in older homes with steel pipe. If you want to tear out the wall in one or two floors, you can replace the damaged pipe. A much more practical repair is to just shut off — and cut off — the pipe and replace (reroute) it with flexible plastic or flexible copper tubing. If it's a short run, say from the basement to the first floor, flexible copper can be threaded up through the wall. If the line is between floors, you will have better luck with flexible plastic. For the latter you can drop a weighted cord down through the wall to which you tie the end of the plastic pipe so it can be pulled up through the wall.

Electrical Safety

Look for the electrical ground connection on any steel pipe you work on; it will be on the cold water side. If you see such a ground wire, replace it immediately after making your repair or connection. If it is heavy wire, it will be from your main electrical supply and is an absolutely necessary connection to assure safe and complete electrical service (it will have no electric current in it). If it is a small ground wire, it will probably be from your telephone, and it is likely that your phone will not work properly until it is reconnected. The cold water line is used as a ground connection because it runs directly into the earth. A hot water line should never be used because it is interrupted through a heating tank, and is possibly even an insulated "dielectric" fitting intended to prevent galvanic action. This fitting could also insulate the electric current from passing to the earth in case of a fault in the electrical system. It will not work even if a ground fault interrupter is included in the wiring system; the GFI still needs to direct current to ground, if only for a mere fraction of a second.

PLASTIC PIPE

Plastic pipe and fittings now are being used by professional plumbers, and plastic is definitely the easiest option for the do-it-yourself homeowner.

As well as being very easy to handle, plastic pipe offers several other advantages: the inside of the pipes are so smooth that they offer much less resistance to the flow of water than metal pipes. In many instances the plastic pipes permit a smaller size of pipe to supply the same volume of water, as compared to some metal pipes. This is obviously a savings in money and material. Plastic also resists the passage of heat much better than metal, so there is less heat loss in hot water lines. In cold water lines the insulating effect works to reduce "sweating" that occurs in summer weather.

There are four basic types of plastic pipe: polyvinyl chloride (PVC), chlorinated polyvinyl chloride (CPVC), polybutylene (PB) which is the newest member of the family, and acrylonitrile-butadiene-styrene (ABS). The latter is used for drain, waste and vent systems. Polyethylene plastic pipe does not have the resistance to pressure and heat that newer plastics such as PB have.

Three of the types of plastic pipe require the use of solvent adhesives; the fourth, PB, cannot be solvent welded and is joined with compression fittings. The one disadvantage of PB pipe is its higher cost, and we have encountered some hardware stores and home centers who do not even carry it because of the higher price tag. For most jobs the solvent-welded plastic pipe is fine, and easy to work.

PB

We have found the added cost of PB to be worthwhile when plumbing in hard-to-reach locations, and when replacing other types of pipe inside a wall where your visibility and space are limited.

PB pipe can be worked very easily; we have pulled a length of it up through a wall with the aid of a "fish wire," much as you would pull a length of electric wire through a wall. The pipe can be used for hot water, as it is rated well above any temperature that will be encountered with an ordinary hot water tank. It also offers a safety factor of several times the pressure that will ever be produced in a normal water supply system, whether from a municipal line or a private pump.

Solvent-welded Pipe

All solvent-welded pipe is handled in much the same manner. You first cut it off cleanly at right angles. This can be done with any fine-toothed saw, including a hacksaw. A good sharp knife will also do the job. A simple miter box will aid in cutting the pipe at a neat right angle. You can also use a tubing cutter designed to

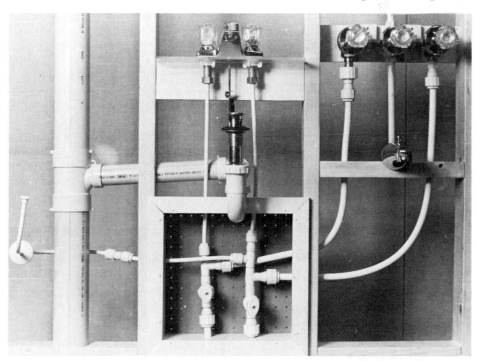

This bathroom "rough in" includes plastic pipes, valves and other necessary fittings for connection to toilet, vanity basin and tub/shower. Shown are CPVC pipe for DWV, along with flexible PB in smaller sizes for water supply.

cut plastic pipe; this is the easiest, most accurate way to cut it. Cutters intended for copper tubing or steel pipe usually will not give a clean edge because the cutting wheels are not sharp enough, and tend to only crease the plastic pipe rather than cut it.

The next step is to remove any burr on the cut end of the pipe, using a sharp knife or sandpaper. A recommended procedure, although not mandatory, is to use a clean rag to wipe some cleaner around the outside of the fitting and the pipe. This will remove any grease, oil or foreign material that would prevent the solvent from reaching the plastic surface. Some craftsmen skip this step, taking a chance that the pipe will clean up by just rubbing it lightly with fine sandpaper. This is not a good idea; the moment or two it takes to clean the plastic is good insurance against a leak later on.

Immediately after cleaning the pipe, and the inside of the fitting as well, apply

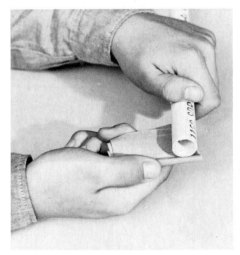

Gently sand cut ends of plastic pipe where they will go into fittings. Pressure ratings are stamped onto the pipe walls.

Brush plastic pipe cement onto the pipe, but not the fitting. Before applying cement, assemble pipe in a "dry" run so you can adjust before cement application.

the solvent adhesive liberally on the pipe and lightly in the socket. Quickly push the pipe into the socket of the fitting, using a quarter turn in order to spread the adhesive. Be sure to align the fitting within a few seconds, as the solvent adhesive begins to set up almost as soon as it is applied. Do not be stingy with the adhesive; any excess will be squeezed out of the fitting when you insert the pipe. The occasional leaks that occur in plastic type are often due to a lack of the adhesive. Try not to overdo it, of course, because the excess cement does not look good, and is almost impossible to remove. Be generous, not sloppy.

Specialty Pipe

While ABS pipe generally is used for drain, waste and vent (DWV) line, one company (Genova Plastic) has a line of PVC fittings and pipe for this application. It is solvent welded in the same manner as the smaller water supply pipe previously described. Genova also has two types of DWV pipe. Their "Schedule 30" pipe will just fit inside a 2x4 wall, while their "Schedule 40" will not. The advantage of the Schedule 30 is that you do not have to build the wall out using 2x6s, as is ordinarily done in a bathroom to provide room for the larger pipe. Both types of pipe have the same inside diameter; the difference between the two types is in the thickness of the pipe wall. Because the Schedule 30 "in-the-wall" pipe is so easy to install, it is accepted by many plumbing codes.

Compression Fittings

Compression fittings used for joining PB pipe consist of a nut, a stainless steel locking ring, and a sealing washer that makes a watertight connection with the fitting — very simple. There is one cau-

PB plastic pipe is joined with compression fittings; it does not take solvent application. One method (Qest) utilizes nut, stainless steel lock ring, sealing ring and fitting. These fittings also can be used on CPVC pipe and copper tubing for watertight connections.

tion with these fittings: the stainless steel locking ring has a razor-sharp edge, so handle it with care.

Slip the first nut onto the pipe or tubing; always have the correct connection size.

Next, add locking ring and sealing rings, which must be flush with pipe or tubing ends. A square cut on pipe or tubing is needed.

Flare Fittings

Most brands of PB and CPVC come in the same sizes as copper tubing, and can be flared to accept standard flare fittings. Using the flare fittings makes it convenient to connect to faucets and other fixtures and appliances. A standard flaring tool is employed after the end of the pipe has been softened in warm water to prevent its cracking when flared. It is necessary to make an absolutely square cut for a flared end, otherwise the flare will not seal in the flare fitting. As with copper tubing, remember to slip on the flare nut before making the flare on the pipe.

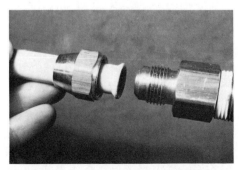

Most PB and CPVC pipe can be flared to accept standard flare fittings used for copper tubing. Warm plastic tubing in water; flare with standard flaring tool.

Cost vs. Convenience

As stated earlier in this chapter, PB pipe and fittings are more expensive than other types of plastic. This additional cost is worthwhile in the savings of time and trouble when connecting plastic pipe to steel or copper. All that is required is to simply remove a section of the metal pipe and slide on the PB fittings. The components fit the metal pipe, and by tightening the nuts at the ends of the fitting, the fitting will clamp onto the pipe to make a watertight seal. A variety of adapters are available to enable connection of PB pipe and fittings (or other types of plastic) to the connectors.

SHUTOFF VALVES

The very first step in your program should be installation of shutoff valves under — or adjacent to — sinks, vanities, toilets and other fixtures.

Shutoff valves enable you to shut off water to whatever fixture you are working on, rather than turning off the water supply for the entire house.

Copper or Steel Plus Plastic

The fastest and easiest way to install shutoff valves in either a copper-tubing or steel-pipe system is with a plastic valve that has compression fittings on the ends. You simply cut out a section of the pipe, slide the compression nuts onto the cut ends, and then slide the valve onto one of the cut ends. The pipe must be pushed aside just a little to slide the nut onto the valve. Then align the pipes and slip the valve onto the other pipe. Once the nuts are turned onto the ends of the valve, the installation is complete.

For either copper or steel pipe, the pipe first should be cleaned with steel wool or sandpaper. We also found it necessary to snug up the nuts about ⅛ turn for three or four days after installation in order to completely stop any seepage. Do not try to tighten the nuts too much when you first install the valve, because a plastic component can be stripped or cracked by overtightening. Just turn it a little more each day to avoid this possibility.

Plastic valves can be used without compression fittings with steel pipe that comes out of the wall under a toilet tank and makes a right angle turn upward to the tank.

First cut the small line that runs upward from the elbow (or disconnect the line at the tank) and unscrew it from the elbow. A right angle plastic valve with pipe threads at one end is now turned onto the pipe coming out of the wall. The opening of the valve that faces upward can be a compression connection for a short length of flexible plastic pipe. The plastic pipe has a ball shape on the top end that is integral with the pipe. It is held by the same nut that originally held the steel pipe (or possibly flexible copper) to the bottom of the tank.

For Steel Pipe

If you have steel pipe, you can cut out a section and replace it with a valve, a nipple and a union. There generally is very little space under a sink or vanity, which means that threading the cut-off pipe in place requires a ratchet pipe die, considerable strength and a great amount of patience.

For Copper Pipe

With copper tubing, you can cut out a section of the pipe and sweat-solder a valve into the line, but here we run into the problem of a hot flame in an enclosed place, and a fire hazard. Yes, it can be done with the proper safeguards: be sure to empty nearby cabinets and place a sheet of metal over any flammable wood.

Kits

You can buy "kits" for installing shutoff valves; they actually are for connecting toilets or sinks, and contain all necessary fittings including valves. The next time you are in a hardware store, look over the display of the plastic plumbing parts and installation kits. Most makers of the plastic pipe and fittings offer free booklets describing how their particular line of

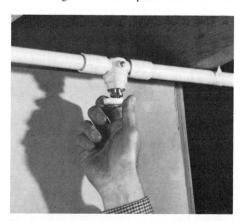

Plastic shutoff valves come in kits and are easy to install, avoiding need to turn off water supply to whole house during repairs.

components should be handled. The booklets are worth picking up just for information on the latest developments.

Location

While it is very convenient to have shutoff valves directly under sinks and vanities, it is not mandatory that they be located there. A practical alternative is to put the valves in the basement under the fixture. The advantage of such a location is that there is more room to work.

EXTENDING PIPES

One practical way to replace the piping is to abandon the old pipes and install new copper tubing or plastic pipe, if your local building codes permit it. Start back at the main shutoff valve that is on the house side of the meter. Disconnect the pipe at this point and check it for plugging. If the pipes up in the bathroom were plugged, the chances are the pipe leading from the meter also will be plugged. The pipe in the ground leading from the meter to the street main also might be partially plugged, but there is not much you can do about it without a lot of expense and trouble.

Start at the shutoff valve and use a reducing bell (coupling) to increase the pipe at least one size larger than the existing pipe. That is, if the present pipe is ¾ inch, replace it with a 1 inch pipe. Run 1 inch pipe throughout the house until it is close to a fixture, then reduce down to the usually required ⅜ or ¼ inch lines that run to the faucets. What the larger pipe does is provide a larger volume of water in the house, which helps reduce loss of pressure due to the partial plugging of the line from the meter to the supply main under the street.

As a word of caution, if the line from the meter to the street main is badly plugged it will have to be replaced. This will require the services of a professional plumber who will need a permit from the water department to do the job. The line from the meter to the main generally is the property of the water department, but you as the homeowner must pay for its repair or replacement.

There are shutoff valves in various sections of the water main, and the water supply is delivered to quite a few homes through one valve. Thus, if a valve is shut off to permit replacing a connection to one home, a number of homes will be without water for a period of time. This is done, of course, and some localities use this procedure whenever a connection to a home must be replaced, or a new hookup is made. Another method sometimes used is to pack the connection to be replaced with dry ice (frozen carbon dioxide) so the water freezes. Once the repair, replacement or new connection is made (quickly) then the water in the line rapidly thaws the frozen spot. With this technique, there is obvious potential for damage due to expansion of the freezing water, so it is not much used.

In some localities the water department may make the repairs or replacement between the meter and the water main, rather than a professional plumber. Check with your water utility to determine the method used in your city or town.

Regardless of how the job is done or who does it, the homeowner is not involved and has no reponsibility until the water reaches the shutoff valve on the house side of the water meter.

Even if you have the line from the main to the house replaced with a new pipe, we recommend that you go at least one size larger from the meter through the rest of your house. This is, as previously stated for the main line; lines to sinks, vanities, tubs and toilets will be a smaller size. We suggest making the branch lines no smaller than ½ inch until it is necessary to make the connection to the fixture. In this way you have the maximum volume of water right up to the fixture.

If you are adding a new bathroom and can work within the wall before the wall surface (plasterboard, paneling, tile backer board) is applied, you can drill down through the wall without too much difficulty. If the bathroom is being remodeled you still may have to remove some of the wall to install the piping.

Substituting Pipe Lines

Where you don't want to remove the wall covering, then we suggest simply abandoning any existing pipes in the wall. This is especially true if the new fixtures will be in different locations than the old ones. For example, if a new vanity cabinet will be installed, place the cabinet in position and drill pilot holes down through the bottom shelf of the cabinet and through the floor. Bore holes for the hot and cold water supply lines and for the drain line.

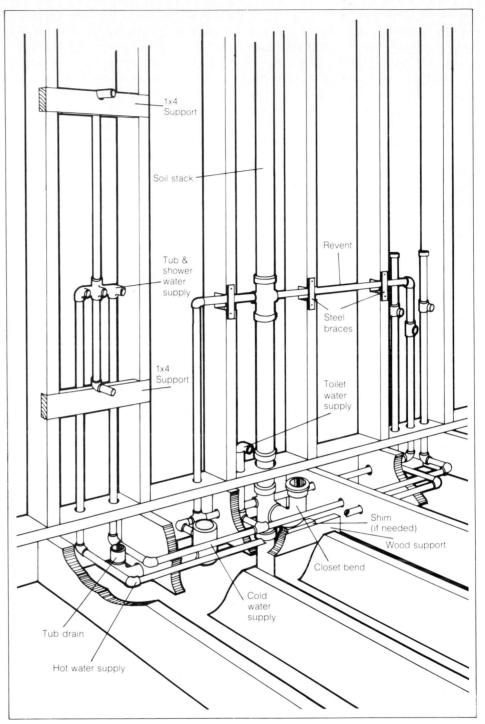

If plumbing will be installed in the wall, open up the existing wall to add larger pipes for drains. Install a vent for new bath and a large pipe up through the roof.

Before enlarging the holes, go down into the basement or crawl space; make sure the pilot holes are not located where the path of the pipe will be interrupted by any obstacle. If the pilot hole is on top of a floor joist, then move it a few inches. Also relocate the hole or holes in the bottom shelf of the vanity cabinet, then drill them a size to accept the pipes. Move the cabinet away from the spot and redrill the holes large enough to provide clearance for the sizes of the pipes you will use.

When the cabinet is replaced in position, and the pipes run up through the floor and the cabinet shelf, they will be out of sight. The same is true of a built-in or recessed tub. The supply line to a toilet will be exposed and must be routed through the floor or the wall. Routing the line through the floor is easier. The hole for the pipe is located once the toilet is temporarily positioned. There is always a chance that the tank connection and the hole in the floor will be a bit out of line, but copper or plastic piping can be bent to accommodate any misalignment. Steel pipe will present problems, and the usual solution is to drill the hole in the floor oversize to allow movement of the pipe, then plug or caulk around the pipe after it is in place. A chrome escutcheon plate then is fitted around the pipe down at the floor juncture, to make the connection neat.

SPECIAL SUPPORT FOR PIPES

Pipes must pass between walls both horizontally and vertically; the most important consideration is maintaining the integrity of the structure so that it will be as strong after it has been modified for passage of the pipes as it was before.

If the wall is load-bearing, provide additional strength by spiking a stud at right angles to the notched one. This is important for load-bearing walls to which you have made cuts.

When notching joists for pipes, the joists must be reinforced more strongly than vertical studs. Notches should be no more than one-fourth the depth of the joist, and near a joist end.

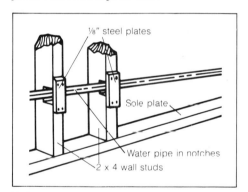

If pipes run through stud wall, notch up to 2½ inches square, but no larger. Or, bore round holes to within 1½ inches of stud edge. Pipe must "thread" through round holes, requiring access to an exposed end stud. Once studs are notched, reinforce openings with ⅛x1½ inch steel flats fastened across the notches.

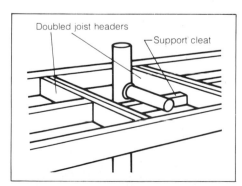

Where a soil pipe passes through the floor framing, add extra support to the opening with doubled headers and a support cleat underneath any horizontal pipe runs.

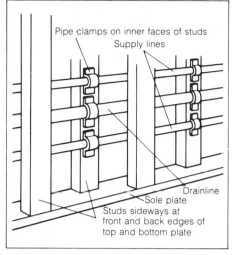

A bathroom wall has enough space for supply and drain lines when the studs are turned edgewise and spiked to the edges of the sole and top plates. The studs are staggered as shown, and pipes are fastened with clamps to the inside faces of the studs.

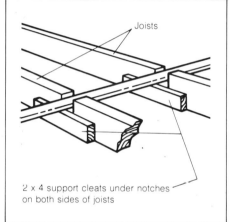

Where it is necessary to notch floor joists to permit running a pipe through them, reinforce them with 2x4 cleats spiked to both sides of the joists, under the notches.

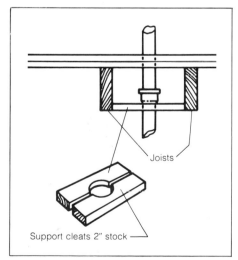

One way to support vertical cast iron soil pipe is use of a "split collar" of 2-inch lumber, which is fitted around the pipe against the pipe hub and then spiked to the floor joists.

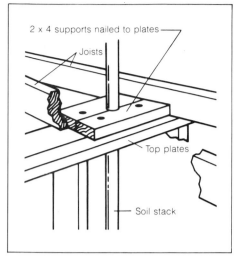

If pipe runs vertically through top stud wall plates, reinforce plates with 2x4s notched to fit around pipe. Nail 2x4s to plates on their inner edges, projecting beyond plate edges. Bore top plates a little larger than the pipes. Cut half-rounds in reinforcing.

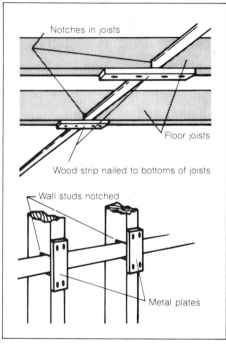

Whether running pipes through joists or wall studs, notch and cover with metal plates. In either situation, and particularly if the pipe is loose, tap wedges or wood strips behind the plates so that pipe does not move under water hammer pressure.

10 Lighting, Wiring, Ventilation

LIGHTING

Two of the most important visual tasks are shaving and putting on makeup. Yet lighting for grooming rarely gets included in bathroom planning, primarily because most people seem unaware of lighting needs. Style need not be sacrificed for function, since a variety of types and styles of good lighting can be used to update or correct light deficiencies in the bathroom. General guidelines about recommended spacing will help you place fixtures where they will do the most good. For shaving and making-up, there should be no shadows under eyes, nose, cheeks, or chin. Lighting for grooming should fall on both sides of the face, top of the head and under the chin.

Placement

Ideally, fixtures capable of a spread of light should extend across the top of the grooming mirror, and down both sides of it to well below chin level. If you cannot have a fixture on both sides of the mirror, stretch out the light by installing a fixture (over the mirror) that is as long as possible, but not less than 24 inches.

Side fixtures should be placed: 28 inches to 36 inches apart and centered, for the majority of people; 60 inches above the floor for those who stand; 45 inches above the floor for those who sit at a dressing table.

Two views are shown for a wrap-around technique. Separate bulbs set in a lighting strip surround three edges of the grooming mirror. Low-wattage opaque bulbs cut down on heat and glare. Covered strip-fixtures for mounting horizontally or vertically come in a wide variety of styles for contemporary or traditional bathrooms. Fixtures can contain as few as three bulbs or as many as seven.

Over-mirror lighting stretches and improves the lighting field when side fixtures cannot be used for some reason. For best results, the ends of the fixture should align with the vertical sides of the mirror (or its frame if it has one). The strip should be 78 inches (on center) above floor level.

Side lighting can be just as effective as wrap-around lighting if the field of illumination extends high enough to include top of the head, and low enough to cludetop of the head, and low enough to

fall shadow-free under the chin. Swaglights arranged to hang along both sides of the mirror can be effective and may be easier to install than wall-mounted fixtures. Free-hanging lamps look especially attractive in large bathrooms. When space is restricted, use wall-mounted side lighting, either long shallow strips or single globes of generous diameter.

Light Diffusion Is Important. Diffusion means spreading light waves over a range of angles so the light produced is softer and does not fall in a single beam. Lighting equipment at the mirror should direct light toward the person and not into the mirror. However, the directed light should not contain pinpoints or spots of glare which can cause eyestrain and discomfort. Grooming lights must have diffuser shields, either built-in or attachable.

Incandescent vs. Fluorescent

Fluorescent lamps are often recommended to those concerned with energy saving because they produce about twice the light that incandescent lamps do — but keep the energy saving in perspective. Most fluorescent lamps can make you

Wrap-around lighting attached to three edges of the grooming mirror (top not shown) furnishes shadow-free illumination.

Bright mirror lighting is given by small bulbs down the sides of the mirror. A fluorescent light is recessed at the top.

If single-bulb fixtures are used beside the mirror, the wattage and diffuser globes should be generous enough to cast even light.

look pretty awful. Incandescent lamps are much kinder, and thus usually are preferred.

For bare-bulb lighting strips, which have no shades or covering, choose bulbs labeled "soft white". These have a translucent inside coating that reduces harsh shadows and glare. Ordinary household light bulbs, with "inside frost," need covers of opaque glass to give soft shadow-free illumination to grooming lights. Moreover, since such bulbs are incandescent, they give off heat. Glass is the only safe cover to use.

Besides creating a more concentrated light, incandescent lamps convert about 80% of the electric energy into heat, while fluorescent lamps change only about 70% of the electricity into heat. In the summer this lowered conversion may be all right, but in the winter the furnace will have to make up that 10% difference, so you really do not save much on energy overall.

There are two types of fluorescent lamps: one is the starter type, now nearly obsolete, that requires a twist in starter. This looks like a small metal can with two pins projecting from one end. The other type of fluorescent is the rapid-start, which uses no starter but does require a special ballast. Both are easy to hook up, since only two wires, a black and a white, extend from the light. For a three-wire circuit, the third wire — which is the ground — connects to the light shell.

Ballasts, which basically are transformers, occasionally go bad and must be replaced. You should have no trouble doing this job if you carefully note which wire goes to which connection, replacing only one wire at a time. Look for the wiring diagram printed on the ballast and follow it carefully.

One other fact about fluorescents should be kept in mind: their life is rated by how many times they are turned off and on. A 40-watt fluorescent lamp (usually 48 inches long) will have a lifespan of about 12,000 hours if burned for at least three hours every time it is turned on. There may be members of the family who do spend three hours at a time in the bathroom, but during the morning "rush hour" when people are getting ready for work or school, this simply is not possible. We feel that incandescent lamps make more sense for bathroom lighting, unless a special effect (such as a light box or lowered ceiling) is desired.

The shapes of fluorescent lighting tubes are suitable for wrap-around combinations, single overhead strips, or vertical-mount side strip lighting. Being cool, their covers or diffuser shades can be made of milky translucent plastics which are lightweight, easy to handle, less apt to break than glass.

When you use fluorescent lighting for grooming use Deluxe colors. Warm White Deluxe is close to incandescent in color, and will not significantly distort skin tones or colors.

Recessed Soffit and Canopy Lighting

When your bath design calls for big expanses of mirror over long vanities and countertops, switch to wide-field over-head illumination for grooming lighting. Recessed incandescent or fluorescent light sources inside a soffit or canopy can provide a wide spread of light over the grooming area and also act as general room lighting if desired.

Dimensions recommended for both soffit and canopy are: the illuminated field should be 16 inches front to back, 8 inches deep (inside the recess), and extend the full length of the mirrored expanse. The translucent shield, or bottom diffuser can be sheets of frosted glass, acrylic panels, "eggcrate" baffles of metal or plastic. The bottom edge of the soffit or canopy should be within ½ inch of the top of the mirror. The top of the mirror should be 78 inches above floor level.

Illumination radiating downward will be augmented by reflection, from the mirror and from the countertop. White and light shades of color are good reflectors. Dark countertops will absorb a good deal of the light. Bulbs or fluorescent tubes may have to be a step or two higher in output to assure full illumination of chin and neck.

Canopy and Soffit Projects. A soffit or canopy is basically a box on the ceiling with an open bottom in which sheets of translucent plastic are fitted. The arbitrary difference between a canopy and a soffit is that a canopy does not necessarily go clear to the ceiling, while a soffit always does. When you build either one, however, keep in mind that at some future time it will be necessary to replace the bulbs. Which means either the plastic panels should be removable, or you should be able to reach over the top of the canopy to remove and replace the lamps. The simplest way to build either lighting enclosure is to have a means of lifting the plastic panels up, turning them and pulling them down out of the way. An alternative is to make a narrow wooden frame that is hinged on one side and held on the other with magnetic latches. The frame is rabbeted around the inside edges to hold the plastic panels. A third method, as with a soffit with a deep frame, is to have enough room so you can lift up one panel and slide it over on top of the other. This will permit reaching one or more lights; following the same steps with the other panel or panels will allow reaching the remaining lights.

Both canopies and soffits are built as

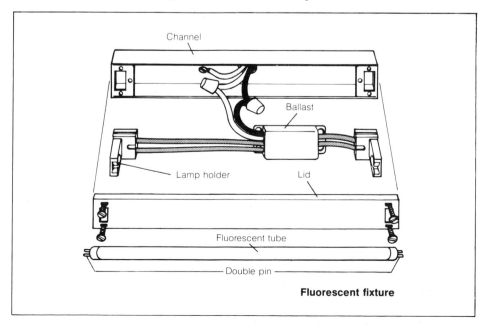

Fluorescent fixture

Channel

Ballast

Lamp holder

Lid

Fluorescent tube

Double pin

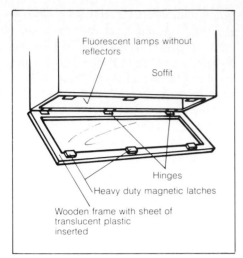

Rabbet narrow wooden frame to hold sheet of translucent plastic. Hinges at back of frame are held in front by magnetic latches. Frame can be narrow, but must be deep for strength.

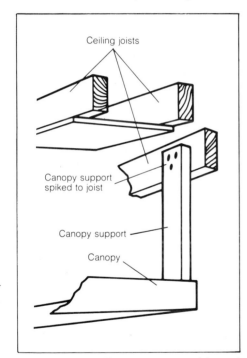

If a canopy or soffit is not supported by end walls, connection attachment to ceiling is necessary. Cut hole in the ceiling; fasten supports to joists and canopy corners. Cover supports with paneling or other material used on canopy framing. Soffit extends to ceiling, to hide ceiling attachment.

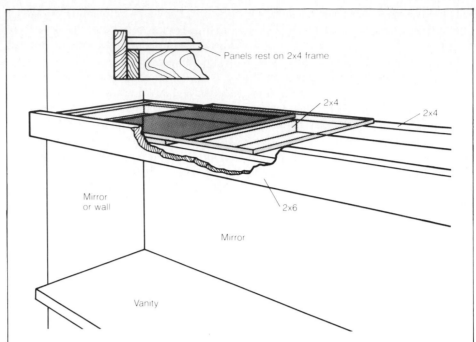

For short spans (under 4 feet) 1x4 and 1x6 stock can be used. Longer spans call for 2x4 and 2x6 stock, with a wider piece at the front of the soffit or canopy. In this assembly, plastic panels lift and slide over each other to permit access to lights. Fluorescent fixtures without reflectors attach to ceiling; paint area above plastic sheets white to reflect light.

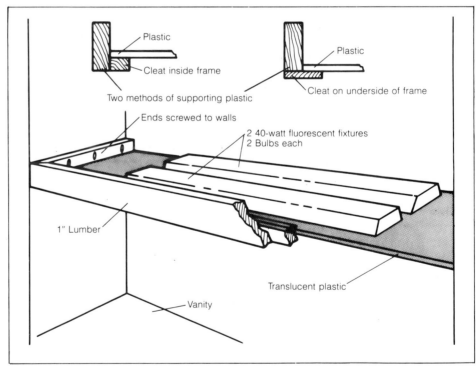

Soffit or canopy of 1x4s or 1x6s between walls attaches to end walls with nails or screws into studs. Cleats, underneath or inside frame member, support plastic sheet. Fluorescent lamps without reflectors attach to ceiling.

boxes; the frameworks are covered with paneling, plasterboard or other material to match the walls and ceiling of the bathroom. If the enclosure is fitted between two walls, then the walls can provide support for the ends of the framework. If the enclosure will be free-hanging, then you will need to attach the framework to the ceiling. With a closed-in soffit, this presents no problems since the necessary cleats on the ceiling will be hidden inside. A canopy open at the top does present

some problems because any cleats will be exposed and visible. One method is to recess the necessary wooden cleats into the ceiling, so they are flush with the plasterboard. For example, you can use ½ inch lumber to be flush with ½ inch plaster. If the ceiling joists are spaced properly, cut holes in the ceiling and at-

tach the supports for the canopy directly on the joists. This will require some taping and plastering on the ceiling around the supports.

For a decorative and strong support, use fancy metal chains, such as those used for swag lamps. The fancy hooks can be fastened to the ceiling with Molly plasterboard or hollow wall anchors, or driven directly into the ceiling joists through the plasterboard or ceiling material.

Finally, for a quick and simple installation, buy one of the framed fluorescent fixtures with a wooden box fitted with a panel of translucent plastic. This fixture can be suspended by chains from the ceiling, or attached directly to the ceiling or to the underside of a soffit.

Ready-made canopies with wood or plastic frames come fitted with plastic diffuser panels and 2 or more fluorescent lamps. The lamp plugs into nearest outlet.

Plant Lighting

Almost all kinds of flowering and foliage plants thrive in the warm humid atmosphere of the bath. If there is no window, or a small frosted one with poor exposure to sunlight, consider artificial light. Special incandescent lights are available for lighting plants as well as stimulating growth, such as Plant-lite by Duro-Test, Grow and Show by G.E., Spot-Gro by Sylvania. Fluorescent lights have been developed that have characteristics most resembling sunlight. Wide spectrum fluorescents come close to having the beneficial rays and plant-stimulating colors of sunlight; full-spectrum fluorescents come closest.

Among the several producers of quality lighting for plants is Duro-Lite Lamps, Inc., which has these notes on lighting plants correctly.

Under full-spectrum lighting, plants appear as they do outdoors; leaf and blossom colors are true. The plants will not look garishly purple or red.

Based on energy costs (the electrical power you pay for), fluorescents are about three times more efficient than incandescent in converting electrical energy into visible light energy. Full-

Set a 2-lamp wide-spectrum fluorescent unit 4 to 9 inches away from plants to illuminate a growing area of 16x21 inches at maximum height.

spectrum fluorescents, unlike common fluorescents, emit a high degree of light energy used by plants.

To determine how much light a plant should have, consider how it grows in its natural state. Ferns, for instance, grow close to the ground under trees and on wet slopes in partial shade. Philodendron grows in full shade. Exotic plants, depending on species, grow in deep jungle shade or bright sunlight. Ask your florist or nurseryman about the plants you buy, then apply these principles to lighting your bath garden plants.

High-intensity Light. Necessary for plants needing lots of light, it can be provided by a four-lamp 40-watt fixture located 8 to 12 inches above the plant. This illuminates a plant area that is 2 by 5 feet.

Medium-intensity Light. This level is provided by a four-lamp 40-watt fixture that is 16 to 30 inches above the plants; or use a two-lamp 40-watt fixture located 8 to 12 inches above the plants. This effectively illuminates an area of 1¼ by 5 feet.

For a plant to maintain its natural shape, it should be lighted from above its middle or central part. If all its nourishing light comes from below, it will tend to become heavier at the bottom and change its natural shape. If light comes from one side, the same growth and shape changes will occur unless you faithfully rotate the plant or plants weekly.

Plants grown under full-spectrum light usually need to be watered more frequently than those receiving ordinary windowsill illumination. Full-spectrum lighting causes added growth.

WIRING

The two major concerns when planning wiring additions or extensions for your

bathroom are: (1) wattage requirements, in order to avoid overloads; (2) safety, to prevent shocks or fires. Most local building codes require that a bathroom electrical service be brought up to code during remodeling in order to lessen the chances of these hazards. Large wiring tasks, such as replacing a service box or installing additional circuits, should be handled by a licensed electrician. However, homeowners often can undertake smaller basic wiring jobs, saving themselves a considerable amount of money. In many areas, the work carried out by a homeowner must be inspected by a licensed electrician, and certain types of wire, electrical outlets, or fixtures, may be specified by code.

Terminology and Materials

Wattage. There are two basic ways to consider wattage. It is a measurement of the amount of power used in a given circuit. By multiplying volts times amps for a given circuit, you will find out how many watts are used ($V x A = W$). Thus, a 15-amp circuit of 115 volts can supply 1725 watts of power. Wattage also is discussed in terms of the rated watts of a given appliance. A 75-watt light bulb will consume 75 watts of energy, converting it to heat and light. A freezer consumes between 300 and 588 watts of energy.

Volts. If you turn on a switch, voltage causes electric current to flow through a wire. The main electric service entering most homes consists of three wires: two live, or "hot," wires and a neutral wire. There are 220-240 volts between the two

The "knob and tube" wiring in older homes is not adequate and is dangerous. Tear it all out, or leave it in place but disconnect it from the service box and from any devices that it powers. You probably should call an electrician.

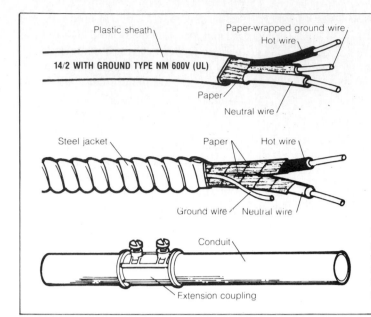

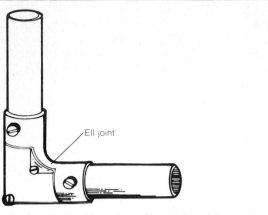

Markings on plastic-sheathed cable indicate (from left to right) cable size and number of conductors, whether or not the cable has a ground wire, the type of cable, and the voltage level. Steel-encased cable is recommended for areas in which wires need more protection, such as within a wall where nails may penetrate. The conduit in a home is usually thin-walled; lengths are joined with connectors.

live wires, and 110 to 120 volts between each of the live wires and the neutral wire. The voltage in most of the outlets in your home is maintained at between 110 and 120 volts, with the exception of special outlets which only accept special plugs and are wired to deliver 220 to 240 volts. Whichever size outlet is involved, the voltage there will be maintained at a reasonably constant level. When your lights dim or brighten because of an unusual circumstance, such as a storm, has suddenly decreased or increased the voltage.

Although the main service to most homes can deliver 220-240 volts, not all service boxes are hooked up to the 220/240 line. If you are uncertain about your service, call your electric company. The larger service is highly recommended, given the electrical demands of most households.

Amps. Amperage measures the number of electrons — the amount of current — that passes through a point in a circuit. Circuits themselves are described in terms of the number of amps — 15, 20, 30, or more — that they can safely handle. Some appliances, although not all, are described in terms of the number of amps of current they consume. Homes with 220-240 service have 100 amps of power available to them.

Circuits. If you work on the wiring in your kitchen, you will be dealing in most cases with 115-volt circuits. These are designed to meet the needs of light fixtures and most appliances, such as hair dryers, fans, or shavers. Because the demands upon a given 115-volt circuit are

not high, it serves several fixtures, which often are located in several rooms. The area a circuit can serve is governed by the size of the wire, fuse or circuit breaker and potential connected load. Typically, it ranges between 375 and 500 square feet per circuit.

Cable Types. There are three basic types of cable for circuits. Inside the cable are three wires that are color-coded. Black (or sometimes red) stands for live wires, white for neutral, and green (or sometimes bare) for ground. The kind of cable in your home may be determined by local code. For any of the projects included in this chapter, find out the code requirements for your particular area.

BX. This cable is enclosed in a flexible metal casing. The black hot and white neutral wires are paper-wrapped; there will also be a green ground wire or a bare ground wire. BX flexes to turn easily around corners. It is good for use in dry indoor locations, especially in areas where wires need protection from nails for later carpentry or decorating projects.

Plastic-coated Cable. This cable is enclosed in a plastic sheath and is sometimes referred to as Romex. All three wires inside are paper-wrapped. It is very flexible. The size of the wire is stamped along the outside of the cable, as are designations for use areas. "T" cable adapts well to a variety of temperatures. "TW" is used in damp settings. "NM" cable is for use indoors in dry settings.

Conduit. In homes with very thin walls, cable is usually enclosed in galvanized steel pipe called thin-walled con-

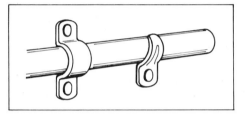

Although conduit is not unusually heavy, long runs should be supported with clamps. Either type will support conduit along wall.

duit or E.M.T. In some areas, conduit is required when more than 3 feet of BX cable is exposed in a basement. When using conduit, run insulated single-conductor wires — black, white and green — through the pipes. Do not try to run plastic or BX cable through a conduit. A conduit can hold a number of cables. It comes in a variety of diameters and in 10-foot lengths. Couplings and joint pieces make it adaptable to most settings.

Wire Types: Solid or Stranded. The wire in the cables of circuits is solid. However, wire in light fixtures is made up of several strands twisted about each other. The distinction is important when splicing two wires together.

Safety System
Before starting any project, turn off the circuit with which you will be working. Go to the service box, where the main service lines of the household divide into circuits, and locate the fuses or circuit breakers. Remove the fuse or switch off the circuit breaker. Never change any switch, fixture or outlet without first breaking the circuit.

Although fuses and circuit breakers

function differently, both serve the same purpose — to limit current flowing through a given circuit. A fuse is a screw-in device constructed with a ribbon of metal that has a low melting point. If the current exceeds the ampere rating of the fuse, the metal ribbon melts and opens the circuit. A circuit breaker performs the same function when its amp rating is exceeded, but it doesn't have to be replaced because its element functions to trip a switch. When the element cools off, the switch can be turned on again.

The amp rating of a fuse or circuit breaker depends upon the size of the wire in the circuit cable. The circuits for living and sleeping areas typically are wired with No. 14 copper wire to provide a maximum for 15 amperes. Some areas of the home are wired with a slightly larger copper wire (No. 12) to provide a maximum of 20 amperes for each circuit. The smallest wire — for the doorbell or the thermostat — is No. 18 copper, which can carry about 6 amperes.

Larger Wire Amperage Ratings * (75°C)

Size (Copper)	Rating
No. 10 wire	30 amp max
No. 8 wire	45 amp max
No. 6 wire	65 amp max
No. 4 wire	85 amp max

*This is based on the 1978 National Electric Code for insulated copper wire.

If a circuit blows its fuse or circuit breaker trips, the device is responding to a current load that the wire cannot safely tolerate. Although the break can be caused by something on the outside of your home, such as an electrical storm, more often the cause for the break is inside.

Aluminum Wiring. In some homes the wires in the circuit cable are aluminum rather than copper. If that is true in your case, you should not attempt to do wiring projects yourself. Aluminum wire is difficult to work with. It presents special problems that should be dealt with by a licensed electrician.

Overloads. Appliances pull the power they need to function correctly. If the black and white wires carry more than the safe amount of current for which they are rated, they are overloaded.

Warning: Use the Correct Fuse Size. If your system has been plagued by burned fuses because of overloaded circuits, do not try to solve the problem by substituting a larger fuse for a smaller one. This can jeopardize the safety of your home. A wire with a high number (such as No. 14) has a lower amperage rating than a wire with a lower number (such as No. 10). If you replace a 15-amp fuse with a 20-amp fuse, when the current goes over 15 amps, the No. 14 wire begins to heat. The 20-amp fuse will not blow until the overload exceeds 20 amps, since it responds only to that level of am-

perage. However, you have created the potential for an electrical fire by allowing too much current in the No. 14 wire, which causes heat generation. The result could be a fire.

Short Circuits and Ground Systems. Current cannot flow in any circuit until there is a continuous conducting path. Normally that path runs from the black wire through a connected device such as a light bulb, and out of the device to the white neutral wire. However, sometimes that normal path is interrupted. If the black wire should come loose from its connection, and come into contact with the metal junction box that houses an outlet or switch, the exposed metal would have the hot side of the 115 volts present on the exposed metal surface. Those volts would take the path of least resistance to ground. If no path existed and you then touched this exposed metal while simultaneously touching a faucet or standing on a carpet fastened with metal staples, you would provide a conducting path for the current to flow and would receive a shock. This can be a fatal situation — especially if you are standing on a damp floor or working with a sink of water. Remember that water (even a damp surface) is a very good electrical conductor.

The above situation, and others like it, are called short circuits. In order to protect your home and its occupants from the dangers of short circuits, the three-

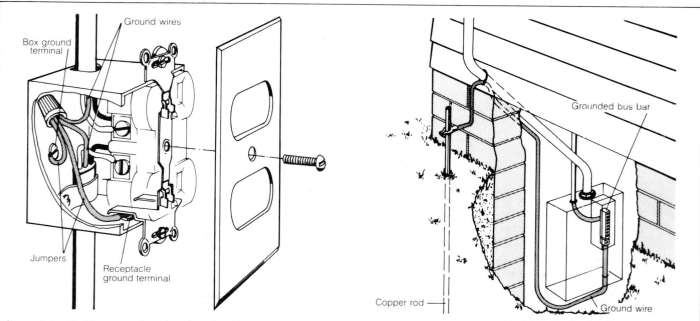

Any metal part of a receptacle or box that should not carry current, but might do so during a malfunction, is given an emergency route to a ground through the cable's ground wire.

If you do not have access to a buried water pipe 10 feet or longer, connect ground system to earth by a steel or copper rod driven a minimum of eight feet into earth.

wire system of your home's circuits — in combination with the supply wires of the electric company — is designed with a ground system with multiple ground connections.

Neutral Wire. Both inside and outside your home the neutral wire carries current. This current, however, is "dead"; it carries no voltage. Outside the home the neutral wire is grounded. It attaches to ground rods driven into the earth at the electric company poles and to one that is right outside your home near the spot where the service wires enter the home. Eight feet long and ½ to ⅝ inches in diameter, these solid rods are usually made of copper-clad, rigid steel. In the service box the neutral wire and the green ground wires of the home's grounding system are connected in what is called a bus bar. Then one branch of the neutral wire leads from the bus bar to the grounded metal water supply pipe. Other branches form an essential part of the house circuits. These branches carry the "dead," or return current.

Green Ground Wire. The green wire in circuit cable is not intended to carry current. Instead it is a built-in safety feature, forming a connection between the grounded bus bar in the service box and the exposed metal parts of all fixtures and appliances, including the plumbing and any other exposed metal.

In a junction box, black and neutral wires are fastened to the outlet or switch. Green wires are fastened to the box itself. In case of a short circuit, the green wire offers a path of least resistance. It carries the excess current to the grounded bus bar (where the fuse or circuit breaker will blow) and then safely into the earth through the grounded neutral wire.

The green circuit wire also connects to all appliances that have special 3-pronged plugs. Any such appliance has a built-in ground wire which leads to the extra prong. That prong in turn fits into a special outlet opening that is wired to connect the prong and the circuit's ground wire. In the event of a short circuit in the appliance, its ground wire sends the excess voltage out through the ground prong to the circuit ground wire, which in turn passes the voltage to ground, blowing a fuse or circuit breaker in the process. (This is why you should not defeat the purpose of the three-pronged plug by using a two-pronged adapter.)

Although the grounding function is primarily the responsibility of the green wire, under certain circumstances the neutral wire attached to the outlet or switch will share or even assume the job. Sometimes the insulation separating the wires in a circuit (which may include an extension cord) wears away or becomes frayed, allowing the black and white wires to touch each other. The hot current is sent directly into the neutral wire, which takes the excess voltage out of the house through the grounded bus bar.

When this or any other short circuit occurs, the resistance offered the current by the wire and the outlets and switches on the circuit is no longer present. Therefore, the current flows to ground very quickly, whether through the green or neutral wires or through a path completely outside the circuit. That surge of current causes the fuse to burn out or the circuit breaker to open.

In addition to the three-wire system, the N.E.C. (National Electric Code) also requires that any room where there is high humidity and water, such as a bathroom, also be protected by a "ground fault circuit interrupter." This device usually is abbreviated GFCI, or GFI for ground fault interrupter.

This device will shut off the current in

A Ground Fault Interrupter is required by National Electric Code for wiring in the bathroom or in any area with high humidity. A GFI can be incorporated with a circuit breaker, or as a separate unit, or it can combine with receptacle. Look for units with a "test" button.

25/1000 of a second if a short circuit occurs and exceeds one-fourth of an ampere. If the current in the short circuit is as little as 5/1000th of an ampere, the GFI reacts more slowly, possibly taking several seconds.

GFI's are not cheap, with simple units such as those that combine a receptacle with a GFI running $80 and up. For a unit to protect all the wiring in a bathroom the cost could be several times that figure. Better-quality units also have a test button built in so you can occasionally check to make sure the device still is protecting the circuit. Any mechanical or electronic device can malfunction and you want to know when it does.

Two-Wire Systems. In older and smaller homes only two wires are in the circuits. There is no green ground wire; grounding is handled by neutral wires and the metal wrapping of the circuit cables. A two-wire system compares poorly to a three-wire one, which provides a separate ground path for faults. In fact, the National Electric Code requires three-wire circuits in all new housing. A two-wire service is usually rated at a maximum of 60 amperes. If your home does not have three-wire service, seriously consider updating your system.

System Updates

If you are remodeling we strongly recommend a larger service box, and one with circuit breakers, to replace a fuse type service box. It is a lot easier to push in a tripped circuit breaker than to replace a fuse.

For maximum protection, run the circuit for the new or remodeled bathroom directly from the service box. Use a combination circuit breaker/GFI. Install a GFI that is rated in volts and amperes to handle the full load of all circuits in the bathroom. It is safest to hire a licensed electrician to install this circuit and its GFI. If you have an older service box with fuses, the GFI will have to be installed in a separate box from the service box, and powered through one of the fuses.

When it comes to the actual location of the switches, receptacles and lights, you need metal or plastic boxes. There is a wide variety of these boxes, and a trip to a well-stocked hardware store would be in order. Before you buy anything, however, draw a sketch showing the locations of the various devices you will need; a rough sketch will do. There will be a light switch just inside the door, turning on a light in the ceiling, or possibly one over the vanity if the bathroom is small. This light may instead be in addition to that on the ceiling, taking a separate switch. There should be a duplex receptacle near the vanity to power electric shavers, hair dryers and so on. There should be *no* receptacles near the bathtub or shower. A ceiling light can be combined with an electric resistance heater or an infrared quartz heater, which is more efficient and requires less electricity. A fan also can be combined with a resistance heater to circulate the warmed air. A combination unit will take heavier wiring, at least 12 gauge, where as lights and light duty receptacles need only 14 gauge wire.

If a bathroom has no windows, as might be the case for one in the basement or attic, building codes generally require an exhaust fan. This fan is quite small, since it does not have to move the volume of air that a kitchen exhaust fan does.

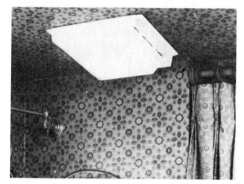

Bathroom exhaust fans help remove moisture and odors, and can reduce heating needs.

Running New Wire

If the bathroom wiring is old, replace it with new wire while remodeling, before adding new surfacing. First shut off the power to the circuit by removing the fuse or pulling the circuit breaker. Start the wire at a connection box near the bathroom and run the new wire by tying it to the old wire. Pull it through the wall. If the old wire is stiff or difficult to pull through, you may be able to cut off the existing wire outside the bathroom and run new wire into it.

If the wall covering has been removed and the studs are exposed, the wiring is run through the studs by boring oversize holes for the wire. This is possible when plastic-sheathed cable (often called Romex) is used, but not when the local building code requires E.M.T. (electrical

metallic tubing). When E.M.T. is used in a wall the tubing is fitted into notches in the studs. Because this weakens the studs, a better method is to run the tubing above the ceiling and route the tubing down between the studs to the location of the switch, receptacle or light fixture. In a two-story house, with the bathroom on the first floor, the tubing can be run up through the wall from the basement.

If the local electrical code requires tubing, stay away from it unless you have had prior experience working with it. It is hard to bend tubing, even with the aid of a tubing bender (usually called a "hickey"). The work can be done, how-

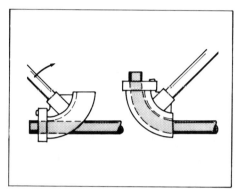

A tubing bender, commonly called a "hickey," shapes and bends thinwall tubing. The hickey comes as curved portion and you provide a length of pipe for a handle. If nonmetallic sheathed cable can be used, don't use thinwall tubing (electrical metallic tubing-EMT).

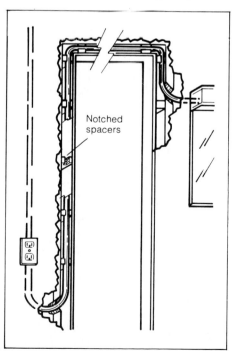

For path around door frame headers, cut 2 notches in upright. Or cut wall access hole; notch header; pass cable through. Slip cable into header notch; repair wall surface. Drill uprights and headers with 18-inch bit.

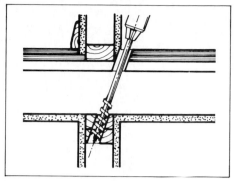

To fish cable, create access from attic or room above. Gently pry off baseboard. Using 18-inch bit and a brace, drill through beams on a diagonal to reach the wall cavity.

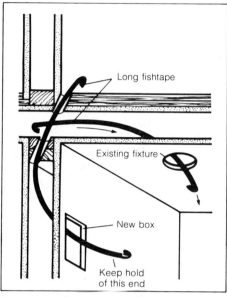

Insert long fishtape into access hole. Push down to box hole in wall. Insert second fishtape into ceiling hole. Hook tapes. Pull both tape hook ends out through ceiling hole.

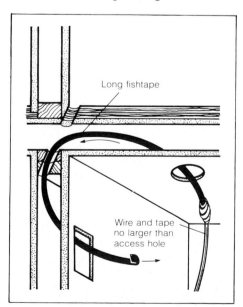

Disconnect tape hooks. Remove 3 inches sheathing from cable. Strip off insulation. Loop wires through hook of long fishtape; tape firmly. Draw fishtape back to box hole in wall.

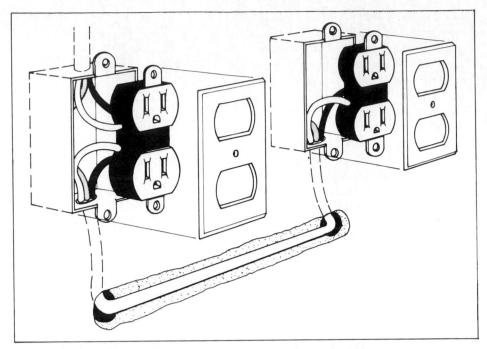

To extend cable from old outlet in a plaster wall to a new one, first cut a channel to hold the cable inside the wall. Punch holes for box connections. Hook up the wires; repair plaster.

ever, if you take your time to practice and allow for some waste. Connections between lengths of tubing are made with compression fittings. Each fitting has a nut that clamps down on a metal ring which, in turn, clamps on to the tubing. Metallic tubing does make a safe and neat job. When all connections are made tightly, the tubing itself becomes a "third wire" that creates a ground.

If you are doing a remodeling job in an older home, rather than a complete remodeling job where wall coverings are removed or the room is a completely new structure, you will be working through enclosed walls. In such cases, try to route all wires through basement joists on the first floor, or through the attic if it is accessible.

Making Wiring Connections. Wire should never be spliced between junction boxes. You can splice wire inside a junction box, but the splice must be made with wire nuts and electrician's tape. The old way of splicing wire — wrapping one wire around another wire and covering the splice with just electrician's tape — is no longer permitted by many codes, because this type of splice is very dangerous. It can cause an electrical fire.

Here are the steps.

Cut the wire to length with wire cutters. Strip away the insulation with a wire stripping tool. Do not use a knife, except to split cable sheathing.

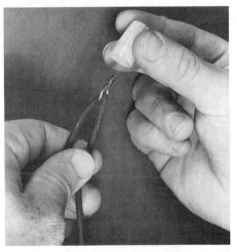

Wire nut connectors are plastic caps lined with threaded metal. Twist the splice tightly together, install the wire nut over the wires and twist the nut.

If the wires are solid, remove 1 inch of insulation from the wires. Hold the stripped ends together, side-by-side. With pliers, twist the ends tightly together.

Screw a wire nut onto the bare joined ends of the wire. Wrap the wire nut and the insulation below the nut with electrician's tape. Give the splice several wraps, so the splice won't pull apart or bare wire become exposed.

If the wires are stranded (many strands), strip off 1 inch of insulation on both wires. Twist the strands tight with your fingers. Hold the wires together — parallel. Then twist the wires together tightly; fold approximately half the splice

over. Now screw on a wire nut and secure the nut with electrician's tape.

To join a stranded wire to a solid wire, strip off about 1 inch of insulation from the solid wire and about 2 inches of insulation from the stranded wire. Twist the stranded wire with your fingers to make the wire as "solid" or tight as you can. Starting at the base of the solid wire, wrap the stranded wire up the solid wire in a spiral fashion. Then bend over half of the splice with pliers. Screw on a wire nut and wrap the nut and wires with electrician's tape.

BX cable. To cut, use a hacksaw, running the saw blade diagonally across one of the steel "rings" about 6 inches in back of the wires encased inside the cable. Be careful not to cut the wires with the hacksaw; just saw through the top layer of steel. Once the initial cut has been made, take pliers and break up the steel layer, pulling the steel apart. The cut end will be

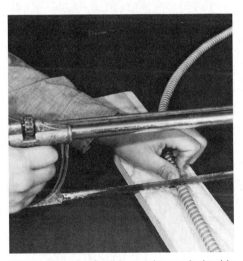

BX, a cable with a flexible metal cover, is durable and can be used for many interior installations. The metal cover must be cut with a hacksaw in order to reach the wires inside.

sharp, so watch your fingers. You can buy a plasticlike insulator sleeve that slides inside the cable to cap the wire. This provides a "finished" end to the cable and also insulates the wires at the cut end.

Plastic-insulated cable. One such cable is Romex. To cut, use wire strippers to make the initial cut, squeezing the handles just hard enough to slice the outer layer of insulation. With a razor knife, split the insulation lengthwise until it meets the cut made by the wire strippers.

Peel off the inner insulation, exposing the wires inside the cable. You can cut the excess inner insulation with a knife.

Conduit. To cut, use a hacksaw. Make

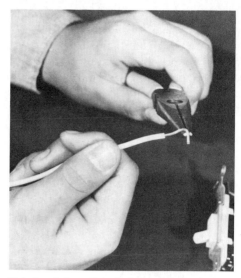

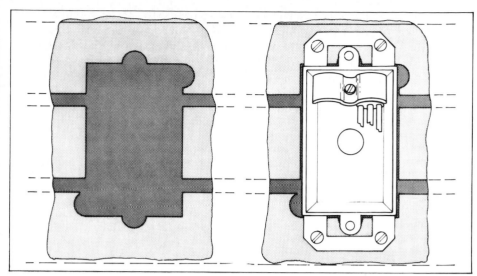

Strip insulation off end of wire at least ½ inch. Bend the wire into an open loop so it fits around screw terminal and stays in place as you tighten.

In an older lath-and-plaster wall, mark around metal box to outline opening for the box. Cut the opening, then determine if the box must be raised or lowered slightly so that center lath is removed completely but the lath above and below is only notched.

Place the wire on the screw terminals in the direction the screw turns. This tightens the wire against the terminal as the screw is turned. Twist stranded wire tight before looping it.

If studs are exposed, it is easy to install a box through which nails can be driven into a stud. Use a deep box with room for wires behind the switch or receptacle.

Always allow at least 6 inches of wire to project from wall opening or box. This permits wiring connections outside of the opening. Attach the box to the wall.

sure the conduit is held tightly while the cut is made. Smooth the cut end of the conduit, if necessary, with a metal file. Conduit may be bent with an electrician's hickey. You can rent a hickey or, if you have a lot of conduit bending to do, consider buying one.

Wire. To cut, use wire strippers which have a built-in wire cutter, or regular wire cutters. No. 9, 10, 12, and 14 wire is solid, single strand wire. No. 0, 1, 2, 4, 6 wire is stranded. Wire above No. 14, also may be stranded. The strands are extremely fine.

Terminal connections. To make them, loop the wire with long nosed pliers to fit around the screw terminal. If the wire is stranded, first twist the strands tightly with your fingers. Wrap the wire (or hook it) around the screw terminal in the direction the screw will be tightened.

Adding a Switch or Outlet

In an older home where the walls are lath and plaster, you can locate a box for a switch or receptacle almost anywhere since the laths are strong enough to support the box solidly. Cut a small opening through the plaster first, then cut completely through the lath at the center of the opening. Notch the laths above and below the center lath. Because of the location of the laths it may be necessary to position the box a little above or below your original location. Once you have opened the wall to find the center lath, use the box as a pattern to mark the opening. Use deeper boxes, rather than shallow ones; it will be easier to work with the wires. Use screw-on connectors to make connection between two wires — these are commonly called "solderless connectors." They provide a secure and insulated con-

nection that can be taken apart if the need ever arises. The connectors have an internal thread that "screws" onto the soft copper wire, and also unscrews. The connectors in various sizes are sold in packages in the electrical department of home centers and hardware stores.

While most light switches are about 40 to 48 inches above the floor, this not necessarily a "standard" height. Originally the switches were located to be above the firestops located halfway up the wall between the studs. Keeping the box above the firestop eliminates the need for notching or boring through the horizontal member. If you have a family of shorter or taller than average people, position the switches accordingly. Do not deviate so much that it becomes obvious, or it could affect the resale value of the house.

If the wall studs are exposed once the

plaster or plasterboard has been removed, you can use one of two kinds of boxes that nail directly to the studs. One type has a projecting flange that is nailed to the face of a stud; for the other type, nails are driven directly through the box itself. In some instances you can install the flange type by knocking a hole through plaster or plasterboard adjacent to a stud and slipping the flange under the plasterboard over the stud. It will be necessary, of course, to patch around the opening after the box has been installed.

When wiring, always allow at least 6 inches of wire to project from a connection, receptacle or switch box. This enables you to strip insulation from the wire ends without interference from the box, and also to connect the wires to a switch or receptacle outside the box. Then push the fixture into the box by bending the

To add a switched light fixture, you must run cable from a power source to new fixture outlet and switch boxes. For a new switch in the middle of the run, the cable begins at the power source and runs to the switch and then to the light. The switch wiring is middle of the run, but the light-fixture wiring is end of the run. Use two-conductor cable with ground wire. The hot black wire of the incoming cable connects at the switch to one terminal and the black outgoing wire connects to the other terminal. Join neutral (white) wires with a cap to give an uninterrupted circuit from the light fixture to the service panel. Join uninterrupted ground wires to the metal box and to each other. The hot wire from the switch connects at the light fixture to the fixture's black wire; the white wire connects to the fixture's neutral wire; the bare ground wire connects to the box.

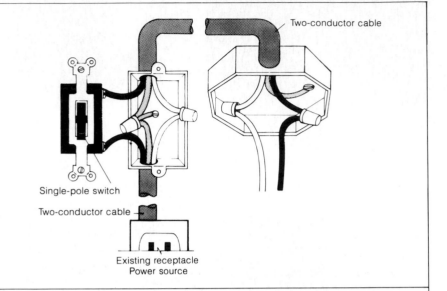

Two-conductor cable

Single-pole switch

Two-conductor cable

Existing receptacle
Power source

When cable runs to the fixture and then to the switch, fixture wiring is middle of the run and switch wiring is a "switch loop." Use 2-conductor cable with ground. For the light, join the neutral wire from the power source to the white fixture wire. Since you need a hot wire to carry power to the switch and back to the fixture, the black wire of the incoming cable joins to the white outgoing wire for power to the switch. Connect black outgoing wire (for power back from switch) to the black fixture wire. For the loop that carries power to the switch and on to the light, fasten the white wire at the switch to one terminal; fasten the black wire to the other.

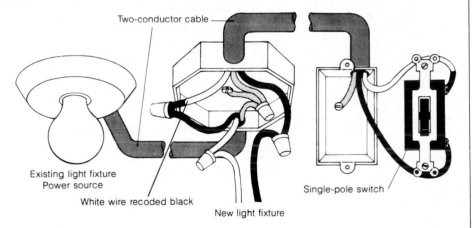

Two-conductor cable

Existing light fixture
Power source

White wire recoded black

New light fixture

Single-pole switch

A circuit from an already installed receptacle, to a switch-controlled light fixture, to an unswitched receptacle, is a combination circuit. Run 3-conductor cable from the switch to the light in order to provide the light's switched hot wire and the receptacle's unswitched hot wire. The neutral (white) and ground wires from the incoming cable connect at the switch as shown for middle of the run (above). The incoming cable's black wire connects with a jumper to the switch and to the black wire of the 3-conductor cable. This black wire will run to the receptacle. The red wire found in the 3-conductor cable will carry power from the switch to the fixture's black wire. Join the white wire in the 3-conductor cable to the white fixture wire and to the white wire that runs to the receptacle. Wire the receptacle as for end of the run.

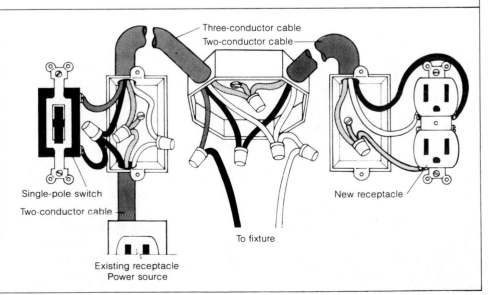

Three-conductor cable
Two-conductor cable

Single-pole switch
Two-conductor cable

New receptacle

To fixture

Existing receptacle
Power source

wires to fit in behind the fixture that screws to the box. Using deep boxes assures there will be plenty of room for the wires, even if more than two wires are required for a particular circuit.

Adding a Ceiling Fixture or Fan

Installation steps for ceiling lights and for recessed fixtures such as fans are the same. First, tap on the ceiling to find the ceiling joists, or drill a few small holes to locate them. When you have found the joists, mark around the junction box for the fixture, making the opening a little larger than the box, since the escutcheon, bezel, or flange will cover a small gap; the extra space will make it easier to work with.

Support the Fixture Box. If you can get above the ceiling, as in an attic, nail two 2x4s between the joists to support the fixture. It is difficult to nail the 2x4s between the joists when working from below — reaching through the opening — although it can be done. Cut two 2x4s for a snug fit between joists. Tap them into place. Mark the inside edges of the joists at the ends of each 2x4. Remove the 2x4s. Cut 2x4 blocks (cleats) about additional 4 inches long, and drive two 8d nails nearly all the way through each one. Put them next to the joists and finish nailing the blocks to the joists. Tap the longer 2x4s into position against the blocks. Toe-nail them to the cleats. Then, after connecting the wires, nail or screw the fixture to the 2x4s.

Fishing the Wire to a Ceiling Fixture. In an older (and some newer) two-story homes you will have to fish wire through a wall and ceiling that are closed in with plaster or plasterboard. For this job you'll need an 18 inch drill bit, usually called an electricians' bit, and 2 fishtapes.

Cut a hole a few inches down from the ceiling into the wall where a switch will be located for a ceiling light or for a fan. Drill diagonally up through the hole through the top plate of the wall into the ceiling cavity.

Cut the opening for the ceiling light. Insert a fishtape up through the hole in the wall, then a second tape through the ceiling opening. It may take some work to have the two tapes interlock so you can pull the wire in the wall up through the ceiling until it shows in the opening in the ceiling. Tape new cable to old; then pull cable across the ceiling to the opening for the switch.

The previous description assumes that the ceiling joists are at right angles to the wall where the switch will be located. If the joists are parallel to the wall, a different technique is required. First, cut the hole for the ceiling fixture or recessed light, heater, combination unit (or whatever). Make the opening for the wall switch, and cut another a few inches down from the ceiling directly above the switch location. Mark a line from the ceiling opening to the wall above the switch.

Now you have to find each of the ceiling joists, usually by tapping or, in an older house you can actually see their locations as dark lines on the ceiling. At each intersection of the joists and your line, chisel out the plaster and notch the joists. Carefully feed the wire above the ceiling and across to each notch. Pull the

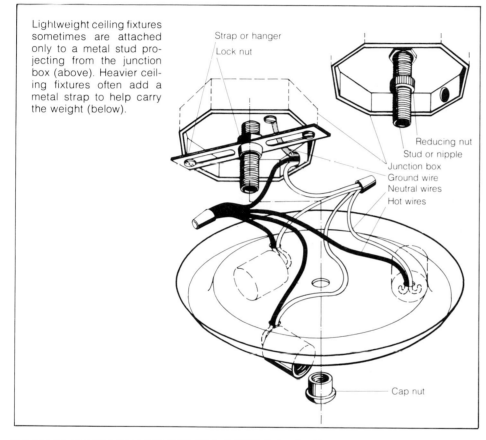

Lightweight ceiling fixtures sometimes are attached only to a metal stud projecting from the junction box (above). Heavier ceiling fixtures often add a metal strap to help carry the weight (below).

Strap or hanger
Lock nut
Reducing nut
Stud or nipple
Junction box
Ground wire
Neutral wires
Hot wires
Cap nut

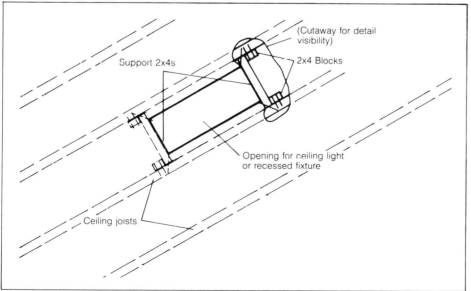

Support 2x4s
(Cutaway for detail visibility)
2x4 Blocks
Opening for ceiling light or recessed fixture
Ceiling joists

Although it is difficult to nail support 2x4s between ceiling joists in a closed ceiling, using blocks enables fairly easy toe-nailing of the support pieces.

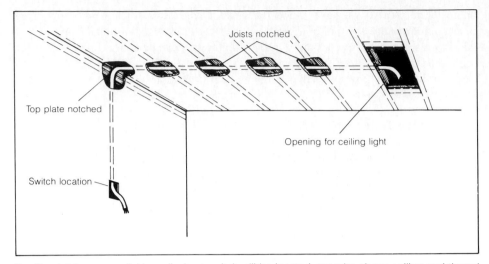

If ceiling joists are parallel to wall where switch will be located, run wire above ceiling and thread under notches in joists. Notch also at joint between ceiling and wall.

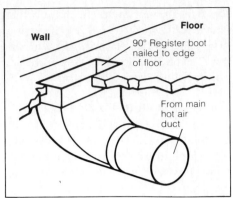

The easiest register installation uses a 90° register boot that comes up through floor near outside wall. A round duct runs to the boot from the main hot air supply duct.

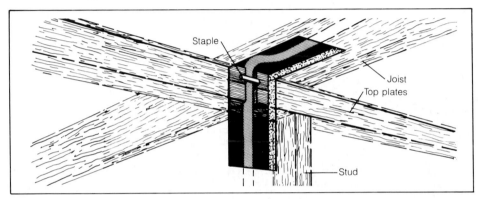

For a wall less than ¼ inch thick, cut a channel in the top plates. Use a keyhole saw for 2 parallel vertical cuts ½ inch deep, ¾ inch apart. Chisel wood out between cuts. Staple cable below top plate edges. For thicker wall, staple cable to top plates, then patch.

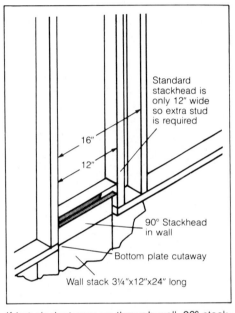

If hot air duct runs up through wall, 90° stackhead directs air into room. Wall stack runs down from the stackhead to duct that runs back horizontally to main hot-air-supply duct.

wire down through the ceiling opening and under each notch. Push the wire back and aim for the next notch and opening. A length of coathanger wire makes the job easier. You'll also need an assistant. When you get to the corner between the ceiling and wall, notch the top plate at an angle and feed the wire down into the wall. The opening near the ceiling will help.

After the wire has been pulled down and out of the opening for the switch, pull the wire taut from the ceiling opening. It also would be a good idea to use a staple, the type made for nonmetallic cable, at each ceiling joist. Use patching plaster at each joist location, and also patch the hole in the wall near the ceiling. The patch may require insertion of a scrap of plasterboard (see Chapter 5).

UL label. When you buy any light, heater or fixture for the bathroom, be sure it is intended for use in the high humidity of a bathroom and that it has an Underwriters Laboratory tag or label. This shows that it has passed all the rigorous tests that this independent testing laboratory employs. Read all instructions and restrictions, and the correct size of wire to be used. It is better to use wire a gauge larger than called for than to use wire that is too small. Undersize wire will overheat in use and can be a potential cause of fires inside a wall or ceiling. All switches and receptacles also must have a UL label. These devices can overheat in use and can then cause fires. A few dollars more for wiring and fixtures will pay off in the long run; appliances will work properly because they receive the full voltage, and risk of fire will be sharply reduced.

HEATING AND VENTILATION
Many bathrooms suffer from lack of heat or inadequate ventilation.

Ventilation
Bathroom ventilation is required in newer homes, and should be included in your remodeling plan. It will help remove moisture and excess heat, as well as odors. Because water either causes or contributes to building material breakdown, a fan prolongs the life of the materials installed in your bathroom. Removal of excess moisture and heat that would otherwise build up in the bathroom using an exhaust fan also lowers energy costs associated with air conditioning. Exhaust fans usually use less energy than dehumidifiers.

Types of Heaters
One practical installation is a baseboard heater. Basically, this is a length of copper pipe with fins attached to it so the heat dissipates rapidly, then the cooled water is returned to the boiler. Baseboard heaters are unobtrusive, take up little space and can be painted to match the walls. If you have any doubts about your plumbing or carpentry skills, have a professional han-

dle this job. Piping should be run from the existing lines, with a valve installed so it can be shut off until needed. Holes should be drilled in the floor to allow the pipes to run up to the location of the radiator or baseboard heater.

A sensible location for a baseboard heater is on the outside wall, under a window if one is located there. This assures that the outside wall is warmed so it does not draw heat from the room.

If you have forced air heat, which is common in houses built in the last few decades, ducts can be run in. "Ducts" — not just one; you must have a hot air supply duct and a cold air return duct to assure complete circulation of the air.

The Hot Air Duct. The hot air duct should run to a register in the outside wall, or in the floor near the outside wall. The duct can be round, but the register in the wall or floor is rectangular, so an adapter called a "register boot" is connected to the round duct where it runs up through the floor or wall. The hot air duct is metal all the way, and one of several kinds of adapters is used to connect to the rectangular main heating duct. Larger mail order houses such as Sears, Roebuck have a complete line of fittings that are shown and described in their catalogs.

The Cold Air Duct. The cold air duct need not be completely metal (depending on local building codes). In some installations the floor joists in the basement or crawl space form the sides of the "duct," while the bottom is a piece of sheet metal. The ends of the cold air duct are made by simply nailing short pieces of 2-inch lumber between the joists, one at each end. An adapter of some type, plus ducting, is used to join the joist section to the main cold air return duct.

In modern installations, the cold air

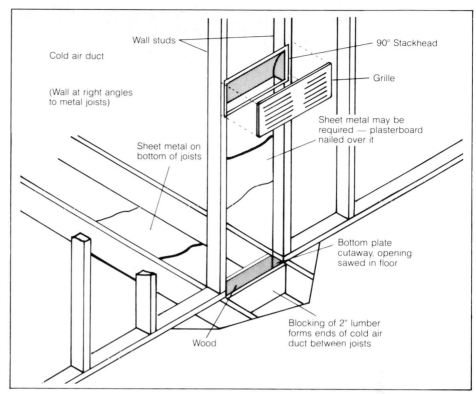

A cold air duct can be run up through wall after covering the bottoms of floor joists with sheet metal to create a duct. Use short lengths of the same stock as the floor joists to block ends of the duct. Depending on local code, you may have to run metal ducts up through wall. If not, use 90° stackhead to direct air into duct from room. The register covers the opening.

register is fairly high on the wall. This is done for two reasons: (1) the warm air rises and is pulled into the return air duct to assure a complete circulation of air; (2) when central air conditioning is installed, the cooled air is discharged into the room through what is normally the hot air register. This cold air tends to stay low in the room, but gradually builds up so that warm air in the upper portion of a room is pushed up and toward the return air ducts. If the cold air register also were low on the wall, or in the floor, the cool air would simply move across the room close to the floor and return to the furnace, without affecting the warm air in the upper part of

the room. The cold air return should be on an inside wall, which means that whenever possible you should arrange the wall studs to meet the floor joists. To do this, the bottom plate must be cut away, and an opening made in the floor.

If the wall you build is at right angles to the floor joists, cutting the opening presents few problems. If the wall is parallel to the floor joists, use round ducts and fittings below the joists. In a basement, where headroom can be a problem, choose shallow rectangular ducting and run it below the joists. In a crawl space that is unheated, insulate both the hot air and cold air ducts.

11 Special Needs: Young Children or the Disabled

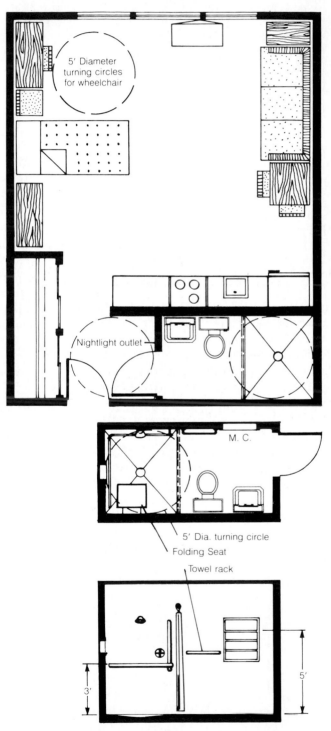

5' Diameter turning circles for wheelchair

Nightlight outlet

M. C.

5' Dia. turning circle

Folding Seat

Towel rack

3'

5'

DISABLED

Whether you remodel or build a new bathroom for the handicapped or disabled, or for a young child, keep in mind in what ways the physical limitations affect the person's mobility and perception. For example, one hand or arm may be weaker than the other, a temporary or permanent tremor in one or several limbs. Shoulder and arm muscles may be strong, but upper torso weakness may restrict the person's ability to sit or stand without something upon which to lean. The person may depend entirely on a wheelchair for mobility, or may be able to stand briefly, to pivot, and to sit on some other chair or stationary support. By understanding what the disabled person can or cannot do for him or herself will give you guidelines for a safe, convenient bathroom.

You must also become familiar with certain measurements and dimensions which are more or less standard guidelines for determining the amount of open floor space, distance between fixtures, height and depth of shelves and countertops, location of storage, placement of safety grab bars and other bathroom features. You will find these dimensions listed at the end of this chapter. Be aware, however, that the measurements are based on guidelines developed for public buildings. These figures represent a composite of all disabilities affecting all types of people. Individual differences will require that you adapt the guidelines to the individual, rather than attempt to force the individual to live with mass standards. That is why it is important to study how the individual moves, using hands, arms, head, legs, or torso.

The person planning the bathroom should have open dialog with the disabled person in order to convey needs to plumbing and electrical contractors, cabinetmakers and carpenters. Some contractors may be reluctant to undertake the project or to give a firm bid. However, if you let them know at the outset that you have worked out a plan with measurements, fixture sources, and accessories, there is a good chance for cooperation.

Always refer to your local codes for barrier-free standards for the disabled so your construction meets all legal requirements.

Supports for Safety

Firm, solid support is more important in bathrooms than elsewhere, so do not scrimp. Institutional-grade grab bars of stainless steel are made for residential use. They are expensive, but will be worth it in the long run.

Towel bars are no substitute for safety bars. They are made of lightweight materials, and the fasteners holding them in place give way if pulled or leaned upon. Also, grab bars should not be used as towel bars. One frantic grasp for a support that is covered with a towel, and both towel and hand may slip off. Pay the price

for well-made bars and place them on doorframes, walls, around toilet, inside tub and shower, wherever the disabled person's experience and your observation reveal they are needed. Almost all shapes, length, and angles of grab bar have been made. A manufacturer's spec sheets will give precise directions for installation, and spell out the kinds of bolts and screws to use for different types of wall material and inner framework. Follow these recommendations because grab bars will be under enormous pull and pressure and so must be securely installed.

All grab bars in bathrooms should be 1¼ inches in diameter because they are easier to grip than thin, slender bars. Also, they should be spaced away from the wall at least 1½ inches to allow for knuckle clearance.

You can save money by making grab bars yourself using 1¼ inch galvanized

plumbing pipe, elbows, and hefty metal flanges for anchoring the pipe to walls. Make sure to bolt the anchor flange to the wall studs or to backing added to the wall. Fastening grab bars to the wall material alone is not good enough. Galvanized pipe is not made to look attractive, so you may want to paint it to match the bathroom colors. Use a rust-inhibiting paint.

A vertical grab bar is recommended for the wall with fittings, close to the front apron, as well as a horizontal bar on the long wall. A grab bar placed near the head end is not desirable.

Installing A Grab Bar

Openings in Existing Tile. There are several ways to install a grab bar on a wall that is covered with ceramic tile. One method requires removal of a tile at each location where a flange will be attached. You then cut the tiles to create an opening through which screws can be driven into the wall. Ideally, you should locate the flanges over wall studs, or backing can be provided for grab bars. Walls may be tiled, but if the tile does not go clear to the ceiling you can find the studs by checking in the area above the tile. You then can use a plumb bob or level to mark down over the tile to locate the flanges for the grab bars. Mark these locations on the tiles before removing them. To remove the tile, scrape out and scratch the grout lines until you reach the wall surface. Then pry gently to lift the tile edges. After the openings have been cut into the tiles, using a tile nipper, reset them into new adhesive.

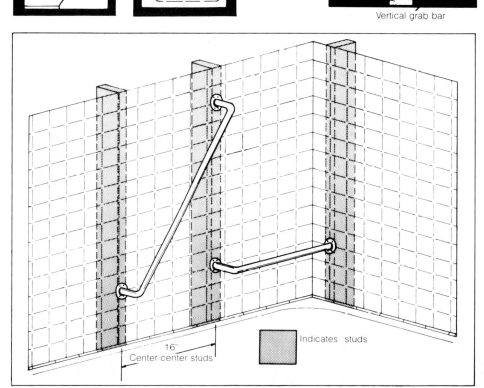

Locate ends of grab bars on wall studs if at all possible. If ends fall between studs, and user is not extremely heavy, Molly bolts can be used. These fasteners allow screws to be removed and replaced; toggle bolts cannot be removed and replaced, and should not be used.

Combinations grab bar/soap dishes and tissue holders are fastened to the wall by inserting them into a mass of mortar.

Using A Masonry Bit. A second method involves use of a carbide-tipped masonry bit to drill through the ceramic tile for the holes through which the screws are driven. The masonry bit is modified as shown, to more closely resemble the shape of a glass drilling bit. If you can find the latter bit, it will serve best, of course; however, it is not always readily available. You can purchase a glass bit by mail order from suppliers of stained glass supplies, and some specialty houses like Brookstone. Glazed tile has a glasslike surface and the glass bits best penetrate the glaze.

Use a variable speed drill motor and start at slow speed until a slight depression is formed. Then increase to a moderate speed. Never use a high speed on glass, ceramic tile or masonry. The bit simply will overheat and become dull. One trick is to use a sharp center punch to lightly tap at the location of the hole you want to drill, just until the glaze cracks, but not the tile. You do run the risk of cracking the tile.

To remove one of the ceramic tiles, first scratch the grout lines around tile until you reach the wall surface, then gently pry around the edges until the tile comes loose. Be sure to mark the desired hole locations onto the tile before you remove it. You then can use a glass bit and a drill press or drill stand to bore the holes. Support the tile on a smooth, flat block of wood while drilling.

If you can transfer the hole locations to the back of the tile, you can use a method employed by some craftsmen to bore the holes. The relatively soft back and inner portion of a ceramic tile are quite easily drilled with a masonry bit. You then have

only the thin shell of glazing to penetrate, which is easier than the front surface approach.

On Walls Without Tile. A third method of attaching a grab bar, useful on a wall without ceramic tile, is that used to install soap dishes, toilet tissue dispensers and other recessed fixtures. In this method an opening is cut in the wall; newspaper is packed around the opening to create a "form." The opening is then packed with mortar, and the bent ends of the grab bar are formed into the mortar. The ends project out through the wall surface and slip into the flange of the grab bar. When the mortar sets up, the fixture is held firmly by the mass of mortar. It does take a considerable amount of mortar (as shown), which may be a problem because the space between studs usually is already filled.

The opening in the wall should be no larger than necessary, and the form created by the newspaper should allow the mortar to extend about 3 inches out around the edges of the opening (inside the wall) to permit a good mechanical grip in the wall.

Use the flanges of the grab bar to correctly space the grab bar. Sink the fixture ends into the mortar, which has been troweled flush with the rest of the wall. Insert the ends on bolts and retrowel the mortar. Press the fixture ends or flange lightly against the mortar and then repack

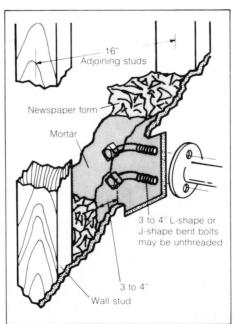

Block of mortar should fit between studs. Newspaper creates form to minimize mortar needed. If tile will be applied to wall, trowel mortar flush with wall, with bolts projecting.

the mortar. When retroweling, don't move the bolts.

Bolts should be at least $1/4$ or $5/16$ inch diameter and bent in an L-shape or a J-shape, as are anchor bolts for holding sill plates in a concrete foundation.

Doors and Doorways

Wheelchair users need 5 feet of turning space (diameter) inside the bathroom. Doorways should have flush sills and a clear opening of 30 to 32 inches for constant wheelchair users, a bathroom lacking these dimensional features must be considered inaccessible until extensive renovations are made, the doorway is widened and some fixtures relocated.

However, if the person can stand briefly and pivot from a chair outside the bathroom to one inside it (a shower chair or typist's chair, for example), a small bath with a narrow door may work. If you and the disabled decide on such a solution, install grab bars on the door frame — inside and outside. Just be sure the grab bars are fastened with bolts, because they will be subjected to enormous weight and pull. Have a bathroom light switch installed outside the door. Place it 30 inches above floor level for wheelchair users, 36 inches if the person is ambulatory.

You should realize too, that a hinged door juts out into open doorway space by as much as two inches. These inches can make the difference between a bathroom that is accessible or not by someone in a wheelchair. Substitutes to swing-out doors are folding doors, pocket doors that slide into a wall recess or a sliding door that is suspended on a wall-mounted track over the doorway. A plain 36 inch flush door, for instance, can be installed to such hardware, permitting it to cover the opening or slide to one side when not needed. This kind of door, to be efficient, needs track hardware (Deluxe By-Pass Wardrobe Hardware track is made by Johnson Hardware Products, Inc., Series 2600F, Size 96 inch).

For the aged and disabled, swing-out hinged doors should open outward. Falling inside the bathroom, a person could block the door on the inside, hampering rescue attempts.

Floor Coverings

Thresholds should be flush so entryway is smooth, free of ridges or bumps over

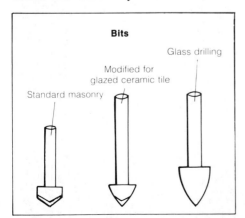

Standard carbide-tipped masonry bit can drill through ceramic tile, but a modified bit does a better job. Special glass drilling bit is best on brittle surface of glazed tile.

which the disabled may trip. Carpeting on the floor outside the bath should extend halfway into the door opening. Then the bathroom floor can be made flush with the carpeting. If the bathroom floor is resilient tile or sheet material, it can be shimmed up level with the carpeting with layers of building felt. Cement one or more layers of felt to the floor, then cement new flooring to the built-up felt. If you are building a new addition, plan to have all floors and thresholds on a smooth continuous level.

The kind of floor covering you choose should help the person move about more easily. If a disabled child or adult can stand and walk however briefly, slick flooring can be a hazard. Select thin, dense indoor-outdoor carpeting. Cut it to cover the entire floor, anchoring all the edges firmly with doublefaced carpet tape. Buy the most economical grade of carpet so you can replace it as soon as wear and tear begins to show.

Wheelchair users, however, can move about more easily on firm, smooth flooring such as resilient sheet or tile than on carpeting. Avoid highly glazed ceramic or quarry tile flooring, and do not use floor polishes, waxes, shag rugs or scatter rugs anywhere.

Fixtures

Sinks and lavatories. These present special problems because they don't project outward far enough to permit close approach for wheelchairs. Furthermore, if the standard lavatory is low enough to be reached across comfortably, a seated person's knees will strike against the bowl. If the washbowl is set high, however, the person may not be able to reach the faucet handles. One solution: replace the bowl with one designed specially for wheelchair users. It resembles a sleek wedge with curved front and a drain offset at the back (see illustrations below). Your plumber can order the basin. It must be installed according to local codes.

Another solution is a countertop sink. You can design and build it (or have it built) any height and width you want. The countertop also provides support for hands and arms, and serves as easy to reach storage space for items usually kept in medicine cabinets. Medicine cabinets should not be considered for some disabled, anyway. They are inaccessible to those who use the basin in a seated posi-

tion; their swing-out doors are difficult to handle; their corners and edges are sharp. Substitutes for medicine cabinet storage are discussed later in this chapter.

The disabled and elderly are best able to handle washbowls that are small and narrow because they are easy to reach across. Plumbers can fit them with an offset drain which will permit adequate knee-space underneath. Select the kind of countertop lavatories you would want for extra-small baths and powder rooms, page 14. They are available in colors and make a bathroom look homelike rather than institutional. American Standard's Spacelyn, for example, measures 20 inches side to side, and is only 12 inches front to back. Kohler's "Boutique" is 21 inches across and 13 inches front to back. The "Farmington", also by Kohler, is 19¼ inches across, and 16¼ inches front to back.

Not every aged or disabled person needs to have a specially designed

Lavatory for wheelchair users has contoured front rim with concealed overflow. It comes with holes for centerset faucet fitting or widespread fittings. Extended wristblade faucet handles help the elderly and disabled.

washbowl. A conventional wall-hung model may be satisfactory. New or existing sinks of this kind can be installed (or re-installed) at a height that is higher or lower than usual, if such an adjustment is considered necessary by the disabled person. However, the sink should be fitted with additional extra-strong support brackets because the elderly and mobility impaired tend to lean heavily on the front edge of the bowl. Use the heavy metal triangular brackets made especially for bathroom sinks. Your plumber will order them, or you may be able to buy them from a plumbing supply dealer. By all means, install such supports if you notice that the elderly or disabled person habitually depends upon the sink for leverage.

Faucet sets and handles. Select fittings according to individual reach and hand-grip capabilities. These can differ in various combinations. Hands and fingers can be strong but the ability to reach may be limited. Conversely, the person may be

Wristblade faucet handles are for those with weak or uncertain grip in hands and fingers.

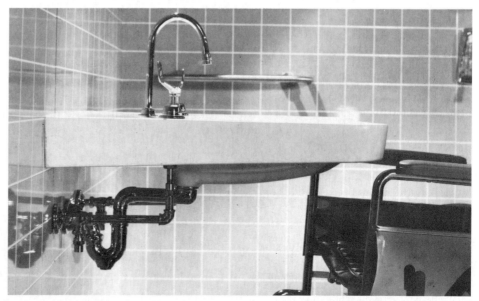

In general, wheelchair users will be comfortable if the top rim of the wheelchair basin is 34 inches above the floor level.

capable of extended reach, but not have the ability to grip and twist a faucet on and off. One side of the body may be stronger than the other. Let the person demonstrate what he or she can and cannot do, then select one of the single-lever faucet sets that are readily available from plumbing suppliers or mail order catalogs. The Spacelyn lavatory mentioned above can be equipped with American Standard's Aquarian II single-lever control which fits on the right or left side of the basin rim. They are convenient for individuals who have more strength in one hand than the other.

If the single knob or lever control faucet might be difficult to operate, consider wristblade faucet handles. They extend up and outward and may be easier to reach. Their flat, wide, wing-like ends make them easy for those with little or no grip strength. Handles can be operated with wrist or heel of an open hand. Decorative handles are usually too small and smooth for the disabled to operate. They can be replaced by wristblade handles manufactured by the maker of the existing faucet set. American Standard, Kohler, and other producers design wristblade faucet handles to be interchangeable with their own products.

Selecting a gooseneck or standard spout becomes a matter of personal preference. Goosenecks look more institutional, and may be rejected for that reason. As a rule, standard lavatory spouts are adequate if the handles are accessible, if the lavatory itself is comfortable and convenient. The gooseneck spout benefits those who want or need a high and wide arc of free space which low-set spouts cannot provide.

Stall showers. Most conventional stalls are too small for wheelchair users. The high step-over lip at the entrance is a barrier that most aged and disabled find difficult to manage. Until recently, roll-in showers had to be custom-built. Now, The Braun Corporation in Indiana produces a molded fiberglass ready-to-install unit that is 4½ feet square. A graded entry and exit lip assures accessibility by wheelchair, yet keeps water from running out. The one piece unit is ideal for new construction; the two-piece unit is for remodeling projects.

Two molded-in storage shelves are an integral part of the shower unit. Doors, shower head and fittings are extra. Be-

cause these units are in the $600 and $700 price range, and fittings are extra, you would be wise to write for illustrated material and spec sheets from the manufacturer in order to plan for and budget your bathroom project. Since the shower stall is spacious and comes in decorator colors it could be a wise investment for the entire family.

A precast terrazzo shower floor with wheelchair threshold is available for builders and home remodelers. The floor of the receptor slopes gently downward from the flush entry toward a center drain. It comes in five sizes, the largest measuring 54 inches front to back, and 42 inches side to side. Prices and shipping require-

This shower/tub kit features molded-in safety bars at several levels to serve as a sturdy, strong grab bar if the occupant begins to slip.

ments vary, so write Creative Industries, Inc. for information.

Molded plastic chairs on wide wheels are designed for use in bathrooms and shower stalls. Shower chairs of this kind make it easier for the elderly and disabled to move around inside the bathroom. They are usually narrow — 21 inches to 23 inches wide — so are less cumbersome than wheelchairs. You will find them in pharmacies which sell health aids and from mail order houses specializing in aids for the disabled. One is Nelson Medical Products, whose address is listed in the source list at the end of this chapter.

Bathtubs. Although most bathtubs are hard, slippery, and difficult to get into and out of, they can be made more accessible, comfortable and safe. For the disabled, one of the best things to come along is the flexible, hand-held telephone-type shower attachment now so widely available in stores and mail order houses. These flexible attachments allow a conventional shower head to be used when desired, and holds a personal shower head on a wall bracket near the bather. The shower hand-set can be lifted off the bracket and used as the bather desires, or it can be set in place to direct water flow at any height the disabled person wishes. Since many disabled people experience a sensation of panic when their heads are covered by an uncontrolled flow of water, the personal shower is an appreciated addition to shower stalls and bathtubs.

Bathtub accessories, furniture and furnishings help make bathing not only more comfortable, but safer. Suction-cup rub-

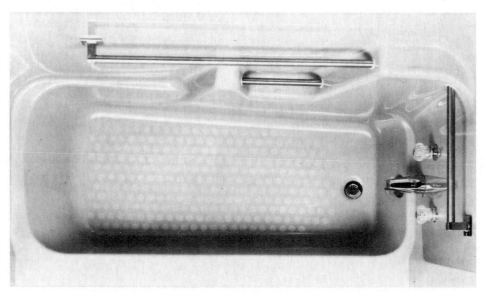

Shown is a top view of the kit's optional nonskid bottom. The surface is permanent, easy to keep clean and its skid resistance meets the needs of HUD's elderly housing standards.

ber mats in the bottom of the tub make slipping and falling less likely. Inside-the-tub chairs of molded plastic with rubber-tipped legs give bathers a feeling of reassurance, making bathing itself more comfortable. When getting in and out of the tub is especially difficult, a transfer bench may help. They fit into the tub and extend beyond the outer rim. Sturdy back support on the bench also serves as a grab bar. The person may sit on or transfer from wheelchair to bench outside the tub, and slide along the bench seat to a comfortable position over the tub. Benches have adjustable legs to accommodate tubs of various heights. One health aid house, Whitaker's, stocks transfer benches.

Toilets. Often the turn-around space needed inside an existing bathroom is blocked by the base of a floor-mounted toilet. Also, for many elderly and disabled, the toilet seat is too low. A wall-mounted toilet might solve both problems.

If most other features about an existing bath work well, you might find it worthwhile to replace the toilet with a new, higher one. In addition to wall-mounts, new 18 inch high floor-mounted models are produced by nationally-known manufacturers, such as the Hygeian by Eljer, the Cadet by American Standard, and the Highline Water-Guard by Kohler. Kohler also can provide a specially designed toilet seat that has securely attached grab-bar supporting arms built into it. It is sold separately; ask for seat model No. K-4655.

An existing toilet might also be made more comfortable and convenient with detachable handrail safety frames available from health aids suppliers, among them Nelson Medical and Whitaker's. These slipover toilet guardrails can be attached to almost any toilet on one or both sides. They are made of chrome-plated tubular steel with plastic armrests and non-skid feet.

In judging toilet accessibility, take into account how the disabled person must mount the toilet, from left side, or right side, or from the front. If a side approach is indicated, the toilet will have to be situated, or re-located, to allow for it. At least 36 inches side-clearance will be needed if the person must transfer from a wheelchair. Eighteen inches to 2 feet at one side or the other may be ample for an ambulatory adult or child. These are the

critical dimensions you should have ready to give plumbers and contractors. With such information, they will know how to plan the bathroom, order supplies, material, and fixtures. They cannot guess at what will be needed. It will be up to you and the disabled person to decide.

Storage. Enough storage space seldom exists in bathrooms for those not disabled. With the extra grab bars and personal hygiene aids the disabled need, there is even less. Add narrow shelves wherever you can. Hang coated wire racks and baskets at convenient levels for toiletries, towels, facecloths and other supplies. Determine levels and heights for holders by actually measuring the individual's reach.

Recessed medicine cabinets above the washbowl are not accessible to anyone who is seated, but you can hang one on the

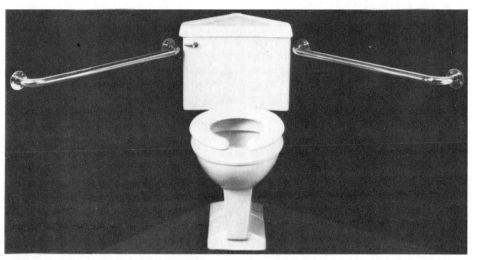
Consider a corner toilet if the arrangement is suitable for movements of the person involved. The seat is 18 inches above floor level.

The Highline Water-Guard measures 18 inches from floor to rim. It flushes with 3½ gallons of water, 36% less than most toilets. Seat with built-in support arms is extra.

Wall-mounted toilets free floor space blocked by base of a floor-mounted toilet. Wall-mounts also permit toilet to be set at higher or lower level than conventional toilets.

An extra-high floor-mount toilet is more comfortable than the conventional, lower height.

back of a door or wall if there is room. Place it low enough for the person to reach without having to twist, turn, or take unnecessary steps. If you take the door off the cabinet, the contents will be even more convenient.

Installation Hints

When installing a toilet, you should locate it, if possible, so a diagonal grab bar can be anchored to the wall just forward of the toilet seat.

When you install a bathtub, provide blocking in the studs to allow attaching a vertical grab bar near the faucets to aid the person to enter the tub. Another grab bar should be positioned diagonally on the back wall to help the disabled to rise from the tub or to take a shower.

In showers, whether in tub or stall, place a recessed soap dish 54 inches above floor level for those who stand, 26 inches above the floor for those who shower when seated. The lower soap dish will be at a convenient height for children, too.

If the washbowl is located opposite the long side of the tub, there should be at least 21 inches between the two fixtures, otherwise a person with unsteady stance could step back and possibly fall into the tub.

When you plan and measure for the placement of grab bars, keep in mind that for greatest safety, they should be anchored to the wall studs. Since studs are centered 16 inches apart, aim for grab bar lengths that will permit spacing of support flanges 32 inches apart . . . in other words, anchored to every other stud.

All of these guidelines, and the space-dimensions that follow, are simply suggestions based on national averages. Above all, work with the disabled person for whom the bath is being designed. Have yardstick and tape measure in your hands as the two of you go through an actual demonstration of how the person moves above and handles the facilities. Shower heads, faucets, light switches, drain lines can be installed anywhere provided the contractor knows where to put them.

DIMENSIONS THAT MATTER

Depending upon the disability, adults and children seated in wheelchairs have a range of reach that helps determine how well they can function independently. The reach chart below will give you an idea of how to arrange spaces, shelves, grab bars, and the like that must be handled from a seated position.

HOW HIGH, HOW WIDE
REACH DIMENSIONS FOR THE DISABLED
Use these dimensions as guides to making a new or existing bathroom accessible, comfortable, convenient.

Doorways   30 to 32 inches wide; 36 inches is ideal
Doorknobs   36 inches above floor level
Horizontal handrails and grab bars for wheelchair users   29 to 32 inches above floor for adults; 16 to 18 inches for children.
Horizontal handrails and grab bars for ambulatory adults   34 to 40 inches above floor level; 30 to 34 inches for children.
Window sills   not less than 28 inches nor more than 36 inches above floor level.
Light switches   30 to 36 inches above floor.
Lavatory vanities and countertops   32 inches (average) between top of surface and floor level. Clear opening between bottom edge of the counter or vanity top and floor must be 30 inches to accommodate wheelchair arms. If the person is an ambulatory adult, vanities and countertops that are from 34 to 36 inches high will be appreciated.
Lavatory vanities and countertops width   (front to back) of 18 inches for most adults and children; 20 inches for those with a long reach.
Toilets   18 inches from floor level to top of rim for most adults, especially the ambulatory elderly. For children, the standard 15 inch toilet will be adequate until full growth is reached.
Bathtubs   if the disability seems to call for a low tub, the 14 inch high receptor tubs mentioned in the section on Small Spaces and Powder Rooms would be adequate. Tubs with higher sides, however, may be needed for leverage or simply to instill feelings of safety. In such cases, the conventional bathtub will probably be advantageous.
Shower stalls   at least 36 by 36 inches; 54 by 54 inches is better.
Towel bars for wheelchair users   29 to 32 inches above floor for adults; 16 to 18 inches for children.
Towel bars for ambulatory adults   34 to 40 inches above floor for adults; 30 to 34 inches for children.
Hanging rods, hooks for clothing for wheelchair users   no higher than 48 inches above floor level for adults; 30 to 36 inches for children.
Mirror, shelves, medicine cabinets for wheelchair users   should be centered quite low; from 30 inches to no higher than 40 inches above floor level.

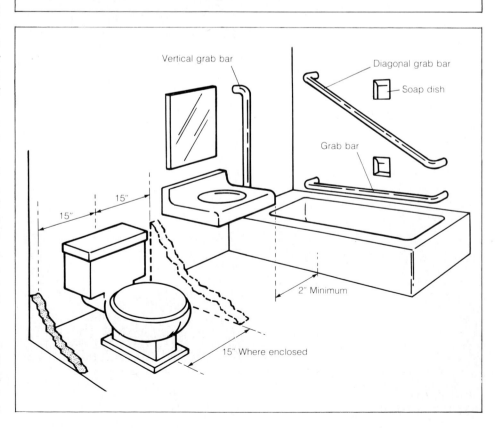

SEATED ADULT REACH*

Reach	Distance	Notes
Vertical	54 to 78 inches	The average is 60 inches
Horizontal (I)	28½ to 33½ inches	One arm extended
Horizontal (II)	54 to 71 inches	Both arms extended from sides
Diagonal	48 inches above floor	One arm extended toward shelf or wall

*A child's reach changes as he or she grows and develops new strengths. A chart of averages, then, would not be of much help. You should take measurements yourself from time to time to adjust the heights and widths of things in the room. Make the room as flexible as you can. Be ready, and willing, to move a hook or raise a shelf from one level to another.

WHEELCHAIR DIMENSIONS

Adult Wheelchair	Dimension	Notes
Length	42 to 44 inches	Unoccupied; footrests attached.
Length	Add 4 to 6 inches	With adult occupant
Width	22½ to 26½ inches	Unoccupied
Width	Add 4 to 6 inches	Allows for elbows and hands
Seat height	19½ inches	Average above-floor height
Seat depth	16 inches	Front-to-back measurement
Arm height	29½ inches	Average above-floor height
Over-all height	36 inches	Average above-floor height to top of backrest
Turning radius (I)	60 x 60 inches	Makes for tight full-circle turns
Turning radius (II)	63 x 63 inches	Preferred amount of turning space

The sizes of wheelchairs and the amount of room they and their occupants need to move about inside a room will help you plan how to place fixtures, doorways, countertops. Children's wheelchairs are smaller. But the size will change as the child grows. For bathroom design, you should have a list of what the chair's dimensions are likely to be. Ask the doctor or therapist who prescribes your child's wheelchair to give you its actual dimensions.

CHILDREN'S BATHS

As with the disabled, the small child experiences difficulties and limitations because of his or her shorter height and less firm grasp. In addition, children often view the bathroom as a nifty place for water games. A bath used by children should therefore contain modifications that have been designed for durability, comfort, and safety, but which can be removed as the child matures.

Materials

Ceramic tile walls and floor best withstand onslaughts of water, food, spills, foot and fingerprints. However, for the duration of active childhood, the floor should be covered in a nonslip material such as studded rubber or cushioned vinyl. Avoid carpeting until the child has passed through the water-fascination stage. Keep in mind that small scatter rugs unfortunately fit nicely into the toilet bowl, so try to do without them for a few years. Also keep the bathmat, towels, and washcloths out of reach, up on shelves, rods or hooks.

Scrubbable paint and strippable vinyl wallcoverings also hold up well during the adventurous years. Most scribblings and fingerprints can be cleaned away, or at least made less conspicuous by lightly scrubbing with spray cleansers and a sponge or a soft cloth.

Furniture Units

Parents and infants need special consideration if the bathroom is used for bathing, diapering, and dressing the baby. Invest in a sturdy changing-and-storage table, and a small plastic tub created for use by babies. You will find these in Infants' Departments in stores and shops. A flexible hose attachment for the tub or washbasin faucet is handy for filling the baby's bath. It's especially important that the changing table be a comfortable height for the parent. Waist-high is preferable. It will be well worth the effort to set the unit on blocks or a platform to assure that it will be high enough. Cut blocks from a section of 4x4 or make a recessed base of 2x4s. Either method allows comfortable toe-space and close approach.

When a baby is able to crawl about, all things at floor level and slightly above represent a new world of wonders to be investigated. Keep base cabinets secure with locks or latches designed to foil young invaders. You will find these locks and latches in hardware stores and in some import shops, with styles in bright-colored plastics. Most do not require a key, but have simple mechanisms that adults can operate but which defy the weaker grasps of children.

Flimsy shelves, chests of drawers, heavy chairs, clothes trees, or floor-standing mirrors can all be toppled easily. These should be removed or placed out of reach until a child is old enough to comprehend the principles of safety.

Lotions, liquids, or powders in glass containers are a special hazard in bathrooms used by children. For the duration of childhood select products packaged in plastic or which can be transferred into unbreakable bottles and jars. All medicines, household chemicals, and sharp objects must be kept secure from prying hands.

Locks. If all this means placing such items under lock and key, so be it. Poison control centers and the National Safety Council can provide tragic statistics which prove that children have no comprehension of the disastrous consequences of an act, as some parents come to realize only when it is too late.

Doors that can be locked from the inside need special attention. There are several ways to avoid a rescue crisis. You can remove turn-locks and hooks. Other alternatives include covering keyholes with

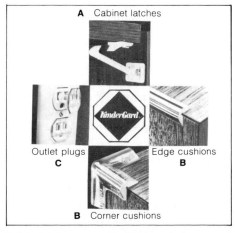

Safety latches, caps, and covers help prevent dangerous explorations by small children. Shown are: A, child-resistant latch for cabinets and drawers; B, edge and corner cushions; C, covers for electric wall outlets.

a solid escutcheon strip, or investing in a door that can be unlocked from the outside even though locked on the inside. Be careful never to keep keys of any kind inside the bathroom.

Just because a door cannot be locked from the inside does not mean that a child will not think he is trapped; he may not be able to open the door simply because he cannot turn the knob. Most door knobs are big, round, and smooth. They often refuse to turn in the grasp of small, wet hands. A lever handle that is long and thick is a definite improvement over a round knob, and may help prevent even short periods of unnecessary terror.

Safe Decor

Even stripped of safety hazards, a child's bath can not only be functional, but also comfortable and attractive. Brightly patterned wallcoverings in water-resistant finishes fill every manufacturer's style book. "Soft toys" of plastic, cloth, and wood are appropriate accessories to give the room color and appeal. Wicker and rattan furnishings and accessories are suitable since they are lightweight, will not shatter into jagged pieces if broken, and can take several dunkings before severe damage begins to show. Modern wicker and rattan are generally inexpensive enough to be used for a few years and then discarded. However, turn-of-the-century pieces are collector items, so a child's bathroom is hardly an appropriate setting for such treasures.

Light switches on walls should be set low enough for a child to reach — from 30 to 36 inches above floor level. This height is handy for adults, too. Lighting fixtures, however, should be high — out of reach and enclosed by diffusers or wire mesh to prevent investigations of the bulb or socket. Avoid pin-up lamps or any lighting fixture that can be lifted off, pulled down or tossed about the room.

Modifications You Can Make

Around the time a child begins to want to do things for himself, he'll find standard sized fixtures are inaccessible. Washbasin and faucets are out of reach, for example. A small step-stool of wood will solve the problem. You can make one of scrap lumber or plywood in your home workshop. Round off sharp corners of the step overhang and add non-skid strips of studded rubber or foam to the legs. Make the

top non skid also with a glued-on piece of carpeting. You can also pad the top with foam or fiberfill covered in a heavy duck or denim, tacked securely in place to the underside of the overhang.

Small step stools are easy to trip over, however, like the perennial roller skate that is always left underfoot. If you want a step that is secure, yet easy to move back and forth, here are two suggestions.

Flip-down Step. This consists of two wood boxes set one atop the other and joined by a continuous hinge. The top box flips down to form a step-up for a child's use, and folds back onto the base (lower box). It is designed to be placed under wallhung basins and countertop lavatories that are open underneath.

The illustration at right shows the assembly in dimensions that allow for a step that is 5 inches high, 5 inches wide, and 16 inches long. Base box dimensions are 5 inches high, 10 inches wide, 16 inches long. You can vary these measurements to suit your own needs depending upon the amount of space beneath the basin. Allow sufficient room for clearance of the top box when it has been flipped over.

The material can be stock lumber, ¾ inch plywood, or a combination of both. To make the top box lighter in weight, and thus easier to flip down or up, you might choose to make it of slats rather than of solid slabs.

The boxes can be finished in brightly colored paint, or given a clear natural finish. Tack or glue a piece of carpeting to two surfaces on the top box that serves as the step. Carpet gives better traction, as well as a soft, warm surface.

Glide-out Step. Installed into a vanity base cabinet, this is your best choice. However, since no standard base cabinets are made with such a pull-out feature, the project is usually one for experienced home carpenters who plan to build their own vanity base. If the step is elongated, it can be used as a bench as well.

If you are building a new vanity cabinet (see the plan in our chapter on "Storage"), or are having one custom built, position the bottom of the cabinet 5 or 6 inches above the floor rather than the usual 3 or 4 inches of the toe space. This will make the toe space a bit high, but not obtrusive or unsightly. Do not run the vertical facing board of the toe space all the way across the cabinet in the usual

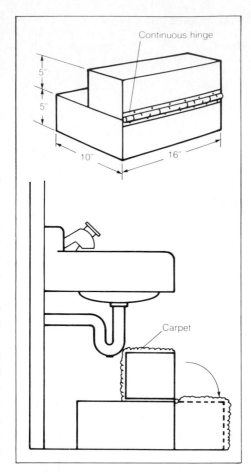

manner, but leave out a section at the center, or in two places if you have two youngsters who will be using the vanity at the same time and if the cabinet is long enough to permit it.

Build a simple box of ¾ inch plywood, glued and nailed together just a bit shorter than the height of the opening in the toe space, about ⅛ inch less, as indicated in the drawing. Sand, finish, and add carpet strips to the top of the box.

You can glue strips of felt or other material onto the bottom edges of the box so it will not scratch the floor, and will slide relatively easily. Do not, however, fit casters under the box, as this will permit it to roll too easily. It may move when a child is standing on it.

If you find that the height of the toe space is objectionable, make the doors long enough to project down over the toe-space — choose a length that will restore the usual 3- to 4-inch space from the floor. If there are drawers, make the front of the bottom drawer project down the same distance, so the lower edges of drawers and door(s) are aligned.

Existing Cabinet. If you are remodeling the existing cabinet, it probably will need to be removed from its original loca-

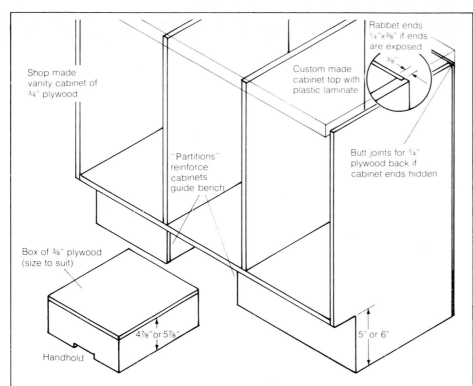

If building a new vanity cabinet, position bottom of cabinet high enough to permit placement of pull-out bench. Cut out a section of the face board of the toe space to accommodate bench. Install partitions front to back alongside the bench opening, for reinforcement and to guide the bench as it is pulled out or pushed in. For toe space at the usual height, make doors long enough to project down below the cabinet bottom to create the 3 or 4 inch height. Drawer fronts for bottom drawers also should extend down to align with bottoms of drawers.

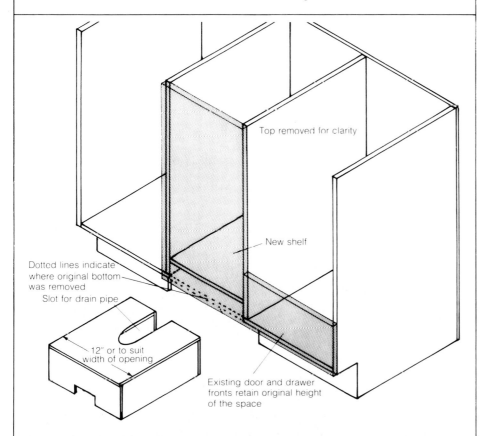

If remodeling an existing vanity cabinet, cut out the center section of the bottom and install a new shelf high enough to allow the pull-out bench. Add partitions to reinforce the cabinet and guide the bench.

tion to permit working on the plumbing or the floor or wall. While it is loose, turn it upside down and saw along the edges of the partitions to remove the bottom shelf. Install a new shelf so its lower surface is 5 or 6 inches from the bottom of the cabinet. Also cut away the facing of the toe space. If necessary, glue and nail strips of wood from front to back to support the partitions.

Make the plywood pull-out box to fit the opening under the new shelf. If the drain line goes into the wall, the box can be made the full depth of the cabinet, or a length that does not contact water supply pipes which come up through the floor.

If the drain goes down through the floor, build the pull-out box with a groove down the middle to fit around the drain. Make it at least ½ inch wider than the diameter of the drain pipe, so it does not bang against it when slid back into the cabinet.

Unlike the custommade or shopmade cabinet, you do not need to make new doors and drawer fronts because the original toe space has been retained, and the door will cover the opening where the pull-out bench is to be stored when not in use.

In the drawing, the doors and drawers as well as the top have been removed for clarity. Note that if one or both ends of the vanity cabinet will be hidden, as in the corner or against another cabinet, the ¼ inch cabinet back can simply be attached to the back edges of the ends. If one or both ends will be exposed, however, rabbet the inner edge of the end that will be exposed so the edge(s) of the back are hidden. This means also that partitions will have to be ¼ inch shorter front to back.

The pull-out box or bench is assembled from pieces of ¾ inch plywood that are glued and nailed together. Cut and smooth a handhold in the front and back ends; children will reverse the little bench on occasion and there will be need to grasp the bench to pull it out. Note that when it is necessary to cut a groove in the bench to fit around a drain pipe, "partitions" are installed along the edges of the slot to reinforce it.

The pull-out step that moves out of the way when not needed can, with minor adjustments, be turned into a storage drawer a few years from now.

12 Enlarging a Bathroom

DESIRABLE OPTIONS

Bathrooms in many older homes (and new ones too) are really too small, but enlarging them would mean taking space from adjacent rooms, and that is not practical. The answer is to extend the bathroom out through the exterior wall. If the bathroom is at the front of the house, check for any local "setbacks." These are local ordinances that determine how far back from a street or sidewalk a structure must be. It is illegal to build beyond a setback line and you could be forced to tear down any structure you had built if it violated this local law. If any part of your house already projects beyond the wall of the bathroom, then it is likely that you can extend the bathroom with no problems.

Where a bathroom is at the end of a house, it can be extended if kept inside a certain distance from the lot line. In most instances this distance is 18 inches. Extending a room at the back of a house seldom creates any problems, as the backyard usually provides ample space for a room extension.

We say "extension" rather than "addition" because if properly done, the new structure will appear to be part of the room. Two basic ways to extend the room are with a bay or with a "hanging closet." A bay has angled sides. It can either be above the foundation or have its own foundation; if it does not have a foundation it should not project more than 3 to 4 feet. A bay always has a preassembled bay window installed in it — anywhere from one to all three sides may have a window.

In one example shown, Bay 1, the existing floor joists are at right angles to the new joists and doubled joists are installed as indicated — with metal joist hangers — for a strong framing. This kind of floor framing does take some skill. If you don't have some carpentry experience, hire a professional carpenter for this job.

In Bay 2 the existing floor joists are parallel, so the floor framing for the room extension is much simpler. The example in Bay 2 is for a situation where the bathroom has been completely gutted so that the floor joists are exposed. The new, longer joists extend beyond the foundation, and their inner ends are on the steel or wooden girder that runs down the center of the length of the house, in the basement or crawl space.

Bay 3 shows how existing joists can be extended by shorter joists that are bolted and/or spiked to the existing joists and allowed to extend (cantilever) beyond the foundation. The general rule is that the

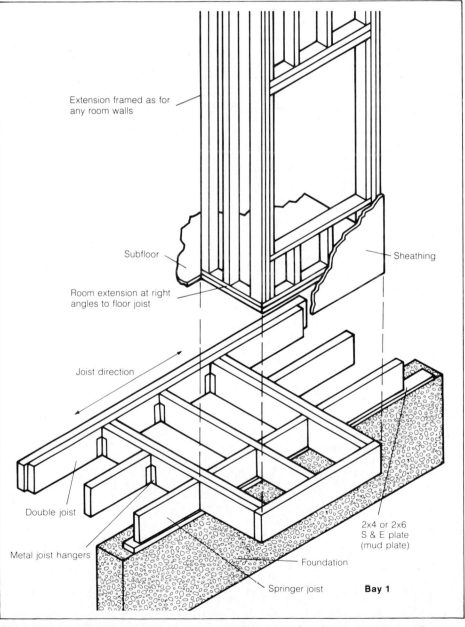

Extension framed as for any room walls

Sheathing

Subfloor

Room extension at right angles to floor joist

Joist direction

Double joist

Metal joist hangers

2x4 or 2x6 S & E plate (mud plate)

Foundation

Springer joist

Bay 1

When room extension is at right angles to existing floor joists, floor framing requires cutting some joists and fitting headers of doubled 2-inch stock to match existing headers. This floor framing requires tearing up bathroom floor.

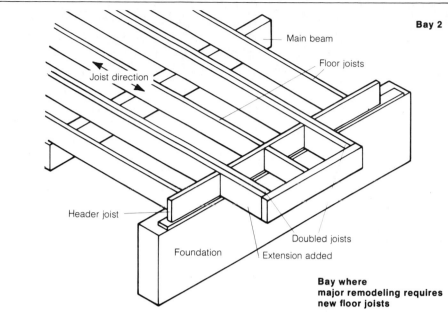

Bay 2

Main beam

Floor joists

Joist direction

Header joist

Doubled joists

Foundation

Extension added

**Bay where
major remodeling requires
new floor joists**

If new joists run parallel to existing joints, double joists can be extended to support the floor. If old bathroom floor is torn up, new long joists can have inner ends resting on main girder under house. It can be done, with difficulty, with floor in place: Fit one longer joist alongside each existing joist at sides of extension; then pull out existing joists and replace with longer ones.

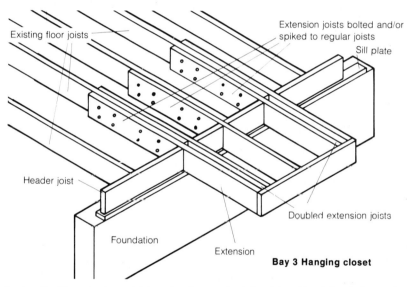

Existing floor joists

Extension joists bolted and/or spiked to regular joists

Sill plate

Header joist

Foundation

Extension

Doubled extension joists

Bay 3 Hanging closet

A practical method has short new joists extending past existing joists. New joists bolt or spike to old joists. This involves cutting out a section of header joists, and only works with joists parallel to old joists.

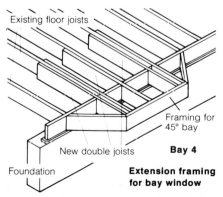

Existing floor joists

Framing for 45° bay

New double joists

Foundation

Bay 4

**Extension framing
for bay window**

If extension has a bay, cut joist ends to match window. New 3-piece header joists close in exposed ends of new joists.

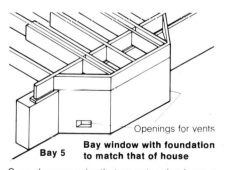

Openings for vents

Bay 5

**Bay window with foundation
to match that of house**

Some bays require that an extension have a foundation and footing to match existing construction. This means pouring concrete footing, and concrete wall, or wall of concrete block. Vents are necessary for elimination of moisture buildup under floor.

length of the overlap is twice the length of the extension. It would be necessary to remove the header joist, which is perpendicular to the floor joist, to install the new joists, but most of the work could be down under the floor in the basement or crawl space, and the floor would not have to be removed.

Bay 4 is a situation similar to Bay 3, but the extension joists are trimmed. The bay is designed to fit a preassembled bay window you will purchase. A three-window bay usually will have a fixed center sash, with sashes on each side that will open for ventilation. The most common bay window will have the side sashes at a 45 degree angle to the center sash, which means the floor framing also should be at 45 degrees.

Bays are available with other angles, and you can have a window assembled from stock sash to fit a particular design. Be sure you have the window before you build the floor framing, to make sure window and floor match in size and angles.

With either a bay or hanging closet, insulate the walls, under the floor and above the ceiling before applying wall surfacing materials.

Step One: Foundation

Your particular home may require a bay or extension set on a foundation. This is especially true if there are other projections on the house, or bays. Construction for such a structure is "standard" with a concrete footing plus a poured-concrete or concrete-block wall on top on which the new wall and floor framing are built. The footing, which is as deep as the foundation wall and twice as wide, extends an equal distance before and behind the wall. The wall should, of course, match the existing foundation wall so the room extension will appear to be part of the original structure. Leave wall openings for the installation of louver vents; these can be formed by placing a block (equal to the size of the vents) in place before pouring the wall. If the wall is of concrete block, just leave out blocks as needed.

Treat the space inside the new foundation like a miniature basement or crawl space, unless you open it up to the existing basement or crawl space. That is, cover the soil with a piece 4 or 6 mil polyethylene plastic and install at least two louver vents in the wall to assure ventilation. If you don't, condensation in the space will saturate the insulation and make it useless. Rotting also will occur in the floor framing.

Step Two:
Adding or Extending Joists

In some cases it is necessary to remove the flooring before adding or extending joists. Removing the bathroom floor might seem like a real housewrecking project, but it really is not. It will not permanently weaken the structure of the house. It will, however, be hard work; care must be taken when tearing up the floor not to inadvertently step into an area where the floor has been removed.

Room Preparation. Shut off the water; remove all the fixtures in the bathroom. At this point you may have to install shutoff valves for each fixture (see Chapter 2), which will require shutting off the main shutoff valve near the meter. Check all the valves and lines to make sure they do not leak, then shut off the water to each fixture.

Stuff a wad of newspaper or rags into the toilet drain once the toilet is removed. This is a large drain; scraps of flooring, nails and other debris can easily fall into it. The same is true of the bathtub and vanity basin. Even if the vanity basin goes into the wall rather than the floor, plug it with a rag. Remove any curtains or drapes, shelves on the wall and, if possible, take glass or mirror doors from medicine cabinets. Use a flat spade to lift off resilient tile or sheet flooring; chip out ceramic tile. Then sweep the floor of the empty room.

Gently pry off any shoe molding and baseboard trim. If your house is quite old, removing the molding and trim may expose the ends of hardwood strip flooring. If so, get your pry bar and start removing it. There will be a subfloor under it, probably of 1-inch lumber, although it may be plywood. In newer homes the subfloor will be plywood or particleboard.

When you get down to the subfloor you will find that it runs under the walls and there are no joints along the walls. This is because in modern house framing the subfloor is nailed down over the floor joists; then the outside walls and interior partitions are built on the subfloor and tilted up into place and spiked to the floor.

Cutting the Floor and Subfloor. If you cannot remove flooring first, you

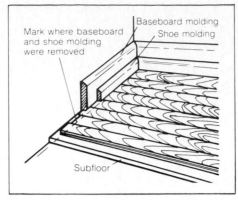

After all fixtures are removed from the bathroom, take off shoe molding (it looks like extra-high quarter round) and baseboard molding. If you have an older home, the ends of the strip hardwood flooring now may show.

must cut flooring and subfloor. Go to the basement or crawl space and check for pipes or wires that attach to the underside of the floor. If there are any, remove them. It is not likely, since any piping or wiring should be fastened to the joists, or run through the joists, but it pays to be sure.

At this point you will need a portable circular saw or, preferably, reciprocating saw. To determine the thickness of the subfloor, measure it next to one of the drain lines. Adjust the saw blade so it projects by the thickness of the floor plus about $1/16$th inch. Position the portable circular saw with the narrow side of the shoe against the wall. You will cut through some nails, so use a "flooring blade" with hardened teeth that will cut through the nails, or use a carbide-tipped blade. The latter blade will require sharpening after the job; the flooring blade usually is "disposable" and is thrown away.

In each corner there will be a few inches that the saw cannot cut. Use a handsaw or an electric jigsaw to finish the cuts. The very last bit of the cut may require a hammer and wood chisel.

For any and all of these operations wear safety glasses. Flying pieces of wood or nails can hit you in the face.

Now begin prying up the flooring. As you remove each piece, drive out the nails and place the flooring back in its original position. This gives a safe platform on which to wall. As you remove each section of flooring, check the joists to see if any are damaged or if there is any rotting near the outside ends where they rest on the foundation.

Extending Floor Joists. If the floor joists run at right angles to the foundation in the bathroom floor, remove the header

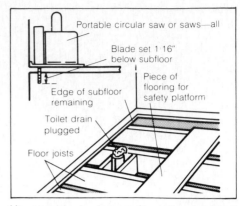

Use portable circular or reciprocating saw to cut flooring. Let blade project thickness of flooring plus 1/16 inch to cut through at all points. In corners, use handsaw or electric jigsaw to finish cuts.

joist that covers the ends of the joists. Whatever the siding of your home, you will want to call a professional to remove the wall before one side of the room can be extended. You may also decide to let the contractor extend the floor joists.

If your home is brick or masonry, or has a brick masonry veneer, let professionals remove the floor and extend the joists. You don't want a wall of masonry to tumble down on you. Not only is it hazardous to your health, but you could seriously damage the structure of your house.

If the floor joists under the bathroom run parallel to the foundation, you again have a problem, because the outside joist under the outside wall is a load-bearing member. Removing it often calls for the skills of a professional to prevent the wall from sagging. Shop around for a small contractor who will do the job for you to the extent of installing the extended floor joists required for your bay or hanging closet. Contract the job with the understanding that when the joists are in place you will take over.

Be sure any contractor you hire has insurance that not only covers his employees (Workman's Compensation), but also liability that covers any added labor and cost to correct damage to the structure should there be a miscalculation during the removal of load-bearing members, as required for installation of the extended floor joists.

If you have determined that the job is within your capabilities, tack-nail pieces of flooring to joists in areas on which you are not yet working so there always will be a safe walkway on which you can work. Keep the bathroom door locked when you are not working in the room; we are creatures of habit and someone might walk into the room and fall through the open floor joists.

Floor joists for the hanging closet or bay are fastened to the existing joists as shown. Clamp the new joists to the old ones, with the upper edges exactly flush. Then drive 16d or 20d spikes through the new joists into the old about every 12 inches, spacing them about 1 inch below the upper edges and 1 inch above the lower edges. Remove the clamps. Drill through both the new and old joists and install ½ inch bolts every 12 inches, keeping the holes 2 inches above the lower edges and 2 inches below the upper edges. Use 4-inch long bolts, with a flat washer at each end against the face of the floor joists, a lock washer and nut.

Stagger the bolts so they are not above and below each other. While it might seem that a lock washer is too much protection against a nut coming loose, keep in mind that a floor flexes. Over the years a nut could come loose and allow the new joists to move. If nothing else, this would cause floor squeaks, and eliminating the squeaks can be as much of a job as building the original floor framing.

Don't be stingy in the length of the new floor joists. If the bay or hanging closet extends 3 feet, then overlap the joists at least 6 feet, which means an overall length of 9 feet for the new joists. Here is a situation where "overbuilding" is almost a must. Make the new joists too long rather than too short, and you won't have problems later. Use Structural Grade No. 2 lumber for the joists, to avoid a springy floor.

Replacing the Flooring. With joists in, replace the flooring. You probably can use some of the flooring you removed, if you were careful not to tear it up too badly. It may be necessary, especially if the subflooring was pieces of 1-inch lumber, to provide a nailing surface around the edges of the floor. This can be done by nailing pieces of 2x4 or 2x6 (or heavier) between joists that are at right angles to the wall, and by nailing lengths of lumber to the closest joist to the wall so they project enough to provide a nailing surface for the flooring.

When nailing lumber between the joists you often can end-nail one end of the pieces, but the other end will have to be toe-nailed from above. Nail a scrap block of lumber, which is the thickness of

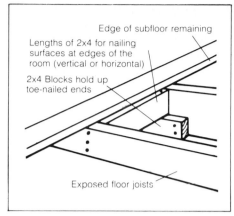

Provide nailing surfaces for edges of replaced subfloor with pieces of 2-inch lumber nailed between joists and shimmed from parallel joists. Blocks hold up ends that must be toe-nailed to joists.

the piece being toe-nailed, to the joist at the upper edge. The block will support the end of the lumber while you toe-nail it.

If new flooring is required, use the same thickness of plywood or particleboard as that removed. If the lumber is the "old fashioned" kind (about 1 inch thick) use 1-inch plywood or particleboard if you can obtain it — or use strips of ¼ inch plywood on the joists as shims for ¾ inch plywood to reach the correct thickness.

If you removed hardwood strip flooring you will have to shim up the joists to allow for it or, better still, laminate two or more thicknesses of plywood to create the proper thickness. To laminate, use plenty of construction adhesive, applied in ribbons from a caulking gun, to glue together the plywood sheets.

Before nailing down the new flooring, frame out for the bay or hanging closet, using a header of doubled 2 inch lumber for adequate support for the opening. Double the joists at each side of the opening. Extend the subflooring onto the floor joists of the bay or hanging closet; this adds strength to the framing. Use construction adhesive on the tops of the joists to help thoroughly join the flooring and joists, in addition to the nails.

Step Three: Framing Walls

After you have the subflooring nailed down for your new room, the walls are framed right on the floor. First sweep the floor carefully to remove all debris, then refer to your working drawing.

Walls are of standard 2x4 stud construction, except wall where a cast iron drain would be located, and this would be of

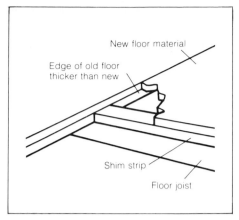

If you can't find material the same thickness as the old flooring, shim floor joists with strips of wood of a thickness that will place new floor at same level as the old—flush with flooring strips that remain at edges of the room.

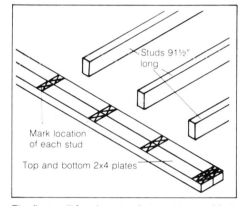

The first wall-framing step is to cut top and bottom plates to length. Then mark locations of all wall studs, including cripple studs under and over windows and doors, and double studs alongside openings.

2x6 framing. Start by laying down two 2x4s the length of the wall framing you will assemble. One will be the top plate, the other the bottom plate. Place them side by side and mark the locations of the wall studs, allowing for window openings, door openings and the like. Around windows and doors you may find that the distance does not divide evenly by 16 inches; for example, there might be 8 inches left over between the last stud and the opening. If so, do not place that last stud as usual. Instead, place two studs at 12 inches each. If the opening without the last stud were 28 inches, the studs would be 14 inches apart.

Cut your studs to length, or purchase ready-cut studs. For a room with 8-foot walls, the studs will be 4½ inches shorter than 8 feet (about 91½ inches). This allows for the thickness of the bottom 2x4 plate (1½ inches) and the double top plate (3 inches). All wall studs must be the same length.

For obvious reasons, the heights of new walls will be determined by the heights of existing walls. When measuring the height of the walls in the existing structure, allow for the thickness of any

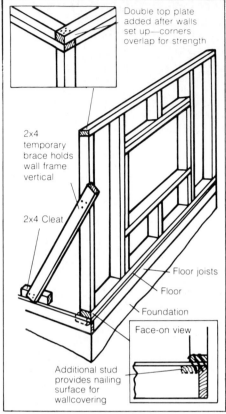

Double top plate added after walls set up—corners overlap for strength

2x4 temporary brace holds wall frame vertical

2x4 Cleat

Floor joists

Floor

Foundation

Face-on view

Additional stud provides nailing surface for wallcovering

Tilt framing upright; temporarily hold it up with 1x4s or 1x6s tack-nailed to framing and to 2x4 cleats on floor. When second top plate is nailed to walls at corner, overlap to strengthen corner joint. Add extra stud as nailing surface in corner. In arrangement shown, wall material nails to narrow edge of a 2x4. Covering is then applied to adjacent wall, which has a nailing surface.

flooring placed over the subfloor, and the thickness of the material used on the ceiling. For example, hardwood strip flooring might be about ¾ inch thick, while the plasterboard on the ceiling could be ⅜ or ½ inch thick.

The thickness of the flooring will have been determined before the joist extension procedures. To find the thickness of the ceiling covering, firmly but gently push an awl or ice pick through the ceiling until it contacts a joist. Holding a finger or thumb on the shank of the awl, withdraw it and measure the length to the tip. If you do this carefully, the small hole will not be noticeable, or easily patched.

Build the wall framing for one wall, working flat on the floor. Raise it to a vertical position, with the help of friends, and tack-nail temporary braces diagonally between the wall frame and the floor to hold the wall in place and vertical. Nail the bottom plate to the floor with 16d or 20d box nails. Build the frame for adjacent wall, stand it up and temporarily brace it in a vertical position. When all wall frames are in place, and nailed to the floor, nail the corners together and remove the temporary braces. Note how the second top plate is overlapped at the corners to help brace the walls; don't forget a "nailing corner", as shown.

Step Four: The Roof

The ceiling joists now should be toe-nailed to the tops of the walls, and usually are spaced 16 inches on center if there is to be a floor above, or 24 inches if there is

not; use 2x10 lumber, or heavier. The ceiling joists tie the walls together and stiffen the framework. The roof framing then is assembled, toe-nailing the rafters with 16d or 20d spikes.

If there is a roof overhang on the house, it might extend far enough for a hanging closet or extension to be built up right under it. The existing roof then will be the roof of the extension. An angled bay will require a 3-sided roof. The framing is a little tricky, but not beyond the capabilities of a homeowner with some carpentry experience and the patience to cut and fit the angled rafters, as shown.

If there is an overhang on the existing roof, there should be one on the roof of the bay, although it need not be as much of an overhang. Try to proportion the overhang to the smaller size of the bay roof.

If the existing roof is flush with the walls of the house, then the roof of the bay should also be flush or nearly so. There should be a few inches of overhang to keep rain and melting snow away.

If the bay projects only about 3 feet from the old perimeter of the room, the ceiling joists can be 2x6 stock, as can the rafters of the roof proper. If the roof projects much more than 3 to 3½ feet, use 2x8 or 2x10 lumber for both ceiling joists and roof rafters. Check the edge of the house roof. If it is boxed in at the edges, the sizes of the ceiling joists and roof rafters determine the height of the boxing; the roof of the bay should have the same kind of edge.

A homeowner/builder will create no

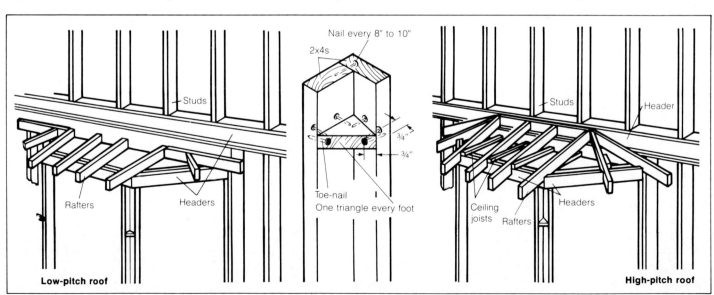

Nail every 8" to 10"

2x4s

Studs

Rafters   Headers

Toe-nail
One triangle every foot

Studs   Header

Ceiling joists   Rafters   Headers

Low-pitch roof   High-pitch roof

Roof and wall framing of bay window extensions are 2x4 stock. Rafters serve as ceiling joists in the low-pitch roof (left). Rafters attach to header on house and to bay framing. 2x4s butt together to make angle corners of bay. Braces are triangular blocks of 2x4. The high-pitch roof (right) uses both joists and rafters. These attach to separate headers on the house but to the same frame header on the bay.

problems by "over building"; that is, using lumber that is heavier than necessary.

For even greater strength in assembling the roof structure, investigate metal fasteners now available for joining all kinds of lumber and timber at various angles. These metal shapes are heavy galvanized sheet metal and are prepunched with nail holes. Some types can be bent at various angles, others are already shaped to hold 2-inch lumber. The devices are sold in larger hardware stores and home centers.

At this point, depending on the weather, you might want to apply the roof decking and cover it with tarpaper, even if you do not apply the shingles. This will assure a relatively protected room in which to work, and the floor and wall framing will be somewhat sheltered from rain and weather. Unless the bay or hanging closet is quite large no rain gutters are required. Local building codes may require a rain gutter if the structure has more than a certain number of feet of roof edge.

Step Five: Exterior Walls

Application of Sheathing. Sheathing now is applied to the outside of the wall framing. There are several types of sheathing in general use, including plywood, solid wood, fiberboard (also called "nail base") and gypsumboard. One of the newest types of sheathing is sheets of rigid insulation.

Solid Wood. Produced in 1x6 or 1x8 strips, solid wood sheathing is not in common use today. When lumber was less expensive and more readily available in longer lengths — and labor was not so expensive — solid wood was applied either horizontally or diagonally. Horizontal placement was preferred, since it went up faster and there was less waste than when applied diagonally. However, horizontal application required let-in corner bracing. The bracing was 1x6 or 1x8 lumber fitted into notches in the wall studs, but now a length of heavy sheet metal is used instead. The latter does not require notching of the studs, and the sheathing goes right over it.

Fiberboard and Gypsumboard. These come in 2x8 foot sheets that are applied horizontally, with end joints staggered. There also are 4x8 feet sheets that are applied vertically. The sheets are fastened with large head roofing nails. Corner bracing is required for fiberboard and gypsumboard; these do not add to the rigidity of the structure, as does plywood.

Plywood. The minimum thickness is $5/16$ inch, but a heavier sheet preferred for quality construction. The sheets in 4x8 foot size (or longer) usually are applied vertically. No corner bracing is required with plywood because it offers a tremendous stiffening to the wall structure. Horizontal application is used on occasion, but short lengths of 2x4 then must be nailed between the wall studs as blocking, to which horizontal joists are nailed.

Rigid Insulation. This type of sheathing is available in sheets 4x8 feet or longer, with a tongue-and-groove along the longer edge. It can be applied vertically or horizontally. It does not require blocking when applied horizontally because of the tongue-and-groove edges. The other edges must meet on a stud for nailing.

If shingles are used for siding over rigid insulation, you must apply horizontal furring strips as a nailing base. The strips are nailed through the board into the studs. Shingles then are nailed to the strips. Bevel, shiplap and similar siding can be nailed directly onto and through the insulation into the studs, as for plywood.

Rigid insulation is frequently used in newer homes that are designed to be energy efficient. Because the insulation is on the outside of the wall framing, heat loss by conduction through the wall framing is eliminated. Because up to 40% or more of a wall is the framing, this is a considerable heat loss or gain. Rigid insulation does cost more than regular sheathing, but can pay for itself in energy savings in just a few years.

Building Paper. Apply building paper over wood sheathing, but not over the other materials. The paper prevents the infiltration of air through the sheathing, but has no real insulation value, despite the fact that some people call it "insulation paper."

Caulking. Modern building practice calls for caulking between sheets of sheathing to prevent air infiltration and to prevent heat loss.

Siding and Windows. Siding on the room extension should match that on the house, of course. As with any major project, sit down and make a rough working drawing with complete dimensions. You then can determine how much lumber and other material you will need. Be sure to

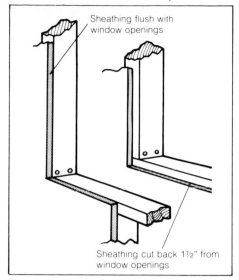

Depending on the style of the window, which you should have on hand before doing the framing and sheathing, apply the sheathing 1½ inches (or more) back from the rough opening, or cut it flush with the edges of the opening

purchase the windows ahead of time, getting a size that will fit in the wall(s) of the proposed extension. With the window on hand you can frame the rough openings and be sure they are the right size.

Buy windows with insulating glazing. The added cost of the double glass will be returned in a few years on the savings in fuel and, especially in a bathroom, you don't want cold drafts from a window.

The windows will be installed in one of two ways: either they will be nailed over the sheathing, with the nails going through the sheathing into the wall studs, or they will be nailed directly to the studs, with the sheathing being cut 1½ inches back from the rough window opening all around. Check the instructions packaged with your windows to determine how they should be installed. Both types of windows are installed from the outside of the rough opening, and are nailed in place from the outside. Modern windows have a vinyl shield over the wooden framing; the vinyl is shaped to provide a nailing flange. The siding overlaps the flange. The nails go through the siding and the flange; the window becomes "self framing" and sealed.

Windows that need sheathing cut back from the rough opening are nailed through the "blind stops" that bear against and are nailed to the framing. Window trim then is nailed to the window so it extends over and seals the joint between the sheathing and blind stops.

Plywood Paneling. If using siding of

plywood paneling, such as board and batten, it may be nailed directly to the wall framing with no sheathing underneath. In this case the siding must be cut back around the window rough openings to allow for windows that are attached by nailing through the blind stops, or trimmed flush with the opening if the window is attached by nailing a flange. Nailing the plywood siding directly to the wall framing does save money, but if you are doing the job yourself we would recommend that sheathing be applied first. It makes the wall stronger and also reduces heat loss.

Aluminum, Steel, Vinyl. If the house has been sided with aluminum, steel or vinyl siding, you will have to match it. There will be instructions packaged with the metal or vinyl siding. You also can check the method of installation of the siding already in place. Usually a starter strip is leveled and attached near the bottom of the wall, then the first strip of siding is applied. From then on each course of siding has the lower edge "locked" into a flange on the preceding course, which automatically levels and spaces the course. Nails are driven through prepunched holes in the upper edge of the siding piece.

In all cases, of course, you must align the new siding with the siding on the existing structure. If it is not possible to exactly align the new and old because the old no longer is obtainable, nail on vertical strips to separate the old and new, so the misalignment will be less obvious.

Unless you will be extending plumbing lines for new fixtures, this is the time —

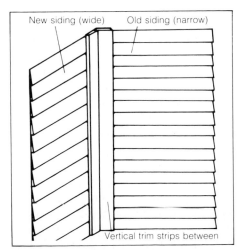

If you cannot match the old siding exactly, insert vertical trim strips between the old and the new. This may be necessary where metal or vinyl siding has been used.

before reinstalling old fixtures — to put down your flooring. If your tub is the type that does not have flooring under it, replace the tub before putting down the flooring.

Once the flooring has been installed, replace the baseboard and shoe molding (or vinyl cove in the case of resilient flooring). If the baseboard and shoe molding were quite old, it might have broken apart when removed. If so, replace them with new wood or plastic molding.

PLUMBING REQUIREMENTS

When you consider an extension for a bathroom, be sure to plan for the location of the various fixtures. If any of them will be located in the extension, allow for the necessary plumbing and wiring. Plumbing might require extra insulation to prevent freezing in cold weather, or you might want to build a foundation with insulation inside the walls and on the floor to prevent freezing. As an alternative, and in combination with insulation, cut two openings in the existing foundation wall (3 to 4 inches in diameter) so warm air is circulated from the basement to warm up the space.

Whenever you add new pipe — or reroute pipe for a more efficient path to the area where you plan to put in new fixtures — draw up a plan before you begin disassembling or installing the pipe. Draw the plan to scale, with ¼ inch or ½ inch equal to one foot, on graph paper. Mark in the existing cold and hot water lines and then make several copies of this drawing. Now you can draw in alternative routings, rearrangements, and branchings. This type of preplanning means that you will not get halfway into the project and then find that your measurements did not take into account the existing pipe, or that you did not leave enough room for air chambers, or some other important omission.

Extending Pipe Runs

The first step is to find the nearest hot and cold water lines and cut into them with a tee pipe connector. As an alternative to cutting pipe — if it is possible — you can disassemble plastic or steel pipe back to the nearest connection and install a tee there. The water must be shut off before you start the job, and when you start cutting the pipes, whether with a pipe cutter or hacksaw, you will have to drain water from the cut. It may be water standing in

the pipes that lead to the first and second floor, or it may be leakage in the main shutoff valve near the water meter. When any valve gets old it will leak a little no matter how good it was to begin with. Main shutoff valves will be metal to metal; that is, both the seat and the face will be metal. Since there is no way to shut off the water from the street main, unless the utility company shuts it off at their connection main, there is no way to replace the washer in order to stop the leakage.

The quickest and easiest way to install a tee connection in an existing pipe is with a plastic fitting that has compression nuts on the ends. The compression nuts will tighten to make a watertight joint on steel pipe, copper pipe or plastic pipe. Polybutylene (PB) can be used for up to 180 degrees and pressures of about 200 lbs. Local codes may dictate which can be used, and they often are not current with the latest developments in plastic pipe. If you use copper pipe it will be necessary to sweat solder a tee, nipple and union in place of a section cut from the supply line. A similar setup is used with steel pipe; the main difference is that all fittings will be threaded; it will be necessary to thread the cut ends of the supply pipes.

If you are working on the plumbing as time permits, your best bet is to immediately install a shutoff valve on the outlet of the tee. Do this for both the hot and the cold water lines. You then can shut off these valves and turn on the main valve so there is water in the rest of the house.

From the tee you have a choice of using any of the three types of supply lines — steel, copper or plastic. Again, and we recommend it where it is not expressly forbidden by code, plastic is the best and easiest product to use. Unfortunately, many codes still assume that plastic pipe is "cheap" and unreliable, although plas-

To keep down costs, rigid PVC or CPVC pipe is used for straight, open runs, but flexible PB is used up through walls. Note that holes are of generous size.

tic plumbing and fittings have been used in industrial applications for decades because it is inert and does not react with chemicals. Another advantage is its resistance to mineral deposits that plug metal pipes. There are both residential and industrial installations of plastic pipe that are 20 years old and older, and which are still in good condition. The same cannot be said for much of the existing metal piping.

Where there is room to work, such as in a basement rather than a crawl space, rigid plastic pipe can be run to the new bathroom. Assemble the piping run "dry" (without cement) first, up to the point where it will connect to a fixture. When you have all the pipe and fittings in place, go back to the start of the run; disconnect each fitting and apply the solvent cement.

You can eliminate many fittings, such as elbows, with use of PB (polybutylene) plastic pipe, which is flexible like a garden hose, and compression fittings designed for use with it. Because PB is flexible, it can be bent around corners to eliminate the need for elbows. There are PB connectors to permit joining the pipe directly to faucets, so that no other kind of piping need be used.

If you want to stay with copper for an existing system of copper, consider flexible copper tubing to run up through the wall or floor. The flexible copper also eliminates the need for fittings to go around corners, reducing the number of points that could leak.

If you insist (or the local plumbing code does) on threaded steel pipe, you will have to cut, fit and thread each length of pipe for each change of direction. When you make your final hookup to a brass faucet (usually chromeplated) you can be sure you have set up a situation where galvanic action will begin occurring the moment you turn on the water.

Warning: Saddle Valves and Saddle Tees. These are a temptation, but should only be used with ¼ inch tubing to supply ice makers, humidifiers, and the like, that require a small volume of water — with absolutely only one appliance per saddle valve and small line. There are larger saddle valves, but they are forbidden by most codes, are hard to find, and take as much time to install as doing the job with the proper fittings. The ¼ inch line will not supply enough volume and tends to

plug up with deposits.

Drain Line Connections. Despite some problems, connecting supply lines is not the major difficulty in an expansion or addition. Adding a toilet fixture will require a main drain of 3 or 4 inches in diameter. If moving the toilet location, the old main drain will have to be connected up to the new fixture. Drains from the bathtub and vanity basin can be connected to the main drain below the toilet, rather than running them back to the main house drain.

Another problem with drains is that older ones will be cast iron, and very heavy. Copper drains are not quite as heavy, but plastic drain lines are the lightest of all and the easiest to install.

If your home has cast iron drains, look for a cleanout in the basement or crawl space to which you can make a connection. You make the connection by using a Y-fitting to immediately provide a new cleanout as well as a connection for the new drains. There should be a cleanout near the bottom end of the drain line in the basement or crawl space; if there isn't, consider having a professional plumber install the connection.

The heavy cast iron drain line runs the full height of the house right up through the roof. These several hundred pounds of cast iron should not be treated lightly (no pun intended). A professional plumber

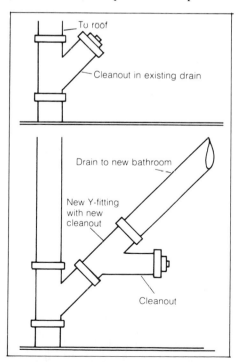

Where there is a cleanout in the main drain in basement or crawl space, fit in a Y fitting to permit connecting new drain.

will have to support the weight of the pipe while it is cut and a fitting installed.

Once the fitting is installed, you can run the drain line yourself using plastic pipe — or steel, copper or cast iron, with the aid of compression fitting. These fittings utilize donut-shape seals for cast iron pipe, or flexible sleeves and stainless steel clamps for connecting straight pipe to straight pipe without bells.

The main drain is run directly to the bathroom wall and run up through the roof, while a tee is run just under the floor

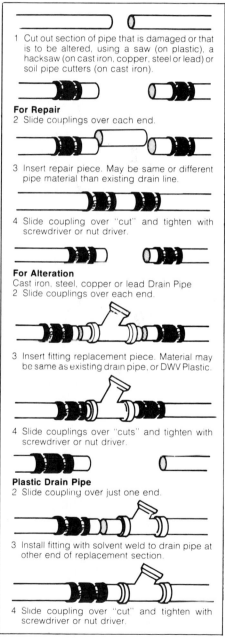

1 Cut out section of pipe that is damaged or that is to be altered, using a saw (on plastic), a hacksaw (on cast iron, copper, steel or lead) or soil pipe cutters (on cast iron).

For Repair
2 Slide couplings over each end.

3 Insert repair piece. May be same or different pipe material than existing drain line.

4 Slide coupling over "cut" and tighten with screwdriver or nut driver.

For Alteration
Cast iron, steel, copper or lead Drain Pipe
2 Slide couplings over each end.

3 Insert fitting replacement piece. Material may be same as existing drain pipe, or DWV Plastic.

4 Slide couplings over "cuts" and tighten with screwdriver or nut driver.

Plastic Drain Pipe
2 Slide coupling over just one end.

3 Install fitting with solvent weld to drain pipe at other end of replacement section.

4 Slide coupling over "cut" and tighten with screwdriver or nut driver.

Use clamp-on fittings to eliminate on-site joints of lead and caulking, sweat-soldering or solvent welding. T-fitting or Y-fitting requires one or both ends fitted wth short pipe for cast iron and copper fittings. Plastic drain line can have fitting solvent welded to it on one end, with clamp-on connector and short pipe piece at other end.

Plastic drain lines come with thick or thin walls. Pipe at left has thin walls, with outside diameter that fits inside standard stud wall of 2x4s. Heavier pipe at right requires shimming out of 2x4 wall, or building wall of 2x6s.

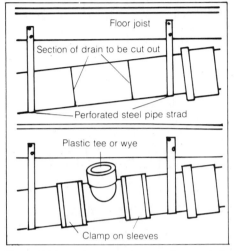

The easiest way to connect new bathroom drain is to join it to an existing drain. Support pipe on either side of section to be removed; leave supports in place after connection is made. New drain needs minimum slope of 1/8 inch per foot, toward existing drain.

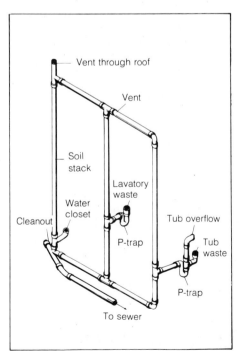

Toilet main drain vents out through the roof. Smaller (1½ or 2 inch) drains from vanity basin and bathtub/shower run into main drain. Tub and vanity also must be "revented" to meet sanitary code and assure good drainage.

to connect the toilet to the drain. The vanity and tub drains are connected to the main drain, and revents are run to the main drain at a point several feet above the fixtures. Another advantage of plastic drain lines is that one type has thinner walls so will fit inside a standard 2x4 stud wall. The heavier plastic pipe, and cast iron or copper, require that the wall be shimmed out to accept the pipe.

Venting and Reventing. The main drain for a new toilet will have to be vented out through the roof. Drains from the tub and vanity require "reventing." Venting and reventing allow atmospheric pressure to enter the drain and prevent a partial vacuum that could cause slow drainage, or even a backup of one drain into another. The need for vents and revents are clearly detailed in any building code, and are required for sanitary reasons. Do not under any circumstances make a drain installation without proper venting and reventing.

Plumbing Rough-in. Plumbing for the new bathroom can be run up through the floor or the wall. Unless the toilet is wall mounted, its drain will come up through the floor. Where a bathroom is being remodeled and wallcovering is not removed on some of the walls, running the pipes up through the floor is simplest. For a neater look, wherever possible,

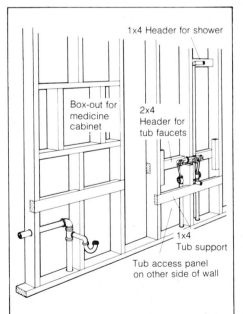

Floor and wall framing must support both supply lines and drain lines, as well as tubs, vanities and medicine cabinets. Standard "rough plumbing" shown has wall open, and lines ready for connection to various fixtures. This is a representative arrangement; many bathrooms will have fixtures in different locations.

keep the pipes in the wall. Pipes for the vanity can be inside the cabinet; those for the tub can be inside a short "stub" wall that has a door in it to permit reaching the plumbing for repairs. The small supply pipe for the toilet can be under the tank and hardly noticeable.

To locate where the pipes should run up through an existing floor or wall, first drill "locating" holes in the floor with a ¼ inch drill bit. Cut lengths of coathanger wire about a foot long and bend a short portion on one end at right angles. The angled piece prevents the wire from falling through the hole when you slip it into the holes you have drilled.

Go down into the basement or crawl space; find the protruding coathanger wires and mark their positions. If you have a helper, have him or her remove one wire at a time, so you can drill a clearance hole for each pipe. The holes should be large enough so the pipes can enter them easily. A ½ inch pipe usually will be the supply line into the bathroom, with an outside diameter of about ⅝ inch; for this, drill a ¾ inch hole.

The hole for the large drain for the toilet will require using a portable electric jigsaw because it will have to be about 4 inches in diameter, or larger. You can, of course, bore all the holes from upstairs, once you are sure the holes are not over floor joists, wires or existing pipes.

To cut openings for pipes, drains, electrical switches and receptacles in new walls, position the wallboard and tap at locations of pipes or electrical boxes to create marks on the back of the board. Use these marks to cut openings on the plasterboard or paneling before attaching it to the wall studs. Careful measurement is required.

After the pipes have been installed, fill in around them with caulking to seal out possible drafts or entries for insects. Where a pipe that comes through the floor is exposed, use a plastic or metal escutcheon plate. There are escutcheons that are split so they can be fitted around an existing pipe.

While any large drain line requires plenty of support, cast iron is so heavy that it requires special framing and support. Vertical vent to roof needs blocking up with V-notched blocks, while a horizontal line to a toilet must be supported to keep the flange rigidly supported under the toilet.

Metric Charts

LUMBER

Sizes: Metric cross-sections are so close to their nearest Imperial sizes, as noted below, that for most purposes they may be considered equivalents.

Lengths: Metric lengths are based on a 300mm module which is slightly shorter in length than an Imperial foot. It will therefore be important to check your requirements accurately to the nearest inch and consult the table below to find the metric length required.

Areas: The metric area is a square metre. Use the following conversion factors when converting from Imperial data: 100 sq. feet = 9.290 sq. metres.

METRIC SIZES SHOWN BESIDE NEAREST IMPERIAL EQUIVALENT

mm	Inches	mm	Inches
16 x 75	⅝ x 3	44 x 150	1¾ x 6
16 x 100	⅝ x 4	44 x 175	1¾ x 7
16 x 125	⅝ x 5	44 x 200	1¾ x 8
16 x 150	⅝ x 6	44 x 225	1¾ x 9
19 x 75	¾ x 3	44 x 250	1¾ x 10
19 x 100	¾ x 4	44 x 300	1¾ x 12
19 x 125	¾ x 5	50 x 75	2 x 3
19 x 150	¾ x 6	50 x 100	2 x 4
22 x 75	⅞ x 3	50 x 125	2 x 5
22 x 100	⅞ x 4	50 x 150	2 x 6
22 x 125	⅞ x 5	50 x 175	2 x 7
22 x 150	⅞ x 6	50 x 200	2 x 8
25 x 75	1 x 3	50 x 225	2 x 9
25 x 100	1 x 4	50 x 250	2 x 10
25 x 125	1 x 5	50 x 300	2 x 12
25 x 150	1 x 6	63 x 100	2½ x 4
25 x 175	1 x 7	63 x 125	2½ x 5
25 x 200	1 x 8	63 x 150	2½ x 6
25 x 225	1 x 9	63 x 175	2½ x 7
25 x 250	1 x 10	63 x 200	2½ x 8
25 x 300	1 x 12	63 x 225	2½ x 9
32 x 75	1¼ x 3	75 x 100	3 x 4
32 x 100	1¼ x 4	75 x 125	3 x 5
32 x 125	1¼ x 5	75 x 150	3 x 6
32 x 150	1¼ x 6	75 x 175	3 x 7
32 x 175	1¼ x 7	75 x 200	3 x 8
32 x 200	1¼ x 8	75 x 225	3 x 9
32 x 225	1¼ x 9	75 x 250	3 x 10
32 x 250	1¼ x 10	75 x 300	3 x 12
32 x 300	1¼ x 12	100 x 100	4 x 4
38 x 75	1½ x 3	100 x 150	4 x 6
38 x 100	1½ x 4	100 x 200	4 x 8
38 x 125	1½ x 5	100 x 250	4 x 10
38 x 150	1½ x 6	100 x 300	4 x 12
38 x 175	1½ x 7	150 x 150	6 x 6
38 x 200	1½ x 8	150 x 200	6 x 8
38 x 225	1½ x 9	150 x 300	6 x 12
44 x 75	1¾ x 3	200 x 200	8 x 8
44 x 100	1¾ x 4	250 x 250	10 x 10
44 x 125	1¾ x 5	300 x 300	12 x 12

METRIC LENGTHS

Lengths Metres	Equiv. Ft. & Inches
1.8m	5' 10⅞"
2.1m	6' 10⅝"
2.4m	7' 10½"
2.7m	8' 10¼"
3.0m	9' 10⅛"
3.3m	10' 9⅞"
3.6m	11' 9¾"
3.9m	12' 9½"
4.2m	13' 9⅜"
4.5m	14' 9⅓"
4.8m	15' 9"
5.1m	16' 8¾"
5.4m	17' 8⅝"
5.7m	18' 8⅜"
6.0m	19' 8¼"
6.3m	20' 8"
6.6m	21' 7⅞"
6.9m	22' 7⅝"
7.2m	23' 7½"
7.5m	24' 7¼"
7.8m	25' 7⅛"

All the dimensions are based on 1 inch = 25 mm.

NOMINAL SIZE (This is what you order.)	ACTUAL SIZE (This is what you get.)
Inches	Inches
1 x 1	¾ x ¾
1 x 2	¾ x 1½
1 x 3	¾ x 2½
1 x 4	¾ x 3½
1 x 6	¾ x 5½
1 x 8	¾ x 7¼
1 x 10	¾ x 9¼
1 x 12	¾ x 11¼
2 x 2	1¾ x 1¾
2 x 3	1½ x 2½
2 x 4	1½ x 3½
2 x 6	1½ x 5½
2 x 8	1½ x 7¼
2 x 10	1½ x 9¼
2 x 12	1½ x 11¼

Acknowledgements, Contributors, Picture Credits

We wish to extend our thanks to the individuals, associations and manufacturers who generously provided information, photographs, drawings, and project ideas for this book. Specific credit for individual photos, drawings and projects is given below with the names and addresses of the contributors.

Allied Chemical Corporation Box 2245, Morris Township, New Jersey 07960 36

American Hardboard Association 20 North Wacker Drive, Chicago, Illinois 60606 65, 66 upper right

American Olean 2583 Cannon Avenue, Lansdale, Pennsylvania 19446 16, 40 lower, 42, 47, 71 upper left, 72 left, 96 lower right

American Standard Box 2003, New Brunswick, New Jersey 08903 111 upper left

Armstrong Cork Company Liberty Street, Lancaster, Pennsylvania 17604 34 right, 41

The Bradley Corporation, Faucets and Special Products Division W142 N9101 Fountain Boulevard, Menomonee Falls, Wisconsin 53051 103 upper and center left

Broan Manufacturing Co., Inc. 926 State Street, Hartford, Wisconsin 53027 131 left

Craig Buchanan, photographer 490 2nd Street, San Francisco, California 94107 37

Monte Burch, Rt #1, Humansville, Missouri 65674 11 lower right, 49, 133 lower right

California Redwood Association 1 Lombard Street, San Francisco, California 94111 62, 63, 64, 99, 100

Chemcraft Box 1086, 54432 Adams Street, Elkhart, Indiana 46515 95

Chicago Specialty Manufacturing Company Skokie, Illinois 60076 121

Childcrest Distributing Inc. 6045 North 55th Street, Milwaukee, Wisconsin 53218 11 upper right

Consumer Lighting St. Louis, Missouri 127 left

Earth Care Company 2572 North Bremen, Milwaukee, Wisconsin 53212 111 upper right

Eljer Plumbing Div. 3 Gateway Center, Pittsburgh, Pennsylvania 15222 143

Fernco Inc. 300 South Dayton, Davison, Michigan 48423 155 right

General Electric Company Lamp Division, Nela Park, Cleveland, Ohio 44112 127 center

Genova, Inc. 7034 East Court Street, Davison, Michigan 48423 115, 118 upper right, 119, 120 lower right, 154 lower right, 156 upper left

Georgia-Pacific Corporation 900 SW 5th Street, Portland, Oregon 97204 59

Klaus K. Kesselhut 208 Farley Drive, Aptos, California 95003 39, 45 left

Kindergard Corporation 14822 Venture Drive, Dallas, Texas 75234 146

Kirsch Company 309 Prospect Street, Sturgis, Michigan 49091 87

The Kohler Company Kohler, Wisconsin 53044 15, 34 left, 46 upper, 102 lower, 108 left, 124 center, 141

Leviton Manufacturing Co., Inc. 59-25 Little Neck Parkway, Little Neck, New York 11352 130

McHale Studio 2349 Victory Parkway, Cincinnati, Ohio 45206 93 lower right

William Manley, Interior Design, 6062 N. Port Washington Road, Milwaukee, Wisconsin 53217 8

Masonite Corporation 29 North Wacker Drive, Chicago, Illinois 60606 33

Richard V. Nunn Media Mark Productions Falls Church Inn, 6633 Arlington Blvd., Falls Church, Virginia 22045 25, 57, 58, 67 left and center, 104, 105, 107, 113 upper right, 114, 116 lower left, 120 left, 132 center and right, 133 left, 143

NuTone Div. of Scovill Madison and Red Bank Roads, Cincinnati, Ohio 45227 37 upper, 95 upper and lower right, 111 lower left, center and lower right

Owens-Corning Fiberglass Corporation Fiberglass Tower, Toledo, Ohio 43659 51, 52, 53 upper left, lower right, 54, 55

Qest 1900 West Hievly, P.O. Box 1746, Elkhart, Indiana 46514 120 center, upper and center right

Quakermaid, A Tappan Division Rt. #61, Leesport, Pennsylvania 19533 92, 93 lower left

Ridge Tool Company Elyria, Ohio 44035 117 center and upper right

Speakman Company, Inc. Box 191, 301 E. 30th Street, Wilmington, Delaware 19899 110 right center, 111 left center

Thomas Strahan Company/Lis King Box 503, Mahwah, New Jersey 07430 35, 82

The Swan Corporation 408 Olive Street, St. Louis, Missouri 63102 53

The Tile Council/Lis King Box 503, Mahwah, New Jersey 07430 16

Universal-Rundle 217 North Mill Street, New Castle, Pennsylvania 16103 142

U.S. School of Professional Paper Hangers 16 Chaplin, Rutland, Vermont 05701 61

Sherle Wagner Corporation 60 East 57th Street, New York, New York 10022 102 upper, 124 left

Wasco Products Inc. Pioneer Avenue, Sanford, Maine 04073 83, 84

James Eaton Weeks Interior Designs, Inc. 223 East Silver Spring Dr., Milwaukee, Wisconsin 53217 14

Western Wood Products Association Yeon Building, Portland, Oregon 97204 23, 97 lower center, 124 right

Tom Yee 114 East 25th Street, New York, New York 10010 9, 12 upper, 13, 38, 43, 44

Yorktowne Cabinets P.O. Box 231, Red Lion, Pennsylvania 17356 85 lower right, 86

1,001 Decorating Ideas Family Media, Inc. 149 Fifth Avenue, New York, New York 10010 11

Material from *How to Create Interiors for the Disabled,* by Jane Randolph Cary, was adapted by permission of Pantheon Books, a Division of Random House, Inc. Copyright © 1978 by Jane Randolph Cary.

Index